ISLINGTON 02/2012

Please return this item on or before the last date stamped below or you may be liable to overdue charges. To renew an item call the number below, or access the online catalogue at www.islington.gov.uk/libraries. You will need your library membership number and PIN number.

3 1 MAR 2012

2 0 AUG 2012

1 0 NOV 2012

2 8 MAR 2013

2 0 DEC 2013

12/15

Islington Libraries

020 7527 6900   www.islington.gov.uk/librarie

FULL of FLAVOUR

MARIA ELIA

Maria Elia was brought up at the stove of her Greek Cypriot father's restaurant in Richmond. Her love of cooking has grown into a passion that has led her to travel the world and incorporate an eclectic range of influences into her cooking style – earning her great acclaim when head chef at Delfina's and the Whitechapel Gallery Dining Room. Maria is currently Executive Chef for Joe's at Draycott Avenue. She is also a contributor to *Olive* and *Good Food* magazine and appears regularly on TV.

www.thisismariaelia.com

FULL of FLAVOUR

Create... how to think like a chef

MARIA ELIA

Photography by Jonathan Gregson

Kyle Books

First published in Great Britain in 2011 by

Kyle Books

23 Howland Street

London W1T 4AY

general.enquiries@kylebooks.com

www.kylebooks.com

10 9 8 7 6 5 4 3 2 1

ISBN 978-0-85783-006-7

Text © 2011 Maria Elia

Design © 2011 Kyle Books

Photographs © 2011 Jonathan Gregson

Author photo (page 1) © Angela Chan

Illustrations © 2011 Kath Harding

Photographer: Jonathan Gregson

Designer and Illustrator: Kath Harding

Project Editor: Jenny Wheatley

Home Economist: Annie Rigg

Prop Stylist: Liz Belton

Copy Editor: Anne Newman

Proofreader: Nikki Sims

Editorial Assistant: Estella Hung

Production: Nic Jones and David Hearn

A Cataloguing in Publication record for this title is available from the British Library.

Colour reproduction by XY Digital Ltd in the UK

Printed in China by C&C Offset Printing Co. Ltd

DEDICATION

To my Mum and Dad, for showing me the path to succeed.

COOK'S NOTES

Butter is unsalted unless otherwise stated

Always make sure fish is from a sustainable source

Eggs should always be free-range and are medium unless otherwise specified

Milk should be organic and semi-skimmed unless otherwise stated

CONTENTS

CREATING WITH FLAVOUR

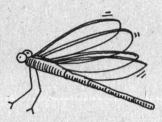

HOW do I combine flavours? Well, over the years I've built up a memory bank of tastes. I combine flavours in my mind and envision how they will taste on a plate. I'll usually sketch the dish and colour it in; thinking about flavour, texture and presentation. Everything is carefully thought about, and cooking in my head and then sketching it helps me to understand a dish before it becomes a reality.

I also like to draw 'mind maps'. I'll think of an ingredient and take it on a mental adventure, noting every possible complementary flavour. Each chapter in this book opens with a simplified version of one of my mind maps, to give an insight into how I've come up with some of the recipes in that chapter.

The recipes in this book are inspired by my culinary experiences and my extensive travels through work and pleasure. Some have been created through experimentation, and some by improvisation.

I want the dishes in this book to help your palate come alive and in turn you can make the recipes your own by taking them on a flavour journey. I've included a 'Take It Further' section at the end of the book, complete with notepaper, for you to take pen to paper and document your own variations.

The challenge in writing this book was transferring what goes on in my head onto a piece of paper! So what I decided to do was to break down my thought process. There are several areas that I focus on when creating a new dish, as follows.

6

THE MAIN INGREDIENT

FOR me, the main ingredient is the starting point when creating a new recipe. That's why I've arranged the book around 18 of my favourite ingredients, including lamb, aubergines and chocolate.

It's important to understand the essence of an ingredient: its flavour, aroma, texture and even appearance. The main ingredient needs respect and should be shown off to its greatest potential.

Consider the ingredient in its raw and simple state. For example, how amazing do freshly picked vine ripened tomatoes taste? All they need is a pinch of salt. From there you can add things like olive oil, basil or some feta, a touch of chilli or some anchovies. You are introducing different flavours that complement that beautiful fragrant tomato. None of the ingredients so far is spoiling the tomato in any way, they are simply taking it on a journey.

The ingredients need to be in season to give the best flavour. How great to shop at a farmers' market as opposed to a supermarket, seeing an abundance of the freshest finest ingredients, talking to the producer and finding out about the provenance.

Working with less familiar ingredients also gets the creative juices flowing – in this book you'll find recipes starring those such as quinoa and pomelo, as well as some underused cuts of meat that won't cost the earth, such as scrag end of lamb and brisket of beef.

COMPLEMENTARY FLAVOURS

OUR palates can detect four basic flavours: bitter, sweet, sour and salty, and a fifth called umami. This is a Japanese word meaning flavour or taste and is described as a savoury or meaty taste. It can be tasted in fermented or cured foods, Parmesan, wild mushrooms and olives, for example. In a nutshell it's a flavour that our palates can't get enough of!

To create with flavour is about understanding the properties of ingredients so you can combine and create a dish that satisfies the palate. Easier said than done, right? Well, the best thing about cooking is that it's a neverending learning experience, that's why I love it; the more you experiment the more you begin to understand what your palate prefers.

Let's take, for example, Slow-roasted Paprika Chicken with Butternut Squash, Smashed Butter Beans and Tomatoes (recipe #6). The sweetness is within the squash, which soaks up the meltingly rich fatty chicken juices. The paprika provides depth of flavour with its smoky earthiness, adding a touch of heat at the same time – complementing the sweet squash. The tomatoes add acidity to liven the dish and bring it all together and the white beans provide a neutral but solid foundation. Lastly, the basil contributes aroma and freshness to perk it all up, and offers the added bonus of vibrant colour.

Hopefully you are beginning to see how flavours are combined; it's about understanding a foundation recipe that works and building upon it. At the same time, it's important not to create confusion. Sometimes less is more, so don't go overboard and add so many elements that you destroy the central flavour. Add ingredients as background notes and let the main ingredient sing its song loud and clear!

USING DIFFERENT COOKING METHODS TO VARY TEXTURE

WHEN I was at the Whitechapel Gallery Dining Room I wanted to create a dish that told a story. So I created 'textures of vegetables' as a main course that evolved through the seasons. For example, it may have been a 'textures of cauliflower' dish. The aim was to create a plate that showed how one ingredient (and to me vegetables seemed the most interesting) could be used in different guises. The characteristics of an ingredient can change dramatically through different cooking techniques.

For cauliflower, I served it raw as a 'couscous' (see recipe #38), adding preserved lemons, mint and pistachio to introduce texture, acidity and a freshness to complement its unique raw flavour. Then I made a soup to which I added lemongrass, a flavour combination I'd been toying with in my mind, and a little ginger and coriander root brought them together. The garnish was a little roasted cauliflower; again the method of cooking gave the cauliflower a completely new flavour. A little savoury panna cotta served cold added interest to the plate with a change of temperature and creaminess. Wafer-thin florets gently fried in olive oil tasted like oyster mushrooms, again a different cooking method to create another flavour.

So, on one plate several textures and flavours of a single ingredient came together in harmony. All I did was add elements to bring out the best of cauliflower.

9

way to roast a bird. Chicken is pretty neutral and combines well with most herbs and spices. So, how about making a summery marinade using chopped dill, with some crushed garlic, olive oil, lemon zest and juice and then marinate as in the recipe. Replace the squash with some lovely baby potatoes, cut in half, toss in oil and season, place the chicken on top and slow roast. To finish, replace the tomatoes with a squeeze of lemon juice (acidic like the tomatoes) and add some fresh blanched peas and broad beans. Lightly crush the potatoes with peas and beans to soak up the cooking juices and again freshen it up with herbs such as flatleaf parsley and mint. Gorgeous!

Or, take the chicken on an Asian flavour journey. Take the predominant flavours of Asian cuisine – chilli, garlic, ginger and coriander root; crush together, mix with oil and rub over the chicken. Use sweet potato and chopped ginger root to replace the squash or even chunks of aubergines. Place the chicken on top and slow roast as normal. Finish by adding lots of chopped coriander, a dash of soy sauce, a squeeze of lime, a splash of fish sauce and some chopped spring onions and chilli.

That's what I'd love you to do with this book – cook the recipes with confidence and then begin to experiment when ingredients are out of season, say, or you need to improvise. Write the changes in the blank 'Take it Further' pages at the end of the book if you loved them and begin to make this cookbook truly yours.

Where space permits I've offered variations for recipes, giving you ideas on how to vary and adapt them to suit your mood or the season. Where a recipe is more complicated, I've offered an alternative, simpler version – perhaps you may only want to take part of a recipe and not even cook the rest. That's exactly how I want you to use this book, it's not at all dictatorial, it's for you to pick and choose how you want to cook from it.

TAKING THE RECIPES FURTHER

I'D LIKE this book is to give you the confidence to develop a recipe and take it further – on your own adventure. Let's go back to the paprika chicken example (recipe #6).

Once you've tried this recipe and you're happy with it you might wonder how you could adapt it for another time of the year when squash is not in season. If it was summer, for example, you'd want something fresher tasting. You've already learnt how to spatchcock a chicken and have seen that slow roasting on the bone is a sensational

FINISHING TOUCHES

CONSIDER whether the dish needs a garnish and, if so, will it serve a purpose?

I believe garnishes should enhance a dish rather than inhibit. For instance, pea shoots used in some of my recipes are an extension of an ingredient being used – yes, peas! Or popcorn with cream of corn (see recipe #39) – it's a garnish but also within the corn family, creating a different texture.

GO FORTH AND CREATE WITH FLAVOUR

I hope the recipes I've provided here give you enough confidence to experiment and go off on a 'culinary adventure'. To me, a recipe is more than just a set of ingredients, it's a fount of information on how to cook various ingredients that in turn guides you towards creating your own exciting dishes and flavour combinations.

I hope you find the recipes and the concept interesting. I will show you how to take them further, but predominantly I wanted this book to be about the reader. I'd like you to take this book, digest it and make it your very own workbook. Pass your recipe variations on to your friends and family and see how they've recreated certain recipes too. That's half the fun of cooking – nurturing, sourcing and tasting ingredients, then creating and entertaining.

So, pour yourself a glass of wine, choose some music to cook to, relax, enjoy and cook – bliss!

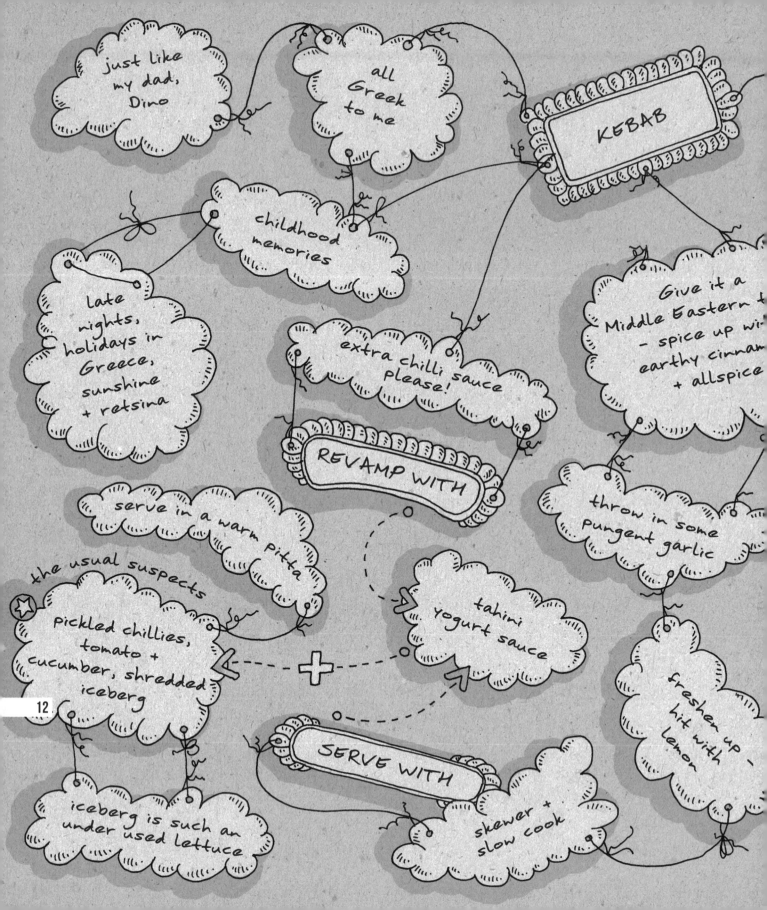

ASIAN BROTH WITH TURKEY MEATBALLS

1 litre chicken stock
1 red chilli, finely sliced
3cm piece of fresh ginger, julienned
2 lime leaves
2 tsp palm sugar
1 bok choy, separated into leaves or baby corn sliced into 1cm pieces
dash of soy sauce
dash of fish sauce

FOR THE MEATBALLS
2 shallots, finely chopped
2 lime leaves, finely chopped
2cm piece of fresh ginger, grated
1 garlic clove, finely chopped
1 chilli, finely chopped
1 small bunch coriander, finely chopped
200g minced turkey
1 egg yolk
dash of fish sauce
2 tbsp light olive oil

FOR THE NOODLES
2 bunches rice noodles
1 small bunch coriander, roughly chopped
½ small bunch mint, chopped
12 Thai basil leaves (optional)
handful of beansprouts
2 spring onions, thinly sliced
1 lime, cut into wedges

First make the broth. Heat the chicken stock, chilli and ginger in pan and bring to the boil. Reduce heat to a simmer, add the lime leaves and palm sugar and cook for 5–6 minutes. Remove from the heat and set aside to infuse while you make your meatballs.

Place the shallots, lime leaves, ginger, garlic, chilli and coriander into a food-processor and pulse until combined. (Alternatively, you can mix by hand; make sure your ingredients are very finely chopped though.) Mix with the turkey mince, along with the egg. Season with a dash of fish sauce (this will replace salt).

Roll the mixture into small balls. Heat the oil in a frying pan, then fry the meatballs for 4–5 minutes on either side or until golden brown and cooked through.

Meanwhile, reheat the broth gently. Once simmering, add the bok choy or baby corn and cook for a minute. Add a dash of soy sauce and fish sauce to taste.

Cook or soak the noodles according to packet instructions. To serve, divide the noodles between serving bowls and arrange the herbs, beansprouts and spring onions on top. Add the meatballs, ladle over the hot broth and garnish with lime wedges.

14

This may seem like a mammoth recipe, but it's really up to you how many of the above to you want to include. The chicken, pancetta chips, croûtons and dressing can all be prepared beforehand. < SERVES 4 >

CHICKEN CAESAR SALAD

Preheat the oven to 200°C/gas mark 6.

Mix the lemon zest, thyme leaves, garlic and olive oil together, rub over the chicken and marinate for at least an hour or overnight. Remove from the fridge half an hour before cooking. Preheat a griddle pan, season the chicken and cook for 8–10 minutes on each side. Leave to rest, then slice.

Lay the pancetta on a baking tray, cover with baking parchment and place another baking sheet on top. Bake for 10–15 minutes, or until browned and crisp. Remove baking sheet and paper and drizzle immediately with maple syrup, sprinkle with black pepper and leave to cool.

To make the croûtons, tear the bread into 2cm rustic chunks and spread over a large baking tray. Drizzle with olive oil and sea salt and mix to coat the bread. Bake in the oven for about 8 minutes until golden and crisp on the outside, but chewy on the inside.

For the dressing, place the eggs, vinegar, anchovies, Parmesan, garlic and mustard in a blender. Whizz to a smooth purée, add the lemon juice and slowly pour in the oil with the motor running.

For the salad, preheat a griddle pan. Halve and quarter the gem lengthways and brush with olive oil. Season with sea salt and pepper, then griddle on both sides, until the leaves have taken on some colour and wilted slightly. Remove from the heat. You can serve these hot or cold.

For the eggs, fill a pan with water, add the vinegar and bring to the boil. Crack the eggs into cups. Once the water is boiling, stir to create a gentle whirlpool. Carefully slide the eggs into the water, one at a time and adjust the heat so the water simmers gently. Cook for 3 minutes, then remove the eggs with a slotted spoon and season.

To assemble the salad, spoon a little dressing on to each plate and place the gem quarters on top. Add a couple of croûtons and the sliced chicken. Spoon over more dressing and top with a poached egg. Scatter over the Parmesan and more croûtons, garnish with the pancetta chips and serve.

zest of 1 lemon
2 tsp thyme leaves
1 garlic clove, crushed
good glug of olive oil
2 boneless, skinless chicken breasts
sea salt and black pepper

FOR THE PANCETTA CHIPS
8–12 thin slices pancetta
2 tbsp maple syrup

FOR THE CROÛTONS
½ ciabatta loaf
good glug of olive oil

FOR THE DRESSING
1 egg
½ teaspoon white wine vinegar
5 salted anchovies
25g Parmesan, grated (plus extra to serve)
1 garlic cloves
1 tsp Dijon mustard
juice of ½ lemon
150ml extra virgin olive oil

FOR THE SALAD
4 baby gem lettuces
olive oil

FOR THE POACHED EGGS
4 eggs

17

#3

I love good old 'poule au pot' and am surprised at how many people have never poached a whole chicken. It is a low-fat method of cooking which keeps the chicken succulent and flavoursome. < SERVES 4 >

POACHED CHICKEN

1 whole medium-sized chicken

4 celery sticks, roughly chopped

1 onion, roughly chopped

2 carrots, peeled and roughly chopped

4 whole garlic cloves

2 bay leaves

few parsley stalks and sprigs of thyme

4 whole black peppercorns

1 glass white wine (optional – you may prefer to drink it!)

Remove any giblets from your chicken and place in a large pot with the celery, onion, carrots, garlic, herbs, peppercorns and white wine. Add enough cold water to cover the chicken well.

Place the pot over a medium-high heat and slowly bring to a simmer, making sure the liquid does not boil, or the chicken will be tough. Cook gently for 1 hour, then remove from the heat, immediately cover and allow to stand for a further hour – the chicken will continue to cook gently.

Remove the chicken from the liquor and leave to cool before serving. Strain the liquor through a sieve, and discard the vegetables, herbs and peppercorns. Skim off any fat and set aside the broth. If you're making in advance, refrigerate the whole chicken in the cooled cooking liquor.

That's the basic recipe, but you're probably wondering what to do with this whole chicken. You can create a world of flavours from this base recipe – read on for ideas.

VARIATIONS

- Use the liquor to poach vegetables and noodles in for an Asian chicken and noodle soup, finishing with fresh coriander, spring onions, Thai fish sauce and a dash of soy.
- The legs can be picked and used in a pasta dish or a risotto.
- The breast can be removed and sliced, and used for Vietnamese Rice Paper Rolls (recipe #46) or in the Chicken Caesar Salad (recipe #2).
- For an Asian twist, replace the herbs with a split chilli, lime leaves, lemongrass, star anise and ginger.
- You can also save the liquor to cook a risotto in; I like to use it to soak dried porcinis in for a double flavour hit if I'm making a chicken and porcini risotto.
- The broth can be made into a 'veloute' the equivalent of a béchamel where the milk is replaced with stock and finished with cream.
- Use the chicken in a fragrant Asian salad dressed with nam jim.
- Poached chicken also makes the best sandwiches!

Hot, comforting and full of goodness - perfect for a winter's day! It's also a great way to use the chicken and poaching liquor from the recipe opposite. < SERVES 2 (REALLY 4, BUT YOU'LL WANT TO GO BACK FOR SECONDS!)>

#4

CHICKEN, BARLEY AND VEGETABLE SOUP

Heat the oil in a large saucepan. Gently cook the onion, leek, garlic, carrot and celery, stirring, until softened. Add the mushrooms and cook for a further 5 minutes. Pour in the cooking liquor or stock and bring to the boil. Add the barley, and simmer for 20 minutes. Add the chicken, season with salt and pepper and cook for a further 10 minutes or until the barley is tender.

Check the seasoning and stir in the herbs, spinach and cream, if using, and serve immediately.

VARIATIONS

- If I'm not adding cream, I like to serve the soup drizzled with olive oil and topped with a little shaved Parmesan.
- If you prefer a tomato-flavoured version, add some peeled and diced tomatoes in the last 10 minutes of cooking.
- Vary your herbs to create your own flavoursome soup.
- Substitute the barley with another grain, such as faro, quinoa or even amaranth – you will need to adjust the timings though, depending on the grain. Pre-soaking speeds up the cooking time.

3 tbsp olive oil

1 large onion, finely chopped

1 leek, finely chopped

2 garlic cloves, finely chopped

2 carrots, finely chopped

4 celery sticks, finely chopped

500g chestnut mushrooms, finely sliced

1.5 litres chicken stock or cooking liquor from a whole poached chicken (see opposite)

180g pearl barley, soaked in cold water overnight, then drained

picked meat from 2 chicken legs or breasts

sea salt and pepper

1 small bunch tarragon, leaves stripped and finely chopped

a handful of flatleaf parsley, finely chopped

2 handfuls of baby spinach (optional)

200ml cream, optional, should you care for a creamy finish

#5 *Hot pitta bread filled with delicious tender chicken, pickled chilli peppers and fresh crisp salad... it's not just because I'm half Greek that I love a good kebab. This one is famous at my annual summer barbecue.* < SERVES 4—6 >

MIDDLE EASTERN KEBAB

FOR THE MARINADE
4 garlic cloves
2 tsp sea salt
pinch of black pepper
juice of 1 lemon
4 tbsp olive oil
1½ tbsp ground cinnamon
2 tbsp ground allspice

12 boneless, skinless
chicken thighs

TO SERVE
warm pitta bread
iceberg lettuce, shredded
tomato, cucumber and red
onions, thinly sliced
pickled chilli peppers
(optional)
Tahini Yogurt Sauce
(recipe #103)

you will need two 30cm
metal skewers to create the
'doner' effect

In a large pestle and mortar, crush the garlic cloves with the sea salt and black pepper, then stir in the lemon juice, olive oil and spices. Place the chicken in a shallow dish, pour the marinade over and coat well. Refrigerate for at least 1 hour or overnight.

Preheat the oven to 160°C/gas mark 3.

Fold a chicken thigh in half and thread widthways on to the two skewers. The skewers should be 3cm apart to make the kebab sturdy. Repeat with remaining 11 chicken thighs to form a solid kebab.

Place the skewered chicken on a hot griddle pan and sear on each side. Transfer to a baking tray and finish in the oven for 40 minutes, turning halfway through cooking. Set aside the cooking juices and pour over the chicken before serving.

To serve, hold the kebab on a chopping board, point-side down, and slice off the meat using a sharp knife.

Serve with the warm pitta breads, salad, pickled chilli peppers and tahini yogurt sauce.

I simply love smoked paprika – the deep, earthy flavours of spice and heat make this dish lip-smackingly great. If you have time, marinate the chicken for at least four hours or the day before. < SERVES 4 >

SLOW-ROASTED PAPRIKA CHICKEN WITH BUTTERNUT SQUASH, SMASHED BUTTER BEANS AND TOMATOES

Preheat the oven to 180°C/gas mark 4.

You need to spatchcock the chicken for this recipe. Calm down, it's not as scary as it sounds! First find your kitchen scissors. Remove the wing tips from the chicken. Place the chicken on a board, breast side down, and then cut along either side of the backbone to remove. Turn the chicken over and then, using the palm of your hand, press down on the chicken to make it flat. There you have it, a 'spatchcock chicken'!

Place the garlic in a pestle and mortar with the salt and crush to a paste. Then add the smoked paprika and enough olive oil to make a runny paste.

Give the butternut squash a wash and cut into large chunks, leaving the skin on. Lay in a roasting tin, sprinkle with sea salt and a drizzle of olive oil.

Massage most of the smoked paprika paste over the breast side of the chicken, getting right into the leg joints, then rub a little on the bone side. Place on top of the squash, breast side down. Leave to marinate in the refrigerator for at least four hours or overnight.

Place the roasting tin in the oven. After 30 minutes turn the chicken over so the breast side is up, and baste with the juices. Lower the oven to 160°C/gas mark 3 and cook for a further 1½ hours, basting every 30 minutes. Remove the chicken from the roasting tin, cover with foil and leave to rest for 10 minutes.

Add the drained beans and tomatoes to the roasting tin and warm through while the chicken rests. Once warm, gently smash the beans with a potato masher or fork, keeping them fairly chunky. Season with sea salt and pepper, toss with the basil and pile on to a large plate. Top with the squash. Cut the chicken in half or into quarters, depending on how hungry you and your guests are, and serve drizzled with those yummy smoky paprika chicken juices.

1 whole 1½–2kg chicken
2 garlic cloves
sea salt and black pepper
2 tbsp smoked paprika – picante or dolce
good glug of olive oil
½ butternut squash, about 1kg
1 x 400g tin of cooked butter beans, or any other cooked white beans
200g cherry vine tomatoes, or plum vine tomatoes
handful of Greek basil or Italian basil, roughly chopped

23

I'm not really an offal fan, but I adore this chicken liver pâté! I first tasted it on a crostini while in Castellina in Chianti many years ago, and was totally inspired. Here is my version of that dreamy dish. < SERVES 4 >

TUSCAN CHICKEN LIVER PÂTÉ WITH FRESH FIGS

500g chicken livers, trimmed of membranes

sea salt and black pepper

4 tbsp olive oil

1 small red onion, finely chopped

4 salted anchovies, finely chopped

225ml red wine

1 tbsp good-quality red wine vinegar, preferably Cabernet Sauvignon

TO SERVE

200ml Cabernet Sauvignon vinegar (optional)

4 slices rosemary or plain ciabatta

drizzle of extra virgin olive oil

handful of rocket leaves

2 fresh figs, cut into 8

Season the chicken livers with sea salt and black pepper. Heat half the olive oil in a large frying pan and gently cook the livers for 2–3 minutes. Remove the livers and set aside.

Heat the remaining olive oil in the same pan and cook the onion until soft. Add the anchovies and red wine and simmer until reduced and syrupy.

Put the livers and the onion mixture in a blender and whizz with the vinegar until almost smooth; season with salt and pepper and then refrigerate until required.

To make a Cabernet Sauvignon syrup, if using, pour the vinegar into a small pan and heat gently until reduced to a syrup (about 3–5 minutes). Store at room temperature.

Drizzle the ciabatta with olive oil, place on a hot griddle pan and cook until crisp on both sides.

To serve, spread the pâté on to the ciabatta slices, top with a few rocket leaves and scatter with figs, then drizzle with olive oil and the Cabernet Sauvignon syrup.

VARIATIONS

- Try adding some garlic and sage to your pâté and serve with fried fresh porcinis instead of figs – just as gorgeous!

One of my all-time favourite ways to cook duck legs! A perfect dinner party dish as you can prepare it up to three days ahead. You can buy the more unusual Asian ingredients over the internet. < SERVES 4 >

RED BRAISED DUCK LEGS

FOR THE BRAISING LIQUOR
120ml light soy sauce

180ml Shaoxing

150g yellow rock sugar

2 strips dried orange peel, or dried mandarin rind, if you have it

1 red chilli, pointed end slit with a sharp knife

2cm ginger, finely sliced

1 stick cassia bark

2 star anise

4 duck legs, about 300g each

FOR THE SAUCE
200g mixed mushrooms, such as king oysters, shimejis, oysters

3 tbsp sesame oil

2 garlic cloves, finely chopped

2 banana shallots, thinly sliced

2cm piece of fresh ginger, peeled and finely chopped

1 red chilli, finely sliced

1 small bunch coriander, finely chopped

TO SERVE
cooked rice

Pickled Enoki (recipe #106) – optional

few leaves Thai basil (optional)

4 baby bok choy, blanched

Place all the braising ingredients except for the duck legs in a deep, large saucepan with 1 litre water. Bring to a boil, reduce the heat and simmer for 15 minutes. Meanwhile, put the duck legs in a separate pan, pour over boiling water and leave for 5 minutes – this will help to remove any blood and excess fat. Drain, then add the duck legs to the red braise and bring back to the boil. Reduce the heat until simmering. Cover the duck with a circle of parchment paper, and place a plate on top that just fits inside the pan. This stops the duck from bobbing up, cooking it evenly (the paper protects the plate from staining). Cook until tender (about 2–2½ hours). Remove duck legs and set aside.

Strain the duck cooking liquor through a sieve into a large jug or pot. If you are planning on making this in advance, leave the cooking liquor to cool before refrigerating. The next day a layer of fat will have set on the surface. If making straight away, ladle off the fat from the surface and continue with the sauce.

Prepare the mushrooms as follows: shiitakes should be destemmed and quartered; larger oysters torn gently in two (leave smaller oysters whole); and shimejis broken up gently from their clumped base. Heat the oil in a wok and, when hot, add the garlic, shallots, ginger and chilli. Stir-fry for 1 minute or so. Add the mushrooms to the wok, give them a quick stir, then add the duck legs and strained red braising liquor. Simmer for 10 minutes or until the duck legs are hot and the mushrooms are tender.

Stir in the coriander and pour into deep bowls. Serve with rice topped with Pickled Enoki, Thai basil and blanched bok choy. Provide some spoons for all that gorgeous liquor!

VARIATIONS

• Make the meal more hearty by adding thin slices of sweet potato or squash while making the sauce.

26

A delicious warming, fragrant and fruity curry. If you don't fancy making your own curry paste, substitute with 2 tablespoons of Thai red curry paste, or even green, and cook as per the recipe. < SERVES 4 >

#9

DUCK, PINEAPPLE AND COCONUT CURRY

Heat the oil in a wok, season the duck with sea salt and pepper and cook over a high heat until browned all over. Pour off any excess fat and set the duck pieces aside.

To make the curry paste, pound or blend all the ingredients together to make a fine paste.

To make the curry, remove the top thick layer of cream from unshaken cans of coconut milk and place this in the wok. When hot, stir in the curry paste and cook for about 2–3 minutes or until fragrant (you are using the coconut 'cream' to fry the paste – something I learnt in Thailand). Keep stirring, so the paste doesn't burn. Then add the rest of the coconut milk along with 300ml water and bring to the boil. Add the seared duck and reduce the heat to a simmer. Cover and cook over a low heat for about 40 minutes or until the duck is tender. Remove the duck and set aside while you finish the curry.

Skim off any excess fat and add the lime leaves, palm sugar and pineapple. Simmer for another 10 minutes or until just warmed through. Finish with fish sauce and coriander.

Slice the duck breasts and divide between four deep bowls. Top with curry sauce and scatter with sliced chilli and Thai basil leaves. Serve with lime quarters on the side along with some steamed rice.

VARIATIONS

- Why not create with flavour by introducing some tamarind?
- Omit the pineapple and use lychees instead.
- For a quick supper, use a pre-cooked Chinese-style duck and warm through in the curry.

4 duck breasts, fat lightly scored
sea salt and black pepper

FOR THE CURRY PASTE
4 red bird's eye chillies
2 shallots, finely sliced
3 garlic cloves, finely chopped
3cm piece of ginger or galangal, peeled and thinly sliced
2 sticks lemongrass, finely chopped
2 lime leaves, finely chopped
6 coriander roots, finely chopped (use ½ bunch fresh coriander if roots unavailable)
1 tbsp coriander seeds, toasted
1 tsp cardamom pods
1 tsp cumin seeds, toasted
1 tsp sea salt
1 tsp green peppercorns, or a little freshly ground pepper

FOR THE CURRY
3 x 400ml cans unsweetened coconut milk
2 lime leaves
2 tbsp palm sugar
500g fresh pineapple, diced
2 tbsp fish sauce
½ bunch coriander, leaves picked
1 green or red chilli, finely sliced
handful of Thai basil leaves
1 lime, cut into quarters

27

Sausage rolls are back in fashion! I wanted to cook a version that used some of my favourite Middle Eastern ingredients and take sausage rolls right out of their box!

< MAKES 2 LARGE SAUSAGE ROLLS OR LOTS OF SMALL ONES >

DUCK SAUSAGE ROLLS WITH A TWIST

Preheat the oven to 200°C/gas mark 6.

Combine all the filling ingredients and season with sea salt and black pepper. Fry off a teaspoon of the mixture to check the seasoning.

Roll the puff pastry out to about 5mm thickness, and cut into two long strips, each about 7cm wide. Divide the filling mixture in two and form into a long sausage down the centre of each strip of pastry – this should be about 2cm wide and 2cm high.

Brush one edge of each strip with a little water and carefully roll the pastry over the filling to create your sausage rolls. Press the sides together to ensure they are joined. You can either leave the rolls whole or cut into portions as shown in the picture.

Brush each roll with egg and sprinkle with seeds. Arrange on a non-stick baking tray and cook for 20–25 minutes until golden.

For the salsa, mix all the ingredients together in a small bowl and serve with the sausage rolls.

FOR THE FILLING

1–2 duck legs, meat removed and minced, or 350g minced duck

2 garlic cloves, finely chopped

1½ tsp ground cumin

½ tsp ground cinnamon

½ tsp ground coriander

½ tsp paprika

pinch of nutmeg

pinch of ground ginger

1 small red chilli, deseeded and finely chopped

small bunch coriander, finely chopped

30g pine kernels, toasted

glug of pomegranate molasses

½ Granny Smith apple, grated

1 small carrot, grated

3 Medjool dates, pitted and finely chopped

sea salt and black pepper

500g puff pastry

1 egg, beaten, to glaze

2 tbsp sesame seeds, hemp seeds or linseeds

FOR THE SALSA

200g cherry tomatoes, chopped

seeds of ½ pomegranate

handful chopped mint leaves

1 carrot, grated

splash of olive oil

splash of red wine vinegar

One of my favourite winter risottos. Italian sausages are made up of pork, spiked with fennel seeds and have the perfect proportion of fat content. If you can't get hold of them, use cooking chorizo instead. < SERVES 4–6 >

ITALIAN SAUSAGE, RED WINE, CHESTNUT AND CABBAGE RISOTTO

275g Italian pork sausages

2 tbsp olive oil

50g unsalted butter

2 banana shallots or
1 onion, finely chopped

400g Arborio rice

200ml red wine

50g cooked chestnuts

2.2 litres hot chicken stock

250g shredded cabbage or
spring greens, pre-blanched

100g Parmesan, finely grated

2–3 tbsp mascarpone

sea salt and black pepper

Remove the skin from the sausages and tear into small pieces. Heat the oil in a pan and fry half the sausage meat until crusty and golden, then drain off the oil and set aside.

Melt the butter in a heavy-based pan, then gently fry the shallots or onion and remaining sausage until softened, but not brown. Add the rice and, using a wooden spoon, toss well until the rice is coated in the buttery shallots and sausage fat. Pour in the wine and allow to evaporate completely before adding the chestnuts and stock.

Add the hot stock to the rice, a ladleful or two at a time, stirring over a medium heat until absorbed. After about 15 minutes, add the pre-cooked sausage and the blanched cabbage.

Continue to cook until the rice is al dente – about 3 minutes. Turn off the heat, add the Parmesan and mascarpone, season with salt and pepper to taste and stir through. Serve drizzled with olive oil.

VARIATIONS

- Add some griddled radicchio, doused with a little balsamic vinegar.
- If you're feeling adventurous, try making this risotto with the cooking juices from a slow-braised oxtail. It's divine tossed with the shredded meat and with a squeeze of lemon to cut through the richness.
- Try using peas or soy beans instead of cabbage or spring greens.

Inspired by Nigella's coke-cooked ham, this warming ginger-beer spiced, sticky ham is great for entertaining as it's easily prepared in advance; and is sure to wow your guests! < SERVES 8 >

GINGER BEER AND TANGERINE GLAZED HAM

Put the gammon, onion, tangerine zest and star anise in a large saucepan. Pour over the ginger beer and top up with water, if necessary, so that the gammon is just covered. Bring to the boil, skim the surface and reduce the heat to a simmer. Cover and cook for 2–2½ hours, until the meat is tender. Leave to cool in the cooking liquor.

Preheat the oven to 220°C/gas mark 7.

Remove the joint from the pan, setting aside the cooking liquor for the lentils. Once cool enough to handle, carefully cut the skin off the ham, making sure to leave a layer of fat. Lightly score the fat into diamond shapes. Line a roasting tin with foil and place the joint on top.

To make the glaze, warm the honey, mustard and ginger beer in a pan and boil until thickened. Spoon over the fat, then stud a clove into the middle of each diamond and bake for 20–25 minutes or until the glaze has caramelised. (You could prepare the ham in advance and finish in the oven at a later stage; if so, remove from the fridge, bring up to room temperature, cover with glaze and increase the above cooking time by 10 minutes.)

Leave to cool before slicing. Make sure you skim off the excess fat before using the liquor for the lentils. The best way to do this if you're using immediately is to add a few ice cubes. The fat will congeal and you can ladle the majority off. Alternatively, cool then refrigerate overnight so the fat settles on the top.

2kg mild-cure gammon
1 onion, halved
zest of 4 tangerines, removed with a vegetable peeler (set aside the juice for the lentils)
4 whole star anise
1.9 litres ginger beer

FOR THE GLAZE
4 tbsp honey
2 tbsp wholegrain mustard
100ml ginger beer
handful of cloves

Chilli and Tangerine Braised Lentils, to serve (recipe #53)

VARIATIONS

- Serve hot or cold. Spice it all up with some additional red chilli.
- Try poaching a whole chicken or duck in the liquor. Brisket of beef or short ribs would also be great cooked in this way.

#13

Overlooked and inexpensive, pork shanks are delicious slow braised with punchy Moroccan spices – ideal for a winter's supper. Inspired by my Moroccan travels.

< SERVES 4 >

MOROCCAN BRAISED PORK SHANKS

FOR THE SPICE PASTE MARINADE

3 garlic cloves, finely chopped

3 cardamom pods

2 tsp coriander seeds

4cm piece of fresh ginger, grated

pinch of saffron strands

1 tbsp sea salt

1 tbsp ground cumin

1 tbsp sweet paprika

2 tsp chilli powder

4 tbsp olive oil

4 small pork hocks, skin removed

FOR THE PORK CASSEROLE

1 onion, diced

2 carrots, diced

1 fennel bulb, diced

1 green chilli, seeds removed, finely chopped

1 large cinnamon stick

1 x 400g can tomatoes, chopped

1 tbsp clear honey

4 strips orange zest

1 litre chicken stock

1 x 400g can cooked chickpeas

1 small bunch coriander, chopped

½ bunch flatleaf parsley, chopped

1 tbsp mint leaves, chopped

sea salt and black pepper

lemon juice, to taste

Using a pestle and mortar, crush the garlic, cardamom and coriander seeds with the ginger, saffron and salt. Add the remaining spices and a little olive oil to form a paste. Rub the paste all over the pork hocks, cover and chill for several hours (overnight if possible).

Preheat the oven to 190°C/gas mark 5.

Heat the remaining olive oil in a roasting tin or casserole dish over a medium heat, and brown the hocks on all sides. Remove from the tin and set aside.

Add the onion, carrots, fennel and chilli to the pan and cook until lightly coloured. Return the ham hocks to the tin, then add the cinnamon, tomatoes, honey, orange zest and chicken stock. Cover the tin with foil and transfer to the oven.

Cook for 1½–2 hours. Add the chickpeas, and cook for a further 30 minutes or until the meat is very tender. Remove the hocks and keep warm. Pour the cooking juices into a saucepan and skim off any surface fat. Simmer the sauce until it has reduced by one quarter. Add the fresh herbs and season to taste with salt and pepper. Add a little lemon juice to taste. Serve with couscous.

This gorgeous Tuscan dish is traditionally made using pork loin, but I prefer using pork belly. The slow roasting and aromatic herbs make it deliciously tender and fragrant. The perfect meal for a lazy Sunday. < SERVES 4–6 >

PORCHETTA WITH ROSEMARY ROASTED POTATOES

Preheat the oven to 200°C/gas mark 6.

To make the porchetta, lay the pork belly skin-side up on a clean, flat surface. Score the pork fat and remove any excess (a craft knife is perfect for this). Crush the garlic in a large pestle and mortar with a good pinch of sea salt, add the fennel seeds, anchovies and sage and bruise.

Transfer to a bowl, and add the rosemary, chilli flakes, lemon zest, capers, olive oil, a good grinding of black pepper and mix. Flip the pork over, so it is skin-side down, then smear the herb and caper mix evenly over it. Set aside to rest for 10 minutes to allow the flavours to develop.

Now you need to carefully roll the meat up widthways and tie it very tightly in the middle of the belly. Continue to tie at 2cm intervals. If any filling escapes just push it back in! Rub a little oil over the joint and season with some sea salt and pepper. Cut the carrot and onion into quarters, place in a roasting tin and put the pork on top. The carrot and onion will act as a trivet and stop the pork from sticking to the tin. Roast for 20 minutes, then cover with foil and reduce the oven temperature to 150°C/gas mark 2. Add the water or stock and cook for 2½ hours.

Start to prepare the potatoes around 50 minutes before the end of the pork's cooking time. Place the potatoes in a pan, add a pinch of salt and cover with water. Bring to the boil and simmer for 10 minutes. Pour into a colander, drain and shake until the potatoes are 'fluffy'. Heat the oil in a roasting tin, then carefully add the potatoes, season with sea salt and add the rosemary. Allow the potatoes to colour a little in the tin, then shake again.

Remove the pork from the oven and set aside in a warm place to rest. Meanwhile, turn the oven up to 200°C/gas mark 6 and cook the potatoes for about 25 minutes, until crisp, while resting the pork.

Heat the pork roasting tin on the hob. Scrape off any caramelised pieces and pour the cooking juices into a jug. Slice the pork carefully, removing the string, and serve with rosemary roasted potatoes and the pork juices.

FOR THE PORCHETTA

1.5kg boneless pork belly
3 garlic cloves
sea salt and black pepper
3 tsp fennel seeds
10 salted anchovies, finely chopped (optional)
½ bunch sage leaves, picked and roughly chopped
2 sprigs of rosemary, picked and chopped
pinch of chilli flakes
zest of ½ lemon
50g capers, rinsed and roughly chopped
1 tbsp olive oil
1 carrot
1 onion
250ml stock or water

FOR THE POTATOES

800g Desirée potatoes, peeled and cut into 3–4cm pieces
sea salt
4 tbsp olive oil
2 sprigs of rosemary, picked

#15

A quick and easy recipe - comforting and bursting with flavour. Experiment with alternative ingredients by using a different meat and fruit pairing - for example you could try lamb with prunes. < SERVES 4 >

SAUSAGE AND BUTTERNUT SQUASH TAGINE

8 Cumberland or 12 merguez sausages

2 tbsp olive oil

1 small onion, finely chopped

2 garlic cloves, finely chopped

pinch of saffron

3 tsp ground cumin

1 tsp ground ginger

2 tsp paprika

2 tsp coriander seeds, crushed

2 x 400g cans chopped tomatoes

300g butternut squash, peeled and diced into about 2cm cubes

1 red chilli, split lengthways

1 cinnamon stick

2 tbsp honey

sea salt and black pepper

100g green pitted olives (optional)

½ preserved lemon, (optional), finely chopped

30g bunch coriander, finely chopped

FOR THE COUSCOUS

300g instant couscous

50g butter, diced

4 tsp finely grated orange zest

sea salt

4 tsp finely chopped green chillies

chopped coriander

Remove the skin from the sausages and roll the meat into balls (a little smaller than golf balls).

Heat half the olive oil in a large pan, add the meatballs and cook over a medium heat for about 5 minutes or until browned. Set aside.

Heat the remaining oil and fry the onion gently until softened. Add the garlic and spices and cook for a further minute until aromatic.

Stir in the tomatoes, squash, chilli, cinnamon stick and honey, season with salt and pepper and cook over a medium heat for 5 minutes. Add sausage meatballs and continue to cook for a further 25 minutes, adding a little boiling water if the tagine looks a little dry.

While the tagine is cooking, prepare the couscous. Put the couscous, butter, orange zest and a pinch of salt into a bowl. Pour over 300ml boiling water, cover the bowl with clingfilm and leave for 2–3 minutes to steam. Remove the clingfilm, fluff up the grains with a fork and stir in the chilli and coriander.

To serve, stir in the olives and preserved lemon, if using, into the tagine and sprinkle with the chopped coriander. Accompany with the warm couscous.

Anise has a natural affinity for pork. Fennel and fennel seeds accentuate the pork's meatiness and add depth of flavour to complement the rich, slow roasted pork belly. Tomato lifts the flavour with an acidic hit. < SERVES 4 >

SPICED PORK BELLY WITH FENNEL PURÉE AND FENNEL AND TOMATO SALAD

Preheat the oven to 200°C/gas mark 6.

Place the pork on a work surface, skin-side up, and use a clean craft knife to score lines into the pork rind, about 1cm apart. Cut through the skin into the fat, but not into the meat. (You can ask your butcher to do this for you). Mix together the fennel and coriander seeds, 1 tablespoon sea salt and the paprika. Rub this all over the skin, pushing it deep into the scored fat. Place the vegetables and thyme in a roasting tin and place the pork on top, skin-side up. Add half the stock and place in the oven. Roast for about 30 minutes, until the skin of the pork has started to turn into crackling.

Meanwhile, prepare the fennel for the purée. Cut the bulbs in half lengthways, then remove and discard the outer layer and core. Place the fennel and garlic on a piece of foil, drizzle with half the oil, sprinkle with salt and form a loose parcel. Place on a baking tray. When the pork has been in for half an hour, reduce the heat to 180°C/gas mark 4. Add the remaining liquid to the meat and place the fennel parcel on another shelf in the oven. Roast for a further hour, until the fennel is tender.

Remove the pork from the oven and rest for 10 minutes. Pass the juices through a fine sieve and skim off any excess fat.

Place the cooked fennel and garlic in a blender. Add the lemon juice, the rest of the olive oil and 2 tablespoons pork cooking liquor. Blend until smooth, then season to taste.

While the pork is resting, make the salad. Cut the fennel in half lengthways, remove and discard the outer layer and core. Thinly slice the bulb horizontally. Place in a bowl with the tomatoes and any wispy fennel tops. Crush the garlic with 1 teaspoon sea salt. Whisk the garlic, vinegar and oils together and pour over salad, toss with some salt and pepper.

Cut the pork lengthways into about 2cm strips and serve on top of the purée, with the salad.

1kg boneless pork belly, skin on
2 tbsp fennel seeds
1 tbsp coriander seeds
1 tbsp sea salt
2 tsp sweet smoked paprika
2 carrots, peeled and halved lengthways
2 celery sticks, halved
1 onion, cut into thin wedges
4 garlic cloves, unpeeled
few sprigs of fresh thyme
700ml chicken stock

FOR THE PURÉE
2 fennel bulbs
1 garlic clove
sea salt
2 tbsp olive oil
juice of ½ lemon

FOR THE SALAD
1 fennel bulb
200g cherry vine tomatoes, halved
100g yellow cherry vine tomatoes, halved
1 garlic clove
sea salt
4 tsp red wine vinegar
8 tsp olive oil
1 small bunch watercress, picked into sprigs

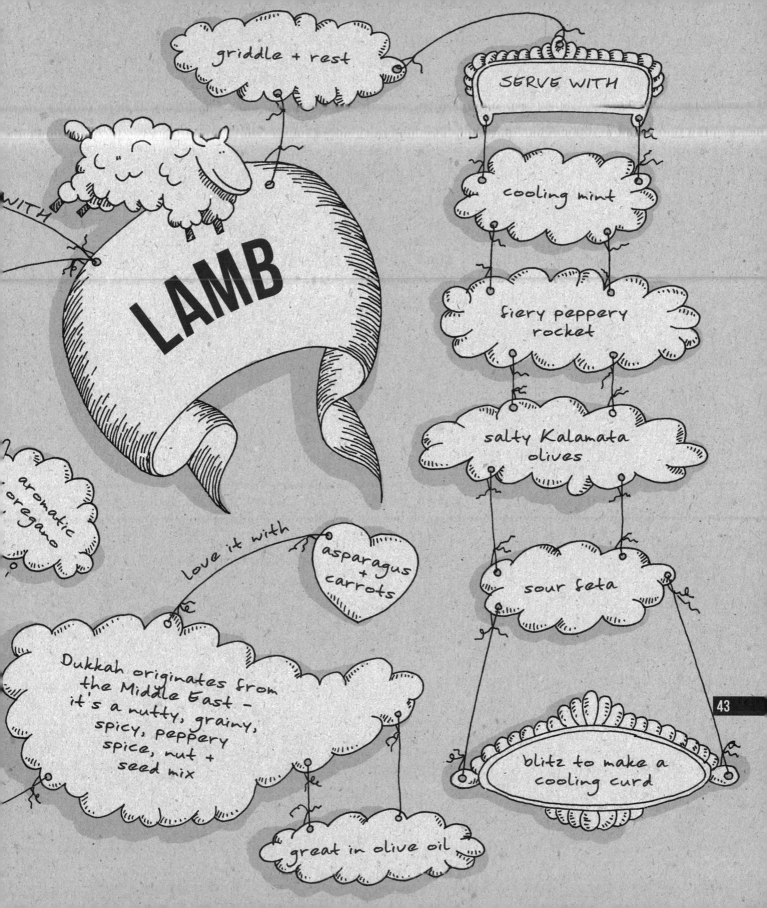

#17

A childhood favourite — lamb meatballs combined with a hint of spice, gently cooked with Dino's Greek peas, tomatoes and unconventional mashed potatoes makes this a super cosy sofa supper. < SERVES 4 >

COSY LAMB MEATBALLS WITH PEAS AND TOMATO SAUCE

FOR THE MEATBALLS
500g lamb mince
2 garlic cloves, crushed
pinch of cayenne pepper
2 tsp ground cumin
1 tsp ground cinnamon
1 tsp paprika
1 tsp turmeric
flour, for dusting
4 tbsp olive oil

FOR THE PEA AND TOMATO SAUCE
2 tbsp olive oil
1 small onion, finely chopped
2 garlic cloves, finely chopped
1 tbsp tomato purée
1 tsp ground cinnamon
1 x 400g can plum tomatoes, crushed
pinch of sugar
1 chicken stock cube
100g frozen petit pois
1 tbsp dried dill
sea salt
½ bunch mint, finely chopped

To make the meatballs, simply mix all the ingredients except the flour and oil together and form into balls. Dust the balls in flour. Heat half the oil in a frying pan and add the meatballs. Cook over a medium heat for 5 minutes. Cook until the meatballs are medium-rare in the centre (about 3 minutes, depending on the size).Then set aside and repeat with the remaining oil and meatballs.

For the sauce, heat the oil in a saucepan and gently cook the onion and garlic until softened. Add the tomato purée and cinnamon and cook for a couple more minutes. Add the tomatoes and sugar and crumble in the stock cube. Bring to the boil, then simmer for 5 minutes. Add the peas and dill along with 200ml water and cook for 15 minutes over a low heat. Add the meatballs and cook for a further 15 minutes, adding a little boiling water if the sauce is a little thick. Season with sea salt, stir in the mint and serve with mashed potatoes.

VARIATIONS

- Serve with flatbread and sprinkle with crumbled feta.
- For an Asian twist, swap the meatball spices for ground ginger, cumin, coriander, a pinch of chilli flakes and turmeric. Omit the cinnamon and the dried dill from the sauce and add some freshly chopped ginger, then finish with chopped coriander and lemongrass.

44

#18

My flatmate and I have an annual summer barbecue. We often get emails from friends asking when it will be so they can plan their holidays around it! This recipe is one of the main reasons they turn up. < SERVES 4–6 >

DILL AND LEMON MARINATED LAMB

3 garlic cloves

3 tbsp sea salt

1 bunch dill, finely chopped, with stalks

6 tbsp olive oil

zest and juice of 2 lemons

1kg boneless leg of lamb, cut into muscle steaks (follow the natural seams in the boneless joint and cut into pieces – you will probably end up with about 4)

Lemon and Dill Braised Broad Beans (recipe #70), to serve (optional)

Pound the garlic and sea salt in a pestle and mortar to form a paste. Transfer to a bowl and mix with the dill, olive oil, lemon zest and juice.

Trim each lamb steak of excess fat and remove any visible sinew. Smear the garlic paste all over lamb and leave to marinate for at least 3 hours or, preferably, overnight in the refrigerator.

Bring the lamb back up to room temperature before cooking to ensure it cooks evenly.

Preheat a griddle or barbecue. Drain and lift the meat out of the marinade and shake off and set aside any excess. Place on the hot griddle or barbecue and cook for about 5 minutes on each side. You can use the excess marinade to baste the lamb while it's cooking.

Set the lamb aside for 10 minutes to rest before slicing. Serve warm with Lemon and Dill Braised Broad Beans.

VARIATIONS

- This is also delicious served with flatbread and Greek yogurt or labneh.
- Create with flavour by varying the marinade ingredients – oregano also complements lemon, as do tarragon and mint.

46

Three of my favourite ingredients in one hit: lamb, feta and watermelon. Juicy medium-rare lamb is marinated in earthy cinnamon with a touch of oregano (keeping it Greek). The dukkah spice mix adds crunch. < SERVES 4 >

DUKKAH ROLLED LAMB, FETA MIND CURD, WATERMELON AND OLIVES

Combine the marinade ingredients, rub all over the lamb necks and leave to marinate for at least 30 minutes, or overnight in the refrigerator. Remove from the fridge 30 minutes before cooking, allowing it to come back to room temperature.

Preheat the oven to 200°C/gas mark 6.

Season the lamb fillets with sea salt, preheat a griddle pan and, once hot, brown the fillets all over. Transfer to an oven tray and roast for 6 minutes, until cooked but still pink. Remove from the oven.

Sprinkle some dukkah on a plate and roll each fillet to coat. Cover loosely with foil and leave to rest for 10 minutes before carving into 5mm slices.

To make the feta mint curd, place the yogurt, feta and garlic in a food-processor. Whizz until smooth, then drizzle in the olive oil, stir in the mint and refrigerate until required. You can make this the day before.

To serve, spread the feta mint curd over the watermelon, top with olives and a few rocket leaves and place the sliced lamb on top. Whisk together the oil and Cabernet Sauvignon vinegar and drizzle over the lamb. Serve immediately.

VARIATIONS

- This is equally delicious with a piece of rare tuna (no need to marinate). It's up to you whether you want to include the dukkah.
- For a vegetarian version, roll the watermelon in the dukkah and top with feta mint curd, olives, rocket leaves, tomatoes, cooked chickpeas and some chopped spring onions.

FOR THE MARINADE
zest of 1 lemon

2 tbsp olive oil

3 tbsp clear honey

2 sprigs of oregano, leaves picked and finely chopped

1 tsp ground cinnamon

2 garlic cloves, crushed

8 tbsp Dukkah (recipe #58)

FOR THE LAMB
4 lamb neck fillets (180g each), trimmed

sea salt

FOR THE FETA MINT CURD
100g Greek yogurt

200g feta cheese, crumbled

1 garlic clove, crushed

1 tbsp extra virgin olive oil

2 tbsp chopped mint

TO SERVE
chilled seedless watermelon, cut into 4 blocks 15cm long, 5cm wide and 1.5cm deep

60g pitted Kalamata olives, roughly chopped

small handful of rocket leaves

3 tbsp extra virgin olive oil

2 tbsp Cabernet Sauvignon vinegar (if unavailable, use red wine vinegar)

47

Add a new dimension to a Sunday roast. Shoulder of lamb is an economical cut and is just right for slow roasting. Minimum preparation that produces maximum results! You'll need some butcher's twine for this recipe. < SERVES 6–8 >

SLOW-ROASTED SHOULDER OF LAMB WITH FENNEL SAUSAGE STUFFING

To make the stuffing, heat half the oil in a frying pan, add the onion and garlic and sauté over a low heat until it begins to caramelise (10–15 minutes). Remove from the heat and transfer to a bowl. Add the fennel seeds and chilli flakes and stir through the breadcrumbs. Leave to cool. Add the sausage meat, season with sea salt and pepper and mix well.

Preheat the oven to 200°C/gas mark 6.

Place the lamb skin-side down on a board and season with sea salt and black pepper. Spread over the stuffing, roll up tightly, secure with twine and place in a roasting tin with 300ml water. Rub with the remaining oil and season. Roast for 20 minutes, then reduce the heat to 180°C/gas mark 4 and cook for 1½–2 hours, basting occasionally with any juices. Remove the lamb from the oven, cover with foil and leave to rest for at least 20 minutes.

For the wilted greens, halve the fennel lengthways, remove the core and slice across as thinly as possible. Heat half the oil in a large frying pan, add the fennel and garlic and cook until tender. Set aside. Return the pan to the heat and add a dash more oil, plus half the mixed greens. Leave to wilt a little, toss with salt and pepper and set aside. Repeat with the remaining greens, then return the cooked greens and fennel to the pan, adjust the seasoning and stir in the lemon juice.

Remove the twine from the lamb and carve into slices. Serve with the wilted greens and drizzle with the lamb cooking juices.

VARIATIONS

- Delicious served with Warm Chickpea Purée (recipe #104), or Spinach with Garlic, Raisins and Pine Nuts (recipe #69) instead of wilted greens.

1 boneless shoulder of lamb, 1.75–2kg

FOR THE STUFFING
4 tbsp olive oil
1 onion, finely chopped
2 garlic cloves, finely chopped
2 tsp fennel seeds
pinch of chilli flakes
180g coarse fresh breadcrumbs
500g fennel or merguez sausages, skins removed
sea salt and black pepper

FOR THE WILTED GREENS
2 fennel bulbs
4 tbsp olive oil
2 garlic cloves
1kg mixed green leaves (such as spinach, rocket, dandelion and chard)
sea salt and black pepper
juice of 1 lemon

49

This dish takes me right back to my childhood, as my mum used to make it frequently. It's a delicious way to prepare lamb, inspired by my dad's Greek Cypriot way of braising meat in a rich, tomatoey sauce. < SERVES 4 >

BRAISED SCRAG END OF LAMB
WITH RUNNER BEANS AND TOMATOES

3 garlic cloves, finely chopped

2 tsp sea salt

zest of ½ lemon

4 tbsp olive oil

1kg scrag end of neck of lamb, on the bone or chops

1 onion, finely chopped

1 celery stick, finely chopped

4 tsp tomato purée

6 fresh tomatoes, skinned and roughly chopped, or 1 x 400g can plum tomatoes, chopped

1 litre chicken stock

½ tsp sea salt and black pepper

1 fresh bay leaf

3cm cinnamon stick

400g medium-sized potatoes, peeled and quartered

4 tbsp parsley, chopped

2 tbsp dill, chopped

300g runner beans, sliced

Crush 2 of the garlic cloves with 2 teaspoons of sea salt to form a paste. Mix with lemon zest, half the olive oil and rub all over the lamb. Marinate for 1 hour or overnight.

Heat the remaining olive oil in a pan large enough to hold the lamb and potatoes. Once hot, brown the lamb in batches and set aside.

Add the onion, remaining garlic and the celery to the pan and cook until softened before adding the tomato purée. Cook for a further minute, before adding the tomatoes and chicken stock. Bring to the boil and season with salt and pepper. Add the bay leaf, cinnamon stick and the lamb. Cover and simmer for 1 hour.

Now add the potatoes, simmer for 20 minutes uncovered before adding half the parsley, the dill and the runner beans. Simmer for a further 15 minutes, until the beans and potatoes are tender.

Serve in deep bowls, sprinkled with the remaining parsley. This dish tastes even better the day after it's made.

50

slow-braise to tenderise until it melts in the mouth – mmmm

has an open, grainy texture

...and the cow

BRISKET

take it on an Asian adventure – braise in ginger, garlic, warming cinnamon, star anise, chilli, soy sauce, shaoxing and dried orange peel

forgotten cuts

oxtail

beef cheeks

= one aromatic, mouth-watering, delicious supper of melting beef

I love tangy flavours and a bit of spice

LUCKY COW!

The combination of veal chops with creamy sage and onion polenta is just sublime! A hint of sweetness from the quince along with sharpness from the Manchego bring this whole dish together. < SERVES 4 >

#22

VEAL CHOP TOPPED WITH MELTED MANCHEGO AND QUINCE, WITH CREAMY SAGE AND ONION POLENTA

Crush the garlic and thyme in a pestle and mortar, mix with the olive oil and lemon zest and rub all over the veal chops. Marinate for 30 minutes or refrigerate overnight.

For the polenta, remove the stalks from the sage leaves and set aside; finely chop the leaves. Melt the butter in a large saucepan and add the onions and sage leaves. Cook over a low heat for about 30 minutes, or until the onions are soft and caramelised.

Meanwhile, heat the milk, 500ml water and the reserved sage stalks together. Once hot, fish out the sage stalks and discard. Add the nutmeg and slowly whisk in the polenta; cook according to packet instructions over a low heat, stirring constantly until thickened. You may need to add a little more hot water if the polenta seems too thick.

Remove from the heat and stir in the caramelised onions, mascarpone and seasoning to taste. Keep this warm while you are preparing the chops.

Preheat a griddle pan, season the chops and cook over a medium heat for 4–5 minutes on each side, depending on their thickness.

Top the chops with the slices of membrillo and Manchego and scatter with plenty of cracked black pepper and some thyme leaves. Place under a preheated grill or in the oven for 1–2 minutes, until golden and bubbling. Divide the polenta between four plates, place a chop on each and serve.

2 garlic cloves

3 tsp thyme leaves, plus
1 tsp for garnish

50ml olive oil

finely grated zest of 1 lemon

4 rose veal chops

120g membrillo (quince paste), thinly sliced

120g Manchego cheese, thinly sliced

cracked black pepper

FOR THE POLENTA

20 sage leaves, finely chopped and stalks reserved

100g butter

400g onions, thinly sliced

500ml milk

pinch of nutmeg

340g instant polenta

100g mascarpone

sea salt and black pepper

VARIATION

- Try topping the veal with a blue cheese, such as *blu di capra* (a delicate blue goat's cheese from Italy) instead of Manchego.

I'm such a snob when it comes to burgers, I'll admit. If I'm going to eat a burger, it's got to be top quality. I think this hits the mark for a great alternative to the traditional beef burger. < SERVES 4 >

VITELLO TONNATO BURGER

FOR THE BURGERS

640g best-quality minced rose veal

1 shallot, finely diced

50g capers, rinsed and roughly chopped

zest of 1 lemon

a handful of flatleaf parsley, finely chopped

sea salt and black pepper

drizzle of olive oil

4 ciabatta rolls, halved

1 bunch watercress, picked or 2 punnets mustard and cress

FOR THE TONNATO SAUCE

2 egg yolks

2 tbsp lemon juice

5 salted anchovy fillets, finely chopped

240ml olive oil

200g canned sustainable tuna in olive oil, drained

1 tbsp salted capers, rinsed

splash of white wine vinegar

squeeze of lemon juice

FOR THE CRISPY CAPERS

3 tbsp olive oil

2 tbsp capers, rinsed and dried

To make the burgers, mix together the veal, shallots, capers, lemon zest, parsley and olive oil. Season with pepper and a little salt (not too much – the capers are salty). Taste for seasoning – if you don't want to try the mix raw, fry off a teaspoon or so then taste. Divide the mixture into four and shape into balls. Refrigerate for up to 1 hour. Shape before shape into burgers about 5–6cm in diameter.

To make the sauce, whisk together the egg yolks, lemon juice and anchovies in a food-processor until smooth. Then, with the motor running, add the oil in a thin, steady stream. You can also do this by hand with a whisk. Add half the tuna and the capers. Pulse, just enough to combine, then fold through the remaining tuna. (If making by hand you may want to roughly chop the tuna and capers to break them down a little). Finish by whisking in a little vinegar and lemon juice to taste. Chill until required – the sauce will keep for up to three days in the refrigerator. (Note: traditionally, the sauce would be made with some of the veal cooking liquor and would use hard-boiled eggs. However, since the vitello in this case is a burger, we don't have any liquor! I apologise to all vitello tonnato purists out there.)

For the crispy capers, heat the oil in a small pan. Once hot, carefully add the capers and fry over a medium heat until crisp (1–2 minutes). Remove from the pan and drain on kitchen paper.

To cook the burgers, preheat a griddle pan or barbecue. Drizzle with olive oil and cook for 2–3 minutes on either side, depending on your preference.

Drizzle the ciabatta rolls with olive oil and lightly toast, then spread with tonnato sauce, layer with some watercress, or mustard and cress, and top with a burger. Garnish with crispy capers, if using. Serve with extra sauce on the side.

#24 I was introduced to Asian braising by my talented chef friend Kim. So underrated, slow braised brisket produces mouth watering results. Hopefully a recipe that will stay in your repertoire for a long time. < SERVES 4–6 >

ASIAN BRAISED BRISKET OF BEEF

1 piece brisket of beef, about 1.5kg

FOR THE BRAISE

150g yellow rock sugar (use palm sugar if unavailable)

4cm piece of fresh ginger, sliced

3 garlic cloves, peeled

2 red chillies, halved lengthways

2 cinnamon sticks

4 star anise

250ml soy sauce

250ml Shaoxing (use sherry if unavailable)

2 shallots, halved

2 pieces dried orange peel

FOR THE BRISKET SAUCE

2 tbsp peanut oil

2 shallots, finely chopped

3cm piece of fresh ginger, finely chopped

1 red chilli, finely chopped

1 garlic clove, finely chopped

6 coriander roots, finely chopped

50g yellow rock sugar

TO SERVE

2 tbsp chopped coriander

1 red chilli, finely sliced

jasmine rice and broccoli or bok choy

Place the brisket in a large pan of cold water, bring to the boil and then refresh under cold running water. Blanching the brisket like this removes the 'scum'. The brisket is now ready for braising.

Place all the ingredients for the braise in a large pot with 2.5 litres water and bring to the boil. Simmer for 20 minutes before adding the beef. Bring to the boil again then simmer, cover with parchment paper and weigh down with a plate that just fits inside the pan. This stops the brisket from bobbing up, cooking it evenly (the paper protects the plate from staining). Continue to cook for 2–3 hours until very tender. Remove the beef and set aside. Skim the fat from the surface and pass the stock through a fine sieve. Leave to cool.

For the sauce, heat the peanut oil in a saucepan, add the shallots, ginger, chilli, garlic and coriander roots and cook until softened. Add the sugar and 700ml of the reserved braising liquor and bring to the boil. Reduce the heat and simmer until reduced by two thirds.

Slice the beef into 2cm steaks and serve on deep plates, topped with lashings of sauce and sprinkled with coriander and red chilli, if desired. Serve with jasmine rice and broccoli or bok choy.

58

While watching early-morning TV in a hotel in Sydney, I saw an amazing meatloaf being cooked. I raced out of bed, grabbed a pen and paper and scribbled down as much as I could. Here's my version. < SERVES 4 (VERY GENEROUSLY) >

#25

MEATLOAF

Preheat the oven to 180°C/gas mark 4.

Cut a large piece of baking parchment and place on a work surface. Place a 21 x 11cm loaf or terrine tin on top and pen mark the length of the tin on the paper.

Lay the prosciutto slices on the baking parchment, overlapping them so as to fill the length of the tin without any gaps. Place the mint leaves on top, then lay the salami or chorizo slices down the centre.

Place the minced meats in a large bowl and mix with the onion, garlic, cheeses, breadcrumbs and herbs. Season with sea salt and black pepper.

Whisk together the mustard, eggs, Worcestershire, brown and sweet chilli sauces and pour over the meat. Mix until well combined. (I like to fry off a little at this stage, so I can check the mix for seasoning before cooking.)

Place the meat mixture (there is a lot of it, don't be concerned) on top of the salami slices and shape into a sausage. Using the parchment paper to help you, roll the meatloaf up into a tight roll. Discard the parchment paper and lay the bacon rashers on top of the roll.

Lay a large piece of clingfilm on the work surface and overlay with six more large pieces of clingfilm, each one slightly overlapping the last so as to form a large, thick piece of film that will encase the meatloaf. Place the meatloaf on top and roll up. Twist the ends in opposite directions and tie to secure. Slide the whole thing into the terrine or loaf tin, and then place that in a roasting tin. Pour about 4cm boiling water into the roasting tin and place in the oven (you are not cooking the meatloaf with direct heat so don't worry about leaving the clingfilm on!) Cook for 1½–1¾ hours.

To check if the meatloaf is done, place a skewer into the centre, press down to release the juices and make sure that they run clear. Remove from the oven and leave to cool for 30 minutes before transferring to a board. Cut one end of the film and pour the juices into a small bowl. Cut away the clingfilm and slice the meatloaf. Serve with creamy mash and a fresh tomato sauce.

8 slices of prosciutto

12 mint leaves

4 slices salami or chorizo

500g minced beef

250g minced pork

250g minced veal (substitute with more minced pork, if you wish)

1 large onion, finely chopped or grated

2 garlic cloves, finely chopped

200g applewood-smoked Cheddar, grated

40g Parmesan, finely grated

250g fresh breadcrumbs

1 tsp dried mint

2 tsp fresh thyme leaves

handful of flatleaf parsley, finely chopped

sea salt and black pepper

1 tbsp Dijon mustard

2 eggs

1 tbsp Worcestershire sauce

2 tbsp brown sauce

2 tbsp sweet chilli sauce or ketchup

6 rashers smoked streaky bacon

This dish brings back fond memories of my time spent working in Tuscany. Tagliata literally means 'to slice'. In Tuscany, they usually make this with sirloin or fillet; personally, I think rib eye works just as well. < SERVES 4 >

TAGLIATA WITH GREEN TOMATOES, OREGANO AND MUSTARD

To prepare the tomatoes, slice them 1cm thick. Gently heat the olive oil in a large frying pan, remove from heat, add the garlic and allow to warm through. Return the pan to the heat and add the tomatoes. Season with sea salt and cook over a low heat for 10 minutes. Add the remaining ingredients and simmer for a further 10–15 minutes, or until the tomatoes have softened but still hold their shape. They should be sweet, but slightly sour. You may need to do this in batches depending on how large your frying pan is.

To prepare the steaks, drizzle them with olive oil and mix together some salt, pepper and the rosemary and rub over the meat.

Preheat a griddle pan and briskly sear the steaks on either side for 2–3 minutes for a medium-rare result. Set aside to rest before slicing.

To serve, place the tomatoes on either individual plates or a large serving dish. Toss the rocket with the olive oil and place on top of the tomatoes. Slice the steak diagonally into 2cm pieces and loosely arrange over the rocket. Serve immediately, with shaved Parmesan, if desired.

400g green tomatoes, cores removed

3 tbsp olive oil

2 garlic cloves, finely chopped

sea salt

3 tsp chopped oregano leaves

pinch of chilli flakes

25–40g demerara sugar, to taste

3 tbsp Savora mustard (if unavailable, use 1½ tsp Dijon mustard)

75ml white wine or cider vinegar

FOR THE STEAKS

2 rib-eye steaks, about 275g each and 2cm thick

olive oil

sea salt and black pepper

leaves of 1 sprig of rosemary, finely chopped

2 handfuls of rocket leaves

shaved Parmesan (optional)

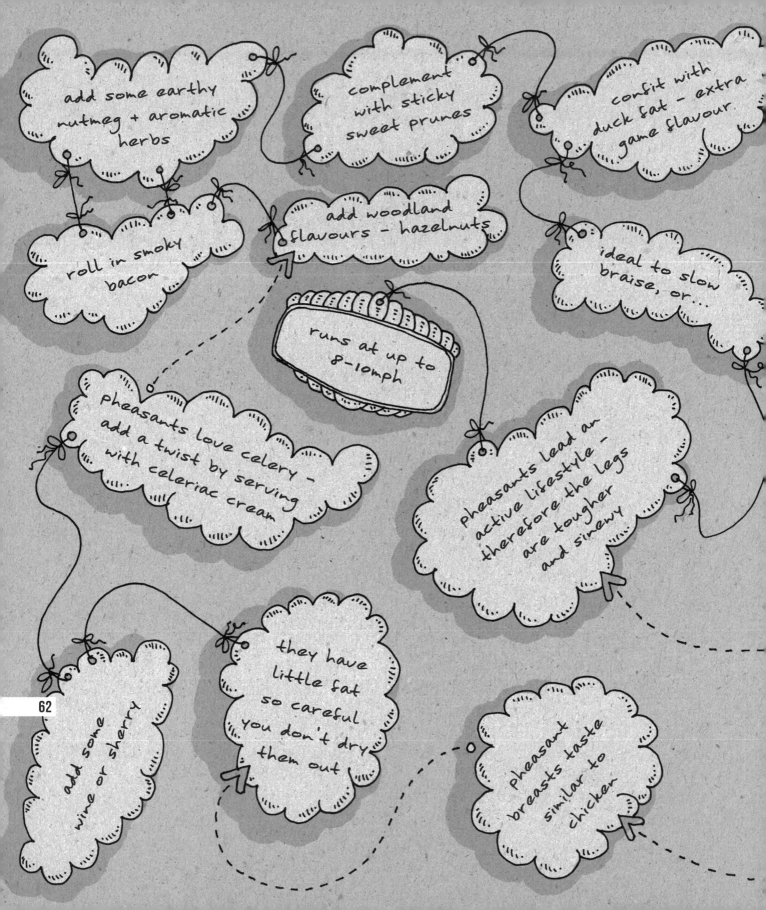

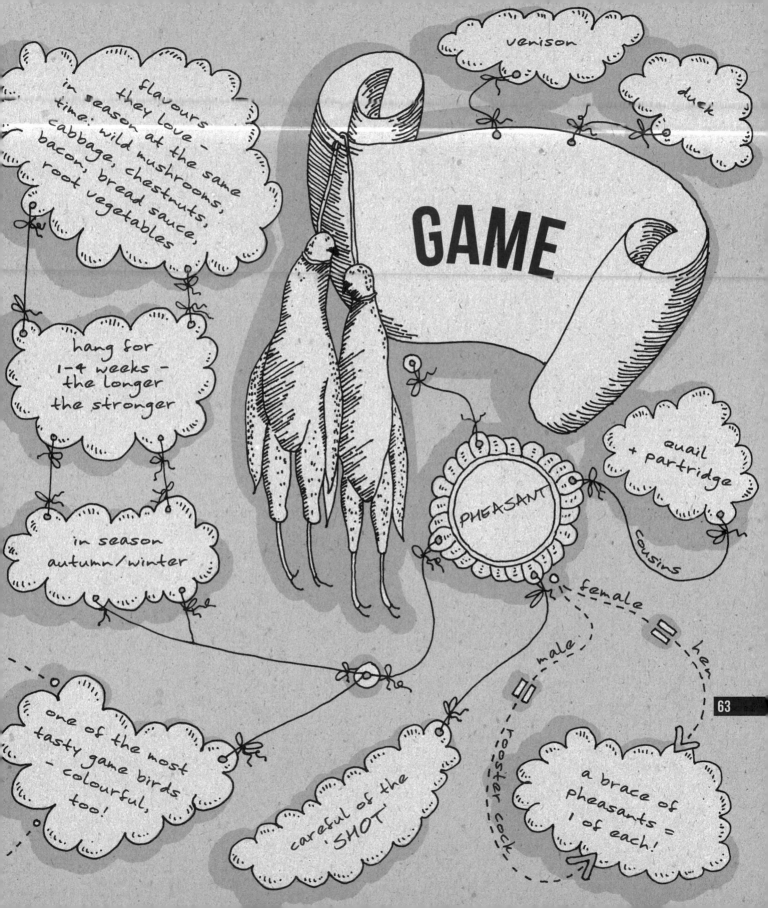

venison

duck

flavours they love – in season at the same time: wild mushrooms, cabbage, chestnuts, bacon, bread sauce, root vegetables

GAME

hang for 1-4 weeks – the longer the stronger

PHEASANT

quail + partridge

cousins

in season autumn/winter

female

her

one of the most tasty game birds – colourful, too!

careful of the SHOT

male

rooster cock

a brace of pheasants = 1 of each!

This traditional Tuscan soup is almost a stew; and since I'm not a traditionalist, I've added rabbit! If you have time, try to make the soup a day ahead to allow the flavours to infuse. < SERVES 4–6 >

RABBIT RIBOLLITA

75ml olive oil

sea salt and black pepper

2 rabbit legs

300g dried cannellini beans, soaked in cold water overnight and drained

1 bay leaf

2 small onions

2 celery sticks

2 carrots

2 garlic cloves, finely chopped

pinch of chilli flakes

2 heaped tbsp tomato purée

1 rind of Parmesan

400g plum vine tomatoes, peeled and chopped

1 bunch Swiss chard, leaves coarsely chopped or 300g cavolo nero leaves, torn

4 slices ciabatta

glug of extra virgin olive oil

shaved or grated Parmesan, to serve

In a large pan, heat a little of the olive oil, season the rabbit legs and sear on both sides until golden. Add the cannellini beans, bay leaf and enough water to cover. Add half an onion, 1 celery stick and 1 carrot chopped in half. Bring to the boil, reduce to a simmer and cook for 1 hour or until the beans and rabbit legs are both tender. Drain, setting aside the cooking liquor and discarding the bay leaf and vegetables. Meanwhile, finely chop the remaining onions, celery and carrot.

Heat the remaining oil in a large pan. Add the chopped vegetables, garlic and chilli flakes and cook over a low heat until tender, for about 15–20 minutes. Add the tomato purée and cook for 2 minutes, stirring over a medium heat. Add the beans, Parmesan rind and tomatoes along with 1 litre of the reserved cooking liquid; bring back to the boil then simmer for a further 20 minutes. Meanwhile, tear the meat from the rabbit legs and shred by hand. Set aside.

Remove the Parmesan rind and place in a blender along with a quarter of the soup and whizz to a smooth purée. Return to the pan along with the chard or cavolo nero leaves and cook for a further 20 minutes.

Season to taste with salt and pepper. The consistency should be stew like; if too thick, add a little more cooking liquor.

Drizzle the ciabatta slices with olive oil and cook on a griddle pan on each side until golden. Divide rabbit meat between preheated bowls, ladle over the hot soup and top with ciabatta, Parmesan and a good glug of olive oil.

VARIATIONS

- If rabbit's not your thing, use pancetta instead – cut into lardons and fry with the vegetables. Chorizo would also be a great alternative.

Gamey rabbit, succulent figs and rich flavourful porcinis: Oh my gosh, a feast for your senses on one plate! Rabbit is an underused meat that makes a great alternative to chicken. < SERVES 4 >

CHICKEN LIVER STUFFED RABBIT WITH CEP BRAISED BARLEY

FOR THE STUFFING

5 tbsp sweet sherry or vin santo

100g dried figs, finely chopped

4 tbsp olive oil

2 tsp fennel seeds

3 shallots, finely chopped

2 garlic cloves, finely chopped

25g pancetta, finely chopped

4 sage leaves, finely chopped

500g chicken livers

sea salt and black pepper

25g breadcrumbs

1 whole rabbit, deboned

sea salt and black pepper

2 tbsp olive oil

1 carrot, roughly chopped

1 onion, roughly chopped

1 celery stick, roughly chopped

700ml chicken or rabbit stock

100ml white or red wine

FOR THE CEP BRAISED BARLEY

1 litre chicken stock

30g dried ceps

50g butter

2 shallots, finely chopped

200g pearl barley

300ml red or white wine

Preheat the oven to 200°C/gas mark 6.

First make the stuffing. Heat the sherry or vin santo in a small pan and then pour it over the figs. Leave to soak. Heat half the olive oil in a large frying pan, add the fennel seeds, shallots, garlic, pancetta and sage and cook until softened and lightly coloured. Transfer to a bowl and leave to cool. Heat the remaining oil and add the chicken livers. Season and cook for 2 minutes until browned. Remove from the heat and leave to cool.

Place the livers in a food-processor with the shallot mixture, figs and breadcrumbs and pulse until just combined. If you don't have a food-processor, finely chop the livers and mix by hand. Season.

Place the rabbit skin-side down on a work surface. Season the cavity. Spread the stuffing evenly over the rabbit. Fold the belly over the stuffing to close, then fold the front and back legs over to form a parcel. Tie with butcher's twine to secure. Heat the olive oil in a small roasting tin. Once hot, sear the rabbit on both sides until golden, then turn off the heat and remove the rabbit. Add the carrot, onion and celery to the tin. Place the rabbit on top and pour in the stock and wine. Place in the oven and cook for 1½ hours, basting every 20 minutes.

Meanwhile, make the cep braised barley. Heat the stock and pour over the dried ceps. In a separate saucepan, heat the butter and fry the shallots gently until softened. Add the barley and cook for a minute, stirring constantly. Add the wine and cook until absorbed. Pour over the hot stock and ceps, bring to the boil, reduce the heat and simmer for 40–60 minutes, stirring occasionally, until the barley is tender and the liquid has been absorbed. Season to taste.

Remove the rabbit from the oven and leave to rest for 10–15 minutes before removing the twine and carving into 2cm-thick slices. Meanwhile, strain the cooking liquor into a small pan, discard the vegetables and reduce to thicken. Skim and discard the fat and spoon the liquor over the rabbit. Serve the rabbit and its cooking juices with the cep braised barley.

It's more economical to buy a whole bird, and the next two recipes offer ideas for using the legs and the breasts. The roast pheasant breast goes beautifully with the Pheasant, Prune and Bacon Rolls (recipe #30). < SERVES 4 >

ROAST PHEASANT BREAST WITH HERBED PUY LENTILS AND CELERIAC CREAM

Rinse the lentils and place in a saucepan. Cover with cold water and bring to the boil. Simmer and cook until tender (about 20–35 minutes), then drain. Heat the olive oil in a saucepan, add the vegetables and simmer until softened. Add the drained lentils, sherry vinegar, herbs and season to taste. Keep the lentils warm.

To make the celeriac cream, place the celeriac, cream and 200ml water in a saucepan with a pinch of sea salt. Bring to a simmer and cook gently for 20–25 minutes, until the celeriac is soft. Add the butter and whizz in a blender while hot to a smooth purée. Season again with salt and black pepper and keep warm.

Preheat the oven to 200°C/gas mark 6.

Heat the oil and butter in an ovenproof frying pan. Season the pheasant breasts with sea salt and pepper, then fry them skin-side down over a medium–high heat until golden.

Turn the pheasant breasts over, sprinkle with thyme and add the wine or sherry. Heat until bubbling, then transfer to the oven and roast for 10–12 minutes or until the juices run clear when the breasts are pierced with a knife. Remove from the pan, add the cooking juices to the lentils and leave to rest in a warm place for 8–10 minutes before serving.

Serve the the roast pheasant breast with the lentils celeriac cream.

VARIATIONS

• I like to serve this dish scattered with a few roasted hazelnuts too – they go beautifully with celeriac and prunes.

FOR THE HERBED
PUY LENTILS
200g puy lentils
2 tbsp olive oil
2 shallots, finely chopped
1 carrot, finely chopped
1 celery stick, finely chopped
4 tbsp sherry vinegar
2 tbsp mixed chopped herbs
(such as chives, chervil and
flatleaf parsley)
sea salt and black pepper

FOR THE CELERIAC CREAM
300g celeriac, cut into about
2cm dice
250ml double cream
sea salt and black pepper
25g unsalted butter, diced

2 tbsp olive oil
15g unsalted butter
4 pheasant breasts
2 tsp thyme leaves, picked
125ml white wine or sherry

Two recipes in one: you confit the pheasant legs a day ahead, then use the flaked meat to make the rolls. Pheasant has a natural affinity for prunes – a little sweetness to pep up the gamey confit flavour. < SERVES 8 >

#30

PHEASANT, PRUNE AND BACON ROLLS

Mix together the coarse salt, peppercorns, thyme, bay leaves, garlic, juniper berries and orange zest to make confit salt. Scatter half the mixture on the bottom of a non-reactive container, place the pheasant legs on top and scatter with the remaining mixture. Cover and refrigerate for 12 hours but no longer!

Preheat the oven to 130°C/gas mark 1. Select an ovenproof dish that will hold the legs and fat snugly. Put the duck fat in the dish and warm over a gentle heat until dissolved.

Rinse the pheasant legs of salt and pat dry. Submerge into the duck fat, and then heat to a gentle simmer.

Cover the surface directly with parchment paper, then cover the dish with foil. Cook in the oven for about 1 hour or until the meat is tender.

Leave the legs to cool in the fat. Remove and flake the meat from the bones, strain the fat and reserve for another use. If making ahead of time, store the pheasant in a clean container covered with fat and refrigerate until required.

When you're ready to make the rolls, preheat the oven to 200°C/gas mark 6. Heat the olive oil in a pan, add the shallots and cook until softened. Transfer to a bowl and mix with the herbs, pheasant and sausage meat, nutmeg, prunes and duck fat. Season with sea salt and black pepper – fry a little of the mixture of to check the seasoning.

Shape into 30g lozenges and wrap each 'sausage' in half a rasher of bacon. Place on a non-stick baking tray and cook in the oven for 12–15 minutes, until golden and cooked through.

VARIATION

- If you prefer, you can serve the confit pheasant legs whole and skip making the rolls. Shake off excess fat and place on a baking tray. Roast in the oven for 10–15 minutes at 180°C/gas mark 4, until the skin is crisp and golden, and serve with celeriac cream and lentils (see recipe #29).

FOR THE CONFIT PHEASANT LEGS

125g coarse sea salt

1 tsp black peppercorns

3 sprigs of thyme, picked

2 bay leaves, roughly chopped

2 cloves garlic, thinly sliced

3 juniper berries, crushed

3 strips of orange zest

4 pheasant legs

300g duck fat

2 tbsp olive oil

2 shallots, finely chopped

3 tbsp chopped mixed herbs, such as sage, thyme and flatleaf parsley

200g sausage meat

pinch of freshly grated nutmeg

150g Agen prunes, finely chopped

1 tbsp duck fat

sea salt and black pepper

4 rashers of smoked streaky bacon, cut in half widthways

69

Bitter sweet flavours complement the exquisite flavour of quail and will make you beg for more!

< SERVES 4 >

POMEGRANATE MARINATED QUAIL, GRIDDLED RADICCHIO AND BITTER LEAF SALAD

4 boneless quail
sea salt and black pepper

FOR THE MARINADE
2 garlic cloves, crushed
pinch of ground cumin
2 tbsp olive oil
4 tbsp pomegranate molasses

FOR THE BITTER LEAF SALAD
1 small radicchio
dash of olive oil
dash of balsamic vinegar
1 red chicory
1 white chicory
8 mint leaves, shredded

FOR THE POMEGRANATE DRESSING
1 garlic clove, crushed
pinch of ground cinnamon
2 tbsp pomegranate molasses
5 tbsp extra virgin olive oil
1 tbsp clear honey

Warm Chickpea Purée
(recipe #104)

Prepare the marinade by mixing all the ingredients together. Add the quail and toss, then marinate for 1 hour or refrigerate overnight.

Preheat a griddle pan over a medium heat. Cut the radicchio in half, then quarters, drizzle with olive oil, season with sea salt and place on the hot griddle pan. Cook until charred on each side, remove and immediately drizzle with the balsamic vinegar. Leave to cool, then cut away core and shred finely lengthways.

To make the dressing, mix all of the ingredients with 2 tablespoons water and store at room temperature.

Preheat a griddle pan, remove the quail from the marinade and season with sea salt and pepper. Place the quail in the pan skin-side down and cook over a medium heat for 3–4 minutes on either side. Remove from the heat and leave to rest in a warm place.

For the salad, halve the red and white chicory and thinly slice on the diagonal. Mix together with the shredded radicchio and the mint. Season, dress and divide between four plates. Spoon a pile of chickpea purée on to each plate and top with the salad. Cut the quails in half and rest one half on top of each salad. Drizzle over the cooking juices and serve immediately.

70

As a kid I remember my mum's Sunday supper tea trolley ~~laden with celery, sandwiches and sardines on toast too~~ Here's my adult version. Sometimes the most simple things in life taste the best! < SERVES 4 >

SARDINES AND CHERRY TOMATOES ON TOAST

Quarter the tomatoes and place in a bowl with the basil leaves, garlic, Parmesan, olive oil and salt. Toss until combined, then set aside.

Drizzle the bread with a little olive oil and cook on a preheated griddle until lightly charred on both sides.

Rub the sardines with a little more oil, season and cook on the griddle for 1–2 minutes per side (skin side first) or until cooked through.

Place an even layer of tomatoes on each piece of toast, top with a sardine (skin-side up), drizzle with olive oil and serve immediately.

500g cherry vine tomatoes
1 small bunch basil, leaves torn
1 garlic clove, crushed
20g freshly grated Parmesan
6 tbsp extra virgin olive oil
sea salt
4 slices ciabatta or sourdough
olive oil, for drizzling
4 large sardines, butterflied

#33 The dressing recipe makes more than you need, but will store in the refrigerator for up to two weeks. You can buy podded soya beans (edamame) in the freezer section of health food shops and some supermarkets. < SERVES 4 >

SMOKED MACKEREL, ASPARAGUS AND NOODLE SALAD WITH GINGER MISO DRESSING

FOR THE GINGER MISO DRESSING
40g fresh ginger, peeled and finely grated
1 garlic clove, finely grated
60ml rice vinegar
1 tbsp soy sauce
½ tbsp caster sugar
75ml sesame oil
2 tbsp yellow or red miso paste

1 bunch asparagus, woody ends snapped off
1 packet soba or buckwheat noodles
dash of olive oil
sea salt and black pepper
4 smoked mackerel fillets, flaked
1 bunch coriander, leaves picked
4 spring onions, thinly sliced on the diagonal
1 avocado, cut into rough 2cm chunks
100g podded soya beans, defrosted
2 tbsp black or white sesame seeds, toasted
1 bunch watercress, picked

To make the dressing, whisk all of the ingredients together in a small bowl with 2 tablespoons water and refrigerate until required.

Bring a large pan of salted water to the boil, add the asparagus and cook for 2 minutes. Remove the asparagus and plunge into cold water. Keep the water boiling for the noodles and cook according to the instructions on the packet. Drain and place in a large bowl, and toss with enough ginger miso dressing to coat.

Preheat a griddle pan, toss the cooked asparagus with olive oil, sea salt and pepper and cook over a medium heat until lightly charred; remove and leave to cool before cutting each spear into three pieces on the diagonal.

Toss the remaining ingredients together with the noodles and asparagus and serve immediately.

76

I had the great fortune of meeting Anissa Helou who taught me the art of Moroccan cooking. Chermoula provides a wonderful fresh taste to contrast with the oily richness of mackerel. < SERVES 4 >

MARINATED MACKEREL WITH CHERMOULA AND CARROT AND OLIVE COUSCOUS

4 whole mackerel (175g each), gutted, heads on or off

2 garlic cloves

1 tsp ground ginger

1 tsp ground cinnamon

pinch of saffron

4 tsp fennel seeds

1 red chilli, finely chopped

2 tbsp olive oil

FOR THE COUSCOUS

150g couscous

50g butter

60g green olives

zest of 1 lemon, finely grated

4 tbsp coriander, finely chopped

pinch of cumin

1 tbsp sumac

1 red chilli, finely chopped

60g chickpeas from a can, drained

50g carrot, grated

FOR THE CHERMOULA

2 garlic cloves

pinch of chilli pepper

2 tsp ground cumin

1 tsp paprika

2 tbsp lemon juice

50g coriander, chopped

pinch of sea salt

80ml light olive oil

Preheat the oven to 180°C/gas mark 4.

Make three diagonal incisions along both sides of the mackerel.

To make the mackerel filling, pound the garlic, ginger, cinnamon, saffron, fennel seeds and red chilli with the olive oil in a pestle and mortar and use the mixture to fill the incisions in the fish. Brush the mackerel with a little olive oil, place on a hot griddle pan and sear for 2 minutes on each side. Place in the oven and cook for about 5 minutes or until the mackerel is cooked through.

Next, place the couscous in a bowl, add the butter and 150ml boiling water, cover with clingfilm and leave to steam for 4 minutes. Fluff with a fork, add the remaining ingredients and season to taste.

To make the chermoula, place the garlic, spices, lemon juice, coriander and salt in a blender and slowly add the olive oil, blending until smooth.

Serve the mackerel with the couscous and drizzle with chermoula.

I'd had a fabulous day out fishing for mackerel with my great friend Stephanie. When we got home we found some gooseberry jelly, a bowl of new potatoes and a bunch of mint in the fridge. And so the dish was born! < SERVES 4 >

MACKEREL WITH GOOSEBERRY JELLY, PINE NUTS AND MINT

Boil the potatoes in salted water until tender. Drain and leave to cool slightly before cutting into 5mm slices. Toss with half the butter and keep warm.

Season the mackerel fillets on both sides with a little salt and pepper. Place in the pan and cook, skin-side down, for 1–2 minutes until the skin is crisp and golden (press on the fillets lightly if they start to curl upwards to get a crisp effect all over).

Turn each fillet over, spoon over the gooseberry jelly and cook for a further minute. If your pan isn't large enough to do all the fillets at the same time, keep the cooked ones warm on a plate.

Serve the mackerel skin-side up. Spoon over the cooking juices and sprinkle with the pine nuts. Serve with warm buttered potatoes and a baby leaf salad.

300g new or Charlotte potatoes

3 tbsp unsalted butter

2 ultra-fresh mackerel, filleted and pin boned

sea salt and black pepper

1 tbsp olive oil

3 tbsp Gooseberry Jelly (recipe #81) mixed with a handful of finely chopped mint

20g pine nuts, toasted

baby leaf salad, to serve

An oldie, but a goldie! This recipe dates back to my Delfina days, and is inspired by Dicky, my sous chef there. A classic flavour combination, delicately brought together on a plate. < SERVES 4 >

#36

HERB AND PINK PEPPERCORN SALMON WITH PEA SAUCE AND SUMMER VEGETABLES

Preheat the oven to 180°/gas mark 4.

Season the flesh side of the salmon fillets.

To make the crust, whizz together all the ingredients in a small blender until they come together. Smear evenly over the salmon fillets and refrigerate until required. If you want to make the crust in advance, place the mixture between two sheets of greaseproof paper and roll out (keeps refrigerated for up to three days or in the freezer for two weeks), then cut to the size of the fish and lay on top.

To make the pea sauce, melt the butter in a pan over a low heat and cook the shallots until softened. Deglaze the pan with the white wine and reduce. Add half the peas, the chicken stock, cream, salt and sugar and cook until the peas are tender. Meanwhile, heat a non-stick ovenproof pan on the stovetop with a dash of olive oil, then add the salmon skin-side down (crust-side up) and cook for 2 minutes until crisp. Remove from the heat, then place in the oven and cook for 4 minutes, depending on the size of the fish (I like to serve my salmon a little underdone in the middle).

Put the remaining peas into a blender and add the hot pea sauce. Whizz until smooth (this helps to keep the bright green colour). Pass through a fine sieve into a small pan, season with sea salt and keep warm while the salmon is cooking.

To serve, divide the hot, buttered vegetables between four deep plates, pour over the pea sauce and lay the salmon on top, garnished with pea shoots.

4 salmon fillets, about 160–180g each

sea salt and black pepper

250g new potatoes

4–8 asparagus spears

100g podded broad beans, fresh or frozen

25g butter

pea shoots, to garnish

FOR THE CRUST

50g mint leaves, finely chopped

2 tsp crushed pink peppercorns

1 garlic clove, finely chopped

100g softened butter

100g fresh breadcrumbs

30g flatleaf parsley, finely chopped

2 tsp sea salt

FOR THE PEA SAUCE

50g unsalted butter

2 shallots, finely chopped

100ml dry white wine

500g frozen petit pois

350ml chicken stock

200ml cream

pinch of sea salt

pinch of sugar

81

Star anise, orange and vinegar bring the earthy beetroot to life; a few orange segments and slivers of raw sea bass add colour and freshness – what a revelation. I love discovering new flavour combinations! < SERVES 4 >

BEETROOT AND SEA BASS CARPACCIO WITH ORANGES

2 oranges, segmented, juice reserved (use blood oranges if they are in season)

100ml red wine vinegar (I like Cabernet Sauvignon vinegar)

2 tbsp caster sugar

2 star anise

2 beetroots, peeled and thinly sliced on a Japanese mandolin

2 tbsp extra virgin olive oil

300g super-fresh wild sea bass fillets, thinly sliced

sea salt and black pepper

pea shoots, sorrel, micro cress or mint, finely torn

Heat the orange juice, vinegar, sugar and star anise in a pan. Stir over a low heat until the sugar has dissolved. Place the beetroot in a non-reactive shallow dish and pour over the liquid. Leave to cool, then refrigerate overnight to marinate.

To serve, arrange the beetroot slices overlapping on a plate. Take 2 tablespoons of marinating liquor, whisk with the olive oil, and spoon over the beetroot. Scatter with oranges and sliced sea bass, then season with sea salt and pepper. Sprinkle with pea shoots, sorrel, micro cress or mint, and serve immediately.

VARIATIONS

- Omit the fish to turn into a vegetarian option – serve with spoonfuls of goat's curd instead along with some crusty bread.

Raw cauliflower couscous combined with preserved lemon, mint and pistachio provides a perfect accompaniment to slightly sweet sea bream. A health conscious dish packed to the 'bream' with flavour. < SERVES 4 >

PAN-FRIED SEA BREAM WITH CAULIFLOWER, PISTACHIO AND MINT COUSCOUS AND CAULIFLOWER PURÉE

To make the couscous, put the pistachios in a food-processor, pulse to a breadcrumb-like texture, then pour into a large bowl. Place half the cauliflower florets in the food-processor and blitz to a couscous-like texture. Add to the pistachios and repeat with the remaining florets. Combine with the remaining ingredients, season with sea salt and add olive oil and lemon juice to taste. Refrigerate for at least 1 hour before serving, to allow the flavours to infuse.

To make the cauliflower purée, place the cauliflower and milk in a small saucepan with the salt. Bring to the boil, simmer and cook until the cauliflower is very tender, then drain, setting aside the milk. Place in a blender, add the butter and lemon juice and whizz until smooth, adding a little of the reserved milk if it is too thick. Season as necessary and keep warm while you cook the fish.

Heat the olive oil in a large non-stick pan (or 2 medium pans), season the fish and pan-fry skin-side down for 2 minutes or until crisp and golden. Flip the fish over and continue to cook for a further 2–3 minutes, depending on the size of the fish.

To assemble, spoon a slick of cauliflower purée on each plate, top with cauliflower couscous and place a bream fillet, skin-side up, next to it. Garnish with pea shoots and a drizzle of extra virgin olive oil.

VARIATIONS

- Try adding some soaked sultanas or chopped medjool dates and a pinch of cumin to the couscous recipe.

FOR THE 'COUSCOUS'
a handful of pistachio nuts, peeled and blanched
½ cauliflower, cut into florets
juice of 1–2 lemons
120ml olive oil
1 bunch mint, finely chopped
1 preserved lemon, cut into quarters, flesh removed, washed and finely chopped
sea salt

FOR THE CAULIFLOWER PURÉE
½ cauliflower, cut into small florets
300ml milk
pinch of sea salt
25g butter
1 tbsp lemon juice

dash of olive oil
4 sea bream fillets, skin scored
pea shoots, to garnish

87

#39

To me, cream of corn and porcinis are a seasonal match made in heaven! I've broken this recipe down into several components; you can make one or all of them – it's up to you how far you want to take the recipe. < SERVES 4 >

SEA BASS WITH CREAMED CORN AND PORCINI POPCORN

FOR THE PORCINI POPCORN
2 tbsp olive oil
50g unpopped popcorn
25g unsalted butter, softened
Porcini Salt (recipe #107)

FOR THE CREAMED CORN
3 ears sweetcorn
50g unsalted butter
2 banana shallots, finely chopped
1 garlic clove, finely chopped
1 chicken stock cube
500ml cream, single or double
sea salt and black pepper

FOR THE PORCINIS
good glug of extra virgin olive oil
500g porcini or mixed wild mushrooms, wiped clean and finely sliced
sea salt and black pepper
1 garlic clove, finely chopped

FOR THE SEA BASS
4 sea bass fillets (weighing 120–150g each)
sea salt and black pepper
dash of olive oil
25g butter
watercress sprigs

Start with the porcini popcorn. Heat the oil in a large saucepan with a tight-fitting lid. Add the corn and cover immediately – it will begin to 'pop'. Cook over a medium heat, moving the pan continuously until the popping stops – this will take about 2–3 minutes. Remove the pan from the heat and leave covered for a minute or else the popcorn will go flying!

Carefully remove the lid, add the butter and porcini salt to taste, setting aside some of the flavoured salt for the sea bass. Toss well to mix. The popcorn can be made ahead of time and stored in an airtight container.

Next, for the creamed corn, remove the corn kernels from the cobs using a sharp knife. Heat the butter in a saucepan and gently fry the shallots and garlic until softened, but not browned. Add the corn and crumble in the stock cube. Stir in the cream, reduce the heat to a simmer, stirring occasionally until the corn is tender – about 25 minutes. Use a hand blender (or potato masher) to blend the mix until semi-smooth, then season with black pepper and salt, if necessary. Keep warm.

For the porcinis, heat the olive oil in a large frying pan. (Cook in batches if you don't have a large pan, otherwise you'll lower the temperature and end up stewing the mushrooms, and that would be sacrilege!) Add the mushrooms and fry over a high heat for 3 minutes. Season with salt and black pepper. Add the garlic and cook for a further 2 minutes, or until the mushrooms are tender. Set aside in a warm place.

Using a sharp knife, score the skin of the sea bass, this will prevent the fish from curling while cooking. Season the flesh side with the porcini salt.

Heat the olive oil in a non-stick frying pan and fry the sea bass skin-side down for 2–3 minutes until the skin is crisp and golden. Turn over, add the butter and cook for 2–3 minutes more, or until the fish is cooked through.

To assemble, divide the creamed corn between four plates, top with some watercress sprigs and the porcinis. Place the sea bass on top, skin-side up and sprinkle over the popcorn. Serve immediately.

This recipe takes strawberries right out of their comfort zone. Their sweet, soft balanced with ginger's gentle spice, acidic subtle rice vinegar and salty fish sauce, combined with aromatic herbs, produce a taste sensation. < SERVES 4 >

FRIED LEMON SOLE WITH THAI SPICED STRAWBERRY SAUCE

Heat 2 tablespoons of the oil in a pan and gently fry the chilli, ginger, shallot and garlic until soft.

In a food-processor, purée the strawberries with 125ml water and the vinegar until smooth. Deglaze the shallots with whisky, if using. Once reduced, add the palm sugar and strawberry purée. Simmer until thickened, then add the lime juice and fish sauce.

Meanwhile, cook the fish. Heat the oil in two large frying pans, mix the cornflour with sea salt, pepper and the Chinese five spice. Coat each lemon sole with seasoned flour and fry, flesh-side, down until golden. Carefully turn the fish over and continue to fry for a further 3 minutes (depending on their size, they should take about 6–8 minutes to cook).

To serve, place each fish on a large plate, spoon over the strawberry sauce, top with the spring onions and herbs and serve with a side dish of steamed jasmine rice.

200ml grapeseed oil for frying, plus 2 tbsp for the sauce

1 red chilli, deseeded and finely chopped

30g fresh ginger, peeled and cut into fine strips

1 shallot, finely chopped

1 garlic clove, finely chopped

225g strawberries, hulled and quartered

75ml rice vinegar

50ml whisky (optional)

25g palm sugar

juice of 1 lime

2 tbsp fish sauce

100g cornflour

sea salt and black pepper

4 tsp Chinese five spice (optional)

2 large whole lemon soles, head and top black skin removed (ask your fishmonger to do this)

2 spring onions, finely chopped on a diagonal

1 small bunch coriander, leaves picked

12 leaves Thai basil or Vietnamese mint

jasmine rice, to serve

#41

I had the most delicious halibut tagine while travelling in Morocco – this is my interpretation of it. You can use any skinless, meaty white fish fillets to replace the halibut if you like. A perfect dish for entertaining. < SERVES 4 >

HALIBUT, ORANGE AND OLIVE TAGINE

pinch of saffron

350ml hot fish stock or water

2 tbsp olive oil

1 onion, halved and finely sliced

2 garlic cloves, finely chopped

2 tsp ground cumin

½ tsp paprika

pinch of ground ginger

1 x 400g can tomatoes, crushed

½ red chilli, deseeded and finely chopped

1 cinnamon stick

1 tbsp honey

zest and juice of 1 orange

1 small fennel bulb, quartered, cored and thinly sliced

4 halibut steaks or 500g skinless halibut fillets, cut into about 50g pieces

sea salt and black pepper

20g pitted olives

20g coriander, chopped

10g flatleaf parsley, chopped

Mix the saffron into the fish stock and leave to infuse.

Heat the olive oil in a large saucepan and gently fry the onion until soft. Add the garlic and spices and cook for 2 minutes. Add the tomatoes, chilli, cinnamon, honey, orange zest and juice and saffron-infused stock, Bring to the boil and simmer for 15 minutes before adding the fennel, then cook for a further 10 minutes.

Season the fish and add to sauce; simmer for 10 minutes or until the fish is cooked. If using halibut steaks, test to see if cooked by moving the bone a little; if there is no resistance, the fish is cooked. If using fillets, the fish will need to cook for about 6 minutes. Stir in the olives and herbs and season to taste.

Serve in deep bowls with couscous or boiled potatoes.

VARIATIONS

- You can vary the fish used – monkfish would make a great alternative, as would red mullet.
- Try adjusting the flavourings a little – substitute lemons for oranges, coriander seeds for ginger and add fennel seeds if you don't have any fresh fennel.

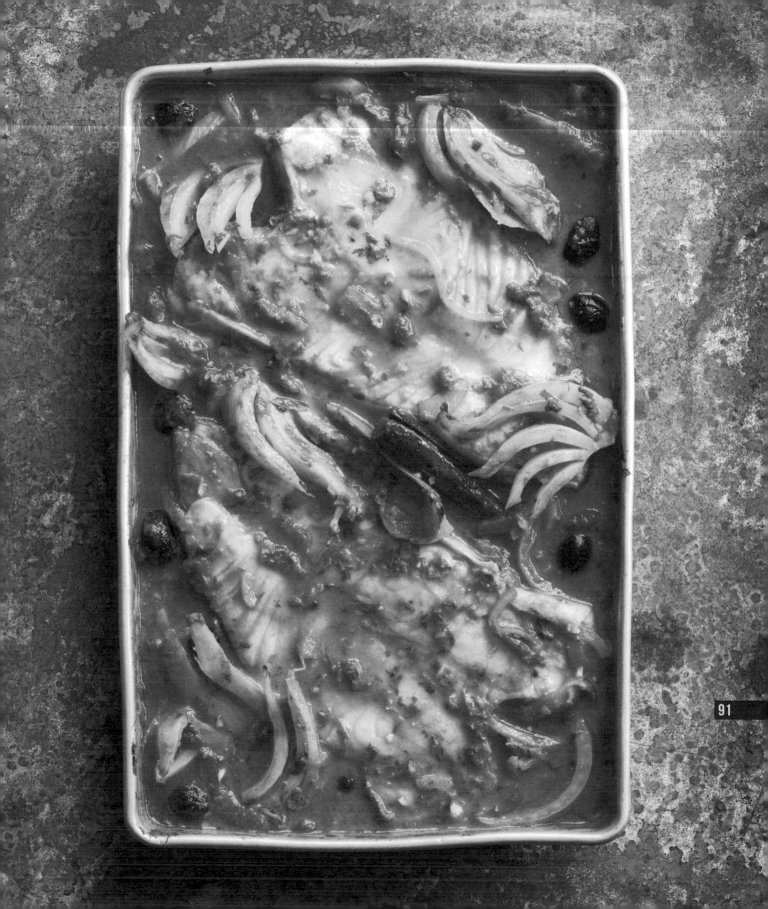

OYSTERS

clean, fresh + sea salty

SEAFOOD

mussels

prawns

clams

CRAB

sweet + meaty, delicate + fresh

claws, brown meat, white meat

pair with vanilla, asparagus + crème fraîche

add to a watermelon curry – gorgeous with a splash of lime + salty fish sauce – liven up with fresh coriander + a hint of chilli

use to freshen up cauliflower soup, add lemongrass to lighten and top with crab meat

Most clams are bought 'purged', meaning their grit has been removed; it's always best to ask, though, before buying. If they haven't been purged, you'll need to rinse and soak them in plenty of cold water. < SERVES 4 >

BAKED CLAMS WITH ROSEMARY, WHITE BEANS AND TOMATOES

Preheat the oven to 200°C/gas mark 6.

Rinse the clams in cold water and shake dry.

Lay a large double layer of foil or greaseproof paper on the counter – it should be big enough to fold over the filling.

Place the clams, garlic, chilli flakes, tomatoes, beans and rosemary on one half of the foil. Drizzle with olive oil and pour over the wine.

Fold the foil or paper over the clams, sealing the edges together to make a neat but loose parcel, making sure you allow enough room for the clams to open up.

Transfer the parcel to a roasting tin and bake in the oven for 10–12 minutes, until the clams are open. Carefully open up the parcels and serve as they are, with crusty bread.

800g clams

2 garlic cloves, finely sliced

pinch of chilli flakes (optional)

12 cherry vine tomatoes, halved

200g cooked cannellini beans, rinsed

sprig of rosemary, leaves stripped

extra virgin olive oil, for drizzling

150ml dry white wine

bread, to serve

VARIATIONS

- This is another recipe for you to take on a culinary journey! For an Asian twist, add aromatics such as ginger, lemongrass, chillies and coriander and omit the rosemary.
- Try cooking these clams on the barbecue.
- You could try using cockles or mussels instead of clams.

#43 The delicate flavour of lemongrass matched with cauliflower combine beautifully to create a soup with finesse; top with sweet crabmeat to add a touch of decadence. < SERVES 4 >

CAULIFLOWER AND LEMONGRASS SOUP WITH CRAB

25g unsalted butter

2 banana shallots, finely chopped

4 sticks lemongrass, tough outer leaves removed and set aside

25g ginger, finely chopped

1 cauliflower (about 700g), outer leaves removed

700ml milk

200ml double cream

sea salt and black pepper

50–60g picked white crabmeat

micro coriander leaves or lemon balm, to serve

Heat the butter in a large saucepan, add the shallots and cook over a low heat until softened.

Finely chop the lemongrass and add to the shallots with the ginger. Tie the reserved tough outer edges together with an elastic band.

Core the cauliflower and break into florets, then finely slice and add to the pan. Add the milk and tied lemongrass and bring to the boil, stirring constantly. Reduce the heat to a simmer and cook until the cauliflower is tender (about 15 minutes).

Add the cream, reheat a little, then remove the tied lemongrass. Blend the soup in batches until smooth (pass through a fine sieve if not smooth enough). Season with sea salt and pepper.

Pour into shallow warmed soup bowls. Top with the crabmeat and a few micro coriander leaves, or some finely chopped lemon balm.

VARIATIONS

- The soup can also be made with scallops instead of crabmeat, if you prefer. Season 8 scallops with a little sea salt and pepper. Add a dash of olive oil to a hot pan, place the scallops in flat-side down and cook over medium-high heat until seared and golden. Flip over and cook for a further minute on the other side (no more). Serve as above.

I can still remember the taste of the most amazing paella I've ever eaten. It was several years ago, in a little shack on Sóller beach in Majorca. My version uses quinoa, a nutty and protein-filled grain. **< SERVES 4 GENEROUSLY>**

SEAFOOD AND QUINOA PAELLA

Combine the stock and saffron in a pan over a low heat and bring to a simmer. Remove from the heat and leave for 5 minutes to allow the saffron to infuse.

Heat the oil in a large paella or frying pan over a medium heat. Add the chicken thighs and brown on each side. Move chicken to the side of the pan and add the onion, red pepper and garlic and cook, stirring, for 5 minutes or until the onion has softened.

Add the paprika and tomatoes and cook for 3 minutes, stirring. Add the quinoa, season with salt and pepper and pour over the saffron-infused stock, bringing it to the boil. Reduce the heat to low and cook uncovered for 15 minutes or until quinoa is almost tender.

Add the beans and cook for 3 minutes. Add the mussels and prawns, pushing lightly into the quinoa, then sprinkle over the peas. Cover loosely with foil and cook for about 8 minutes or until the prawns have changed colour and the mussels have opened. Turn off the heat and leave to rest for 5 minutes.

Discard any unopened mussels and serve straight from the pan, sprinkled with parsley and with the lemon wedges on the side.

1 litre chicken stock

large pinch of saffron

2 tbsp olive oil

4 chicken thighs, skin on and bone in

1 small onion, finely chopped

1 red pepper, deseeded and finely chopped

2 garlic cloves, finely chopped

1 tsp smoked paprika

3 vine-ripe tomatoes, peeled and finely chopped

300g quinoa

sea salt and black pepper

150g green beans, top and tailed and halved

400g mussels, debearded

12 king prawns, shells and heads on

100g frozen peas, defrosted

large handful of flatleaf parsley, coarsely chopped

lemon wedges, to serve

#45

One of my favourite ways to eat squid.
It's fresh flavoured without the usual deep-fried
preparation — perfect for a summer barbecue.
I'm salivating as I write! < SERVES 4 >

CLEMENTINE AND CHILLI GRIDDLED SQUID

FOR THE MARINADE
4 red chillies
finely grated zest of
2 clementines
4 tbsp olive oil

**FOR THE SMOKED CHILLI
AND CLEMENTINE DRESSING**
juice of 6 clementines
75ml olive oil
dash of Chardonnay vinegar
(if unavailable, use white
wine vinegar)

8 medium-large squid tubes
½ cauliflower, cut into florets
300ml milk
sea salt and black pepper
25g butter
sea salt and black pepper
micro coriander, to serve

First, make the marinade. Pierce the chillies with the point of a knife and cook on a hot griddle pan until the skins are blackened. Remove from the pan, leave to cool, then peel away the charred skins. Cut in half lengthways, scrape away the seeds and discard. Finely chop the chillies, setting aside half for the dressing. Mix the clementine zest with the remaining charred chillies and olive oil. Set aside while you prepare the squid.

Remove the wings and outer skin of the squid. Using a knife, make a split lengthways along one side of each squid to open up the tube. Scrape out and discard any guts and cartilage. Lightly score incisions in a criss-cross fashion (at about 5mm intervals). Place the squid tubes in the marinade, mix well and marinate for at least 30 minutes or overnight.

To make the dressing, heat the clementine juice and reduce by half or until it's syrupy. Remove from the heat and whisk with the chillies set aside earlier, olive oil and vinegar. Season with a pinch of sea salt. This dressing will keep in the refrigerator for several days.

Next, make a cauliflower purée. Set aside three florets and cut the remaining ones into small even-sized pieces. Place in a saucepan with the milk and a pinch of sea salt. Cook over a low heat until the cauliflower is tender. Drain the cauliflower, setting aside the milk; liquidise the cauliflower until smooth, adding the butter, seasoning and enough of the milk set aside earlier to make a nice, smooth consistency. Keep warm.

Thinly slice the reserved florets lengthways on a mandolin. (They need to be wafer thin, so mind your fingers.)

Remove the squid from the marinade, season with sea salt and cook on a preheated griddle pan, scored-side down. As the squid cooks, it will slowly roll into a tube. Turn the squid over after about 3–4 minutes and cook on the other side.

Serve the squid on cauliflower purée, drizzle with clementine chilli dressing and sprinkle with shaved cauliflower and micro coriander.

Juicy peaches, brimming with flavour and refreshing Thai herbs, prawns and chilli – a quintessential summer lunch in itself. If you don't have rice paper rolls, just toss in a bowl with dressing and serve as a salad. < MAKES 16 ROLLS >

PRAWN, PEACH AND THAI BASIL VIETNAMESE RICE PAPER ROLLS

Cook the rice noodles according to the instructions on the packet. Drain and rinse thoroughly with cold water so they don't stick together, then set aside to cool.

Fill a large, shallow bowl with warm water. Dip one rice paper into the water to soften (this will take 10–40 seconds, depending on how thick they are). Remove and lay on a damp tea-towel. Arrange three prawns down the centre with some herbs, noodles, peanuts, peach and lettuce. Don't overfill or it will be too fat and impossible to roll.

Fold the edge of the paper closest to you over the filling, fold in the sides, then roll up tightly to make a neat parcel. Set aside on a tray while you repeat with the remaining rice papers and fillings. Cover the rice paper rolls with a damp tea-towel until you are ready to eat.

To make the dipping sauce, place the chilli, garlic and palm sugar in a mortar and grind to a smooth paste. Stir in the remaining ingredients, alog with 1 tablespoon of water.

Serve the sauce in little dipping dishes with the rice paper rolls.

VARIATIONS

- The shredded smoked paprika chicken from recipe #6 makes a great alternative to prawns.

50g rice vermicelli noodles

16 round rice papers

48 large cooked peeled prawns

½ small bunch mint, leaves picked

small bunch coriander, leaves picked

32 leaves Thai basil or Vietnamese mint

50g unsalted roasted peanuts, coarsely chopped

1 peach, halved, thinly sliced, then julienned

1 baby gem lettuce, halved, finely shredded, lengthways

FOR THE DIPPING SAUCE

1 small bird's-eye chilli, deseeded and finely chopped

2 small garlic cloves

1 tbsp palm sugar

juice of 2 limes

4 tbsp fish sauce

1 tbsp rice wine vinegar

101

#47 *Sea salty fresh oysters paired with subtle bitter and delicate aromatic beer – here are two flavours that really love one another. I've added a zesty fresh and crisp salad to complement them.* < SERVES 4 >

OYSTERS WITH BEER JELLY, GREEN APPLE, AND LIME AND CORIANDER SALAD

12 oysters

250ml Belgian beer (I like to use Duvel)

3 sheets leaf gelatine, soaked in cold water

FOR THE APPLE SALAD

1 Granny Smith apple

zest of 1 lime and juice of ½ lime

micro coriander, or 2 tbsp finely chopped coriander, to garnish

1 tsp finely chopped green chillies, seeds removed

dash of extra virgin olive oil

crushed ice, to serve

Open the oysters using an oyster knife and strain the liquor through a sieve into a saucepan. Remove the oysters from their shells and refrigerate. Rinse the bottom shells and set aside for serving.

To make the jelly, add the beer to the oyster liquor in the pan and bring to a simmer over a medium heat. Remove from the heat.

Squeeze the soaked gelatine leaves to remove any excess water and stir into the hot beer mixture until completely dissolved. Pour through a fine sieve into a shallow plastic container. Leave to cool, then refrigerate for about 2 hours or until set.

To make the salad, thinly slice the apple, preferably on a Japanese mandolin if you have one, and cut into fine strips. Combine the apple with the lime zest and juice, coriander and chillies and dress with a dash of extra virgin olive oil.

To serve, cut the jelly into fine dice and divide between the 12 oyster shells you set aside. Place an oyster on top of each and garnish with salad. Serve the oysters on crushed ice.

VARIATIONS

- Use agar agar to set the beer as opposed to gelatine.

102

You may have gathered by now that I have an obsession with watermelon which, in the case of this recipe, makes a delicate, refreshing curry; one of my most talked about recipes – perfect for a balmy summer's evening. < SERVES 4 >

WATERMELON AND SEAFOOD CURRY

To make the curry, liquidise 1.5kg of the watermelon in a blender or food-processor until smooth. Cut the remaining watermelon into 1cm cubes and set aside.

Heat half of the oil in a large frying pan. When hot, gently cook the onion, ginger and garlic until soft. Add the chilli, lemongrass and spices and cook for a further minute. Add the liquidised watermelon, bring to the boil, then simmer until reduced by half. This should take about 20–30 minutes.

To prepare the seafood, heat the remaining oil in a large frying pan. Season the squid with salt and pepper and fry in two batches over a high heat for 3 minutes per batch. Set aside.

Once the curry has reduced, add the squid, crabmeat, coriander and the diced watermelon that you set aside and gently heat through. Add fish sauce and lime juice to taste – the curry should be hot, sweet and sour. Serve immediately.

2kg watermelon (the seedless variety works best), rind and seeds removed

2 tbsp grapeseed oil

1 onion, finely chopped

30g ginger, finely chopped

1 garlic clove, finely chopped

1 red chilli, deseeded and finely chopped

1 lemongrass stick, finely chopped

1 tsp turmeric

2 tsp ground coriander

1 tsp cumin seeds

pinch of cayenne pepper

500g cleaned squid, sliced into rings

sea salt and black pepper

100g meat from crab claws

1 bunch coriander, finely chopped

dash of fish sauce, to taste

juice of 1–1½ limes, to taste

add tomatoes, garlic + herbs to create your own baked beans

absorb flavour like a sponge

finish with herbs, cherry tomatoes, feta – fav or sourdough toast or with lamb

cook in orange or apple juice for extra flavour

high in protein + contains all the amino acids needed for good health

comfor

cook for breakfast – just like porridge!

use in sweet or savoury dishes

QUINOA

is an ancient food native to South America

pronounced 'keen-wah'!

Italians eat lentils on New Year's Eve – they symbolise money + good fortune for the coming year

Italy

Greec

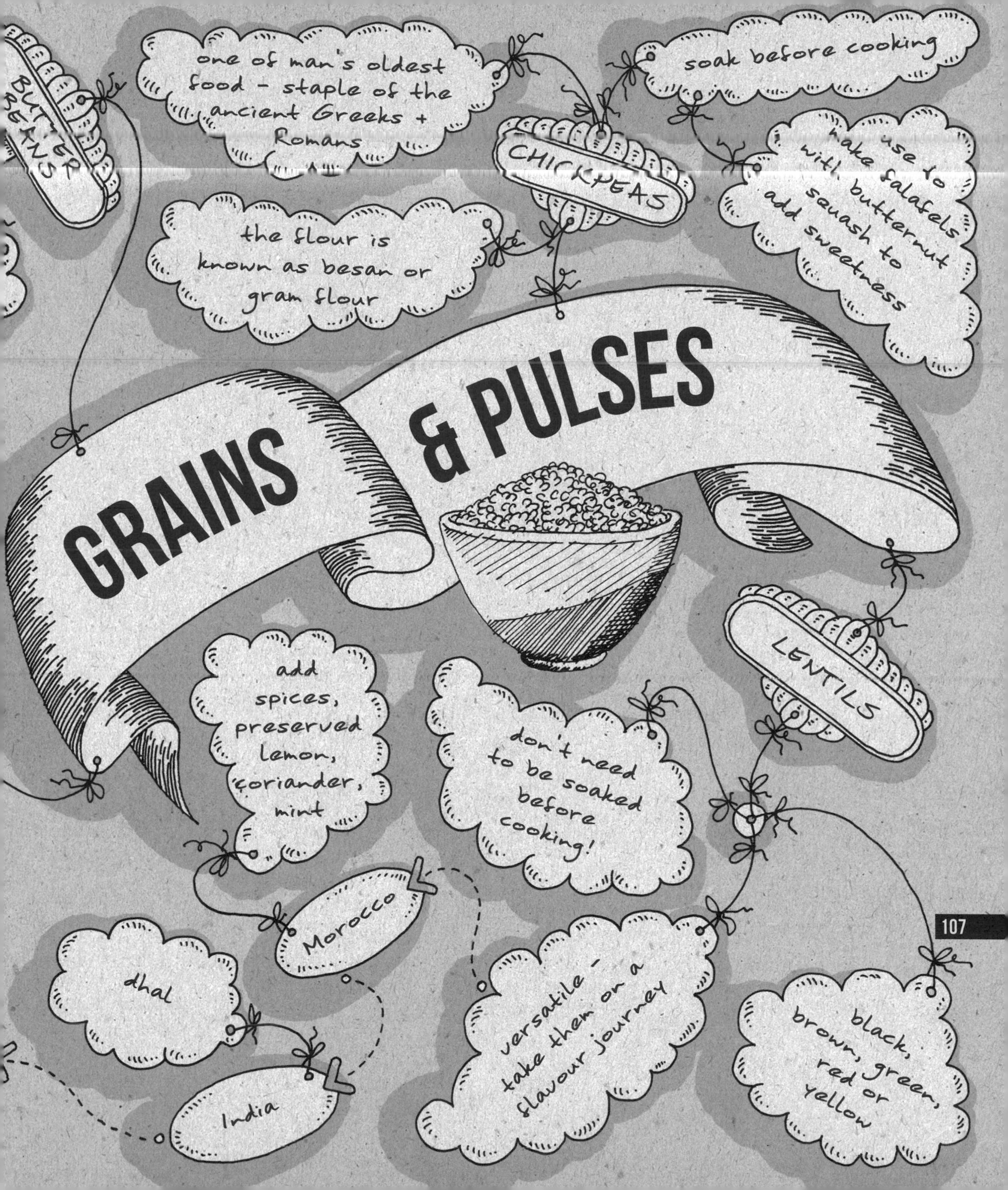

BUTTER BEANS

one of man's oldest food – staple of the ancient Greeks + Romans

soak before cooking

CHICKPEAS

the flour is known as besan or gram flour

use to make falafels with butternut squash to add sweetness

GRAINS & PULSES

add spices, preserved lemon, coriander, mint

don't need to be soaked before cooking!

LENTILS

dhal

Morocco

India

versatile – take them on a flavour journey

black, brown, green, red or yellow

#49 *Pretty much a store-cupboard soup. I had to put together a last-minute starter one day – and this soup was the result! Fab for summer.* **< SERVES 4 >**

CHILLED WHITE BEAN AND GREEK BASIL SOUP WITH PRAWNS, LEMON AND CHILLI

2 tbsp olive oil

3 shallots, peeled and thinly sliced

2 garlic cloves, finely chopped

2 x 400g cans cannellini beans

450ml light chicken stock

handful of Greek basil, roughly chopped

sea salt and black pepper

pinch of chilli powder

juice of 1 lemon

FOR THE PRAWN TOPPING

2 tbsp olive oil

16 raw tiger prawns, peeled

sea salt and black pepper

pinch of chilli flakes

1 lemon, segmented and chopped

1 tbsp Greek basil leaves

Heat the olive oil in a saucepan, add the shallots and garlic and cook over a low heat until softened (about 10 minutes). Add the beans and chicken stock, bring to the boil, then reduce the heat to a simmer and cook for 10 minutes.

Leave to cool a little before blending in batches, adding the basil to each batch, until smooth. Season with sea salt and pepper, and add a pinch of chilli powder and lemon juice to taste. If the soup seems too thick, add a little water. Leave to cool and refrigerate, covered, until required.

To make the prawn topping, heat the oil in a frying pan, and season the prawns with sea salt, pepper and chilli flakes. Cook the prawns for 2 minutes until translucent. Transfer to a bowl and toss with lemon and basil leaves.

Top the chilled soup with the prawn mixture and drizzle with olive oil. Serve immediately.

VARIATIONS

- Sorrel would make a great substitute for the Greek basil; you will need about 10 leaves, deveined, for the soup.
- Tangerine flavoured olive oil is gorgeous drizzled on top of the soup instead of regular olive oil.

108

#50

GREEK BEANS ON TOAST WITH FETA AND TOMATOES

Soak the beans overnight in plenty of cold water.

Next day, drain and rinse the beans and place them in a large saucepan. Cover with plenty of cold water and bring to the boil. Reduce the heat and simmer until just tender (about 50 minutes).

Preheat the oven to 150°C/gas mark 2.

Drain the beans, setting aside both the cooking liquor and the beans.

Heat the olive oil in an ovenproof pan. Add the onion and garlic and cook until softened over a medium heat. Add the tomato purée and cook for a further minute. Add the plum tomatoes, sugar, reserved beans and 700ml of the liquor set aside earlier. Season with salt and pepper, cover with foil or a lid and cook for 30 minutes. Remove the cover, then stir and cook for a further 30 minutes until most of the liquor has been absorbed and the beans are tender.

Season to taste, stir in the herbs, cherry tomatoes (if using) and serve warm on toasted sourdough sprinkled with feta and drizzled with olive oil.

500g dried butter beans

150ml olive oil

1 onion, finely chopped

3 garlic cloves, finely chopped

1 tbsp tomato purée

1kg vine plum tomatoes, skinned and roughly chopped

1 tsp sugar

sea salt and black pepper

15g parsley, finely chopped

10g oregano, finely chopped or 3 tsp dried

100g cherry tomatoes, halved (optional, but I like the contrast of cooked and fresh tomatoes)

200g feta cheese, crumbled

toasted sourdough, to serve

olive oil, for drizzling

111

#51 When I first tasted quinoa I thought the health benefits outweighed the taste. I decided this needed to change and experimented cooking it in flavoured stocks and fruit juices. Here's the result of one experiment. < SERVES 4 >

ORANGE AND SUMAC SCENTED QUINOA

2 tbsp olive oil

1 carrot, finely chopped

1 celery stick, finely chopped

1 small onion, finely chopped

120g quinoa

finely grated zest of 1 orange

240ml freshly squeezed orange juice

sea salt and black pepper

25g flaked almonds, lightly toasted

½ bunch coriander, finely chopped

½ bunch mint, finely chopped

1 avocado, diced into 1cm cubes

shiso sprouts, if available

2 tsp sumac, plus a pinch for garnish

Heat the oil in a medium pan. Add the carrot, celery and onion and cook over a medium heat until tender. Add the quinoa and cook for 1 minute while stirring.

Add the orange zest and juice, and bring to the boil. Reduce to a simmer and cook for 10–15 minutes until the quinoa is tender and the orange juice has been absorbed. Season with sea salt and pepper.

Leave to cool a little before stirring through the almonds, coriander, mint, avocado and sumac. Garnish with shiso sprouts if available and sprinkle with a pinch of sumac.

VARIATIONS

- I like to serve this with oily fish, such as mackerel.
- It's also delicious served chilled with prawns or on its own.
- Great with chilli-roasted feta too.
- try cooking the quinoa in apple juice instead of orange juice.

112

#52 I'm constantly being told to eat more protein to maximise the benefits of working out. Whether you exercise or not though, here's your very own 15-minute protein fix. And it's quick and easy to make, too. < SERVES 4 >

MOROCCAN SPICED LENTILS WITH PAN-FRIED SALMON AND AVOCADO CREAM

FOR THE LENTILS

1 tbsp light olive oil

1 onion, finely chopped

2 garlic cloves, finely chopped

1 tbsp grated fresh ginger

2 tsp cumin

1 tsp cinnamon

2 tsp paprika

1 tsp ground coriander

175g pre-cooked brown or puy lentils

100ml chicken stock or boiling water

small bunch coriander

½ small bunch mint

juice of ½ lemon

4 salmon fillets, skin on

sea salt

1 tbsp grapeseed or olive oil

25g raisins, presoaked in hot water to plump (optional)

1 preserved lemon, quartered, flesh removed, rinsed and finely chopped (optional)

1 tbsp chopped green/red chilli (optional)

FOR THE AVOCADO CREAM

1 ripe avocado

juice of 1 lime

dash of milk

Heat the oil in a medium saucepan. Add the onion and cook over a medium heat until softened. Add the garlic, ginger and spices and cook for a further 2 minutes.

Meanwhile, cook the salmon. Season the salmon flesh with salt. Heat a large non-stick pan over a medium heat, add a little oil and, when hot, carefully place the salmon skin-side down in the pan.

Add the lentils to the saucepan with the spicy onion mix and add the stock. Cook over a gentle heat for about 5 minutes.

Now make the avocado cream. Halve the avocado, remove the stone and scoop out the flesh. If you've got a hand blender, whizz all the ingredients in a jug with a pinch of salt and purée until smooth. You want a yogurt-like consistency (add a little extra milk, if necessary). If you don't own a hand blender, mash the avocado with a fork or potato masher or pass through a sieve, then mix with the lime juice and milk and season with salt.

Return to the salmon. Turn the fillets over – the skin should be crispy by now.

Finely chop the herbs and add to the lentils. Season to taste and finish with a squeeze of lemon juice. Add raisins, preserved lemon and chilli, if you fancy.

Serve the lentils topped with salmon and a spoonful of avocado cream.

VARIATIONS

- Serve with roasted butternut squash, griddled courgettes with lemon and mint or purple sprouting broccoli with pine nuts and tahini yogurt.
- These lentils are great served cold the next day with some flaked smoked mackerel or crumbled feta, or even just on their own with a little Greek yogurt.

Earthy puy lentils jazzed up with citrus and spice – a perfect partner for Ginger Beer and Tangerine Glazed Ham (recipe #12). If you have any leftovers, try serving with some pan-fried shredded squid. < SERVES 4–6 >

CHILLI AND TANGERINE BRAISED LENTILS

Heat the olive oil in a large saucepan over a medium heat. Add the carrot, onion, celery, garlic and chilli and cook until the vegetables begin to soften (about 5 minutes).

Meanwhile, place the lentils in a fine mesh colander and rinse well under cold water. Drain before adding to the vegetables.

Add the hot stock and about two thirds of the tangerine juice. Bring to the boil, then reduce the heat and simmer for 20–25 minutes or until the lentils are al dente and most of the liquid has been absorbed. Add a little more stock if the lentils look a little dry during cooking.

Remove from the heat and stir in the tangerine zest and remaining juice. Season, then leave to cool a little before stirring through the crème fraîche and parsley. Serve warm or at room temperature.

VARIATIONS

- If serving with Ginger Beer and Tangerine Glazed Ham (recipe #12), use the hot ham cooking liquor to cook the lentils instead of chicken or vegetable stock.

- Finish with chopped fresh mint or coriander. Or vary the recipe by replacing the lentils with fresh borlotti beans – you'll need to cook for an additional 30–40 minutes, so will need a little extra stock or water.

- Lentils are one of the most versatile ingredients, so try taking them on a flavour journey, from Morocco to the Mediterranean: omit the ginger and spices, add a dash of tomato purée, some fennel seeds (optional), cherry tomato halves and continue to cook as above. Finish with lots of fresh basil and parsley, a squeeze of lemon and a glug of extra virgin olive oil. Stir through a spoon of ricotta the next day, or serve topped with a little grated Parmesan.

2 tbsp olive oil

1 carrot, finely chopped

1 onion, finely chopped

1 celery stick, finely chopped

1 garlic clove, finely chopped

1 red chilli, deseeded and finely chopped

225g puy lentils

550ml chicken or vegetable stock

zest of 2 tangerines and juice of 6 tangerines

sea salt and black pepper

2 tbsp crème fraîche

small bunch flatleaf parsley, finely chopped

115

My autumnal version of falafel — sweet and lightly fragranced with fresh coriander. The salad adds freshness and colour. Great as a snack or light lunch.

< MAKES ABOUT 24 >

BUTTERNUT SQUASH FALAFELS

Preheat the oven to 200°C/gas mark 6.

Cut the butternut squash into 2–3cm chunks. Place in a roasting tin and drizzle with the olive oil, season with sea salt and cook for about 20 minutes or until tender. Leave to cool.

When cool, place the butternut squash pieces in a food-processor, together with any juices. Add all the remaining ingredients, except the flour, and blitz to a rough paste. Season to taste. Transfer to a bowl and add enough flour to make a smooth mix. Refrigerate for up to 1 hour to firm the mixture up.

The mixture should be sticky rather than really wet, so add a little more gram flour if necessary. Wet your hands and form into balls about 2–3cm in diameter. Roll in the remaining gram flour, place on a tray lined with floured baking parchment and refrigerate until required.

Heat the oil to 175°C and fry the balls in batches for 3–4 minutes until golden. Remove from the oil and drain on kitchen paper.

For the salad, wash and shave the fennel using a mandolin or sharp knife. Drizzle over the pomegranate molasses, scatter and toss with the pomegranate seeds, spring onions, parsley and salad leaves. Season with salt and pepper.

Serve the falafels with the salad, tahini yogurt sauce and pitta bread on the side so your guests can build their own sandwiches.

700g butternut squash, peeled and deseeded

2 tbsp olive oil

sea salt

2 garlic cloves, finely chopped

2 tsp ground cumin

½ tsp ground coriander

pinch of cayenne pepper

½ tsp baking powder

1 x 400g can chickpeas, rinsed and drained

20g coriander, finely chopped

1 tbsp lemon juice

100g gram (chickpea) flour, plus 50g for dusting

vegetable or groundnut oil, for frying

FOR THE FENNEL, PARSLEY AND POMEGRANATE SALAD

1 fennel bulb

2 tbsp pomegranate molasses

seeds of 1 pomegranate

2 spring onions, finely sliced

20g flatleaf parsley, leaves picked

2 handfuls of mixed salad leaves, such as mizuna and baby red chard

sea salt and black pepper

Tahini Yogurt Sauce (recipe #103)

pitta bread, to serve

117

Ooooh, roasted sweet butternut squash, earthy lentils, fresh mint, sour salty feta, mint and sticky caramelised spiced onions – what more could you ask for? Delightful! < SERVES 4 >

ROASTED BUTTERNUT SQUASH FILLED WITH CARAMELISED PUY LENTILS AND FETA

2 small butternut squash, about 600g each

4 tbsp olive oil

sea salt and black pepper

150g puy lentils

2 onions, halved and thinly sliced

2 garlic cloves, finely chopped

2 tsp cumin seeds

2 tsp ground cumin

1 tsp ground cinnamon

½ tsp sweet paprika

pinch of cayenne pepper

90g feta cheese, crumbled

30g pine nuts

2 tbsp chopped mint

1 tbsp chopped flatleaf parsley

juice of 1 lemon

seeds from ½ pomegranate, to garnish

Heat the oven to 200°C/gas mark 6.

Wash the butternut squash and carefully cut them in half lengthways. Using a spoon, scoop out the seeds and fibrous centre and discard. Put the squash halves on a baking tray cut-side up, drizzle with 1 tablespoon olive oil, season and roast in the oven for about 35 minutes or until the flesh is tender. Remove from the oven and leave to cool slightly.

While the squash is cooking, simmer the lentils for about 30 minutes, until al dente, and drain.

When the squash is cool enough to handle, scoop out some flesh, leaving a border of 1cm, then roughly chop the flesh and put it in a bowl.

Heat 3 tablespoons olive oil in a large frying pan, add the onions and garlic and cook until beginning to caramelise (about 15 minutes). Add the spices and cook for 2 minutes more. Add the lentils, squash flesh and 200ml hot water and simmer for 8 minutes, until most of the water has been absorbed. Remove from the heat and stir through the feta cheese, pine nuts, herbs and lemon juice. Season to taste with salt and pepper.

Spoon the mixture equally between squash halves and cook in the oven for 10–15 minutes. Serve garnished with pomegranate seeds.

VARIATIONS

- You could use 200g precooked lentils, or cook the lentils ahead of time. As another time saver, the filling can be prepared in advance.

118

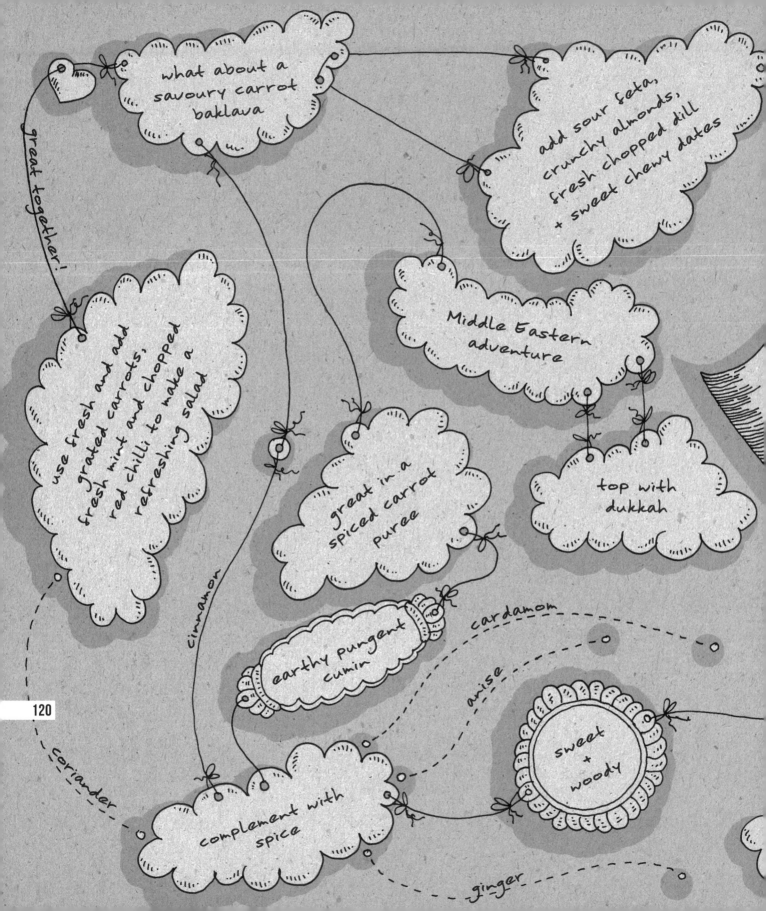

what about a savoury carrot baklava

add sour feta, crunchy almonds, fresh chopped dill + sweet chewy dates

great together!

use fresh and add grated carrots, fresh mint and chopped red chilli to make a refreshing salad

Middle Eastern adventure

great in a spiced carrot puree

top with dukkah

earthy pungent cumin

cardamom

anise

sweet + woody

cinnamon

coriander

complement with spice

ginger

120

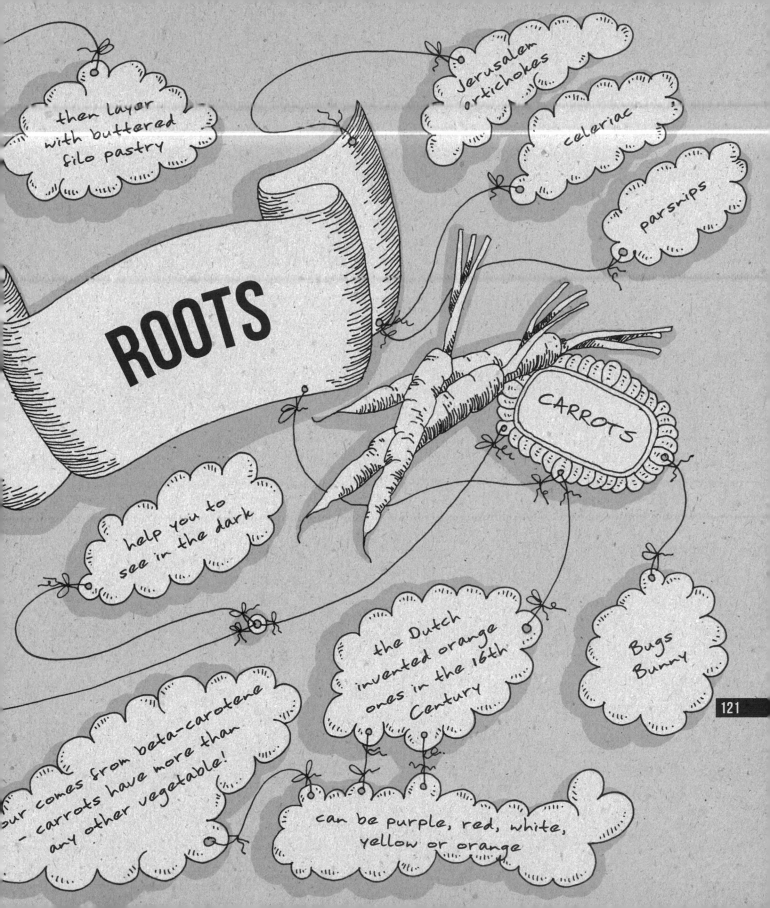

then layer with buttered filo pastry

Jerusalem artichokes

celeriac

parsnips

ROOTS

CARROTS

help you to see in the dark

the Dutch invented orange ones in the 16th Century

Bugs Bunny

our comes from beta-carotene — carrots have more than any other vegetable!

can be purple, red, white, yellow or orange

I experimented combining mozzarella and Porcini Salt and it was a complete revolution. This flatbread recipe was designed to showcase their harmonious relationship.

#56

< SERVES 4 GENEROUSLY>

NEW POTATO FLATBREAD
WITH ROCKET, MOZZARELLA AND PORCINI SALT

In a small bowl, combine the yeast, sugar and water and leave in a warm place until foaming (about 10 minutes).

Combine the flour and salt in a mixing bowl, and pour in the olive oil and yeast mix. If you have a food-processor with a dough hook attachment, use this to form a dough; otherwise, get mixing by hand until the dough is cohesive. Turn out on to a lightly floured surface and knead until smooth and elastic (about 10 minutes). The dough will be quite sticky at first, but it'll come together once you start kneading – rubbing a little olive oil into your hands will make this easier.

Place the dough in a clean, oiled bowl, cover and leave in a warm place until doubled in size (about 1–1½ hours).

Preheat the oven as high as it will go.

Cook the potatoes in salted water until just tender. Drain, leave to cool, then cut into 5mm slices. Place a large upturned baking tray in the oven.

Turn out the dough and knock back. On a lightly floured surface, roll and gently stretch the dough into a rounded rectangle to fit the baking tray. Place on a piece of baking parchment, drizzle with olive oil and lightly season with Porcini Salt and pepper. Top with mozzarella and potato slices, then season again with Porcini Salt and pepper. Carefully slide on to the hot upside-down baking tray and bake in the middle of the oven until the base is crisp (about 10–12 minutes).

Remove the flatbread from the oven, top with the rocket leaves, then drizzle lightly with olive oil and serve.

VARIATIONS

• These flatbreads are really good with a poached egg on top.

FOR THE FLATBREAD

10g active dried yeast

10g sugar

250ml warm water

420g plain flour

2 tsp sea salt

1 tbsp extra virgin olive oil, plus extra for drizzling (or use truffle oil)

FOR THE TOPPING

200g Jersey Royals or new potatoes, washed

3 tbsp olive oil, plus extra for drizzling

Porcini Salt (recipe #107)

freshly ground black pepper

250g ball of buffalo mozzarella

handful of rocket leaves

The earthy Jerusalem artichokes and spicy sweet chorizo complement each other beautifully. Deep undertones also run through from the chestnuts, and the caramelised apples add a bit of 'zing'. A luxurious soup. < SERVES 4 >

JERUSALEM ARTICHOKE AND CHESTNUT SOUP WITH CHORIZO AND APPLE

50g unsalted butter

4 shallots, thinly sliced

2 garlic cloves, thinly sliced

2 tbsp chopped thyme leaves

1kg Jerusalem artichokes, peeled, sliced and placed in acidulated water

50ml sherry

55g cooked chestnuts (I use the vacuum packed ones)

1 litre chicken stock

sea salt and black pepper

½ Bramley apple, peeled, cored and cut into 1cm dice

10g caster sugar

knob of butter

olive oil

1 cooking chorizo

200ml cream (optional)

2 tbsp chopped flatleaf parsley, to serve

Heat the butter in a large pan. Add the shallots and cook over a low heat for 10 minutes until softened and slightly caramelized. Add the garlic, thyme and Jerusalem artichokes and cook for a further 5 minutes. Add the sherry, chestnuts and chicken stock and bring to the boil. Reduce to a simmer, season with salt and pepper and cook until the artichokes are tender (about 15–20 minutes).

Meanwhile, preheat a frying pan, toss the apple in the sugar and pour into the hot pan. The sugar will start to caramelise as it hits the pan; add a knob of butter and cook for 1 minute over a high heat until golden. Set aside.

Wipe the pan with kitchen paper and preheat again. Slice the chorizo and cook in the hot frying pan with a little olive oil for 3 minutes and set aside.

Blitz the artichoke mixture in a blender until smooth, then return to the pan, adding cream if desired. Check the seasoning and warm through. Add a little extra stock or water if it's too thick.

Divide the soup between four bowls. Top with the chorizo, drizzle with chorizo oil and scatter with apple and a sprinkling of parsley. Serve with crusty bread.

124

#58

I love food like this! I normally make my dukkah with hazelnuts, but I think the almonds provide a better combination with the carrot purée.

< SERVES 8 >

SPICED CARROT PURÉE WITH DUKKAH

FOR THE DUKKAH
100g almonds, blanched
50g coriander seeds
20g cumin seeds
75g sesame seeds
sea salt and black pepper

FOR THE CARROT PURÉE
1kg carrots, cut into 2cm pieces
100ml extra virgin olive oil, plus more for drizzling
2 tbsp lemon juice
1 tbsp harissa
1 tsp ground cinnamon
pinch of ground ginger
sea salt and black pepper

To make the dukkah, toast the almonds in a medium pan over a medium heat until golden. Transfer to a work surface to cool a little, then finely chop. Transfer to a bowl.

Add the coriander and cumin seeds to the pan and toast until fragrant (about 2 minutes). Transfer to a pestle and mortar, leave to cool completely, then coarsely grind and mix with the almonds.

Toast the sesame seeds until golden, leave to cool, then grind, together with 2 teaspoons sea salt. Add to the almond mixture and season with black pepper.

To make the carrot purée, cook the carrots in a large saucepan with water until tender. Drain and return the carrots to pan over a medium heat to dry thoroughly (about 1 minute). Remove from the heat and mash the carrots with a potato masher or whiz until smooth in a blender.

Gradually, blend in the olive oil, lemon juice, harissa, cinnamon and ginger. Season with sea salt and pepper.

Transfer the carrot purée to a large, flat bowl. Using the back of a spoon, smooth the surface, raising a little at the edges, drizzle with olive oil and sprinkle with the dukkah. Serve at room temperature with hot Turkish or pitta bread or a flatbread.

VARIATIONS

- Substitute the carrots for butternut squash or use a green pumpkin; roast in the oven until tender, then follow recipe above.
- For flavour variations, add some chopped dried apricots to the carrot purée or blend with some cooked red lentils. Finish with chopped coriander or mint for a fresher, less earthy flavour.

126

A simple summer salad that, served with Carrot Baklava (recipe #63), lends additional texture along with colour. Alternatively, you could serve it with Pomegranate Labneh (recipe #105). < SERVES 4 AS AN ACCOMPANIMENT >

#59

CARROT AND HERB SALAD

Lightly peel the carrots, cut off the roots and trim the carrot tops to 1cm in length. Place in a pot of cold salted water and bring to the boil. Simmer until just tender (about 6 minutes). Drain and cut in half lengthways.

Whisk together vinegar, oil and honey, and pour over the hot carrots, Season, toss with herbs and serve immediately.

VARIATIONS

- To make this salad go further, serve with Orange and Sumac Scented Quinoa (recipe #51) or with Middle Eastern Kebab (recipe #5).
- Additional extras to add to the salad: flaked almonds, chilli-roasted feta, spiced sunflower seeds and cooked barley.

8 baby carrots (if you can get a variety of colours, so much the better)

few carrot leaf tops

10ml Chardonnay vinegar (if unavailable, use white wine vinegar)

20ml extra virgin olive oil

1 tbsp clear honey

sea salt and black pepper

½ bunch purslane, if available (if not, use baby spinach)

few sprigs flatleaf parsley, picked

By cooking the parsnips in various ways you will not only create different tastes, but textures that will complement each other beautifully. This is a perfect salad to serve as a starter or as a light lunch. < SERVES 4 >

TRUFFLED PARSNIP SALAD

First, peel, core and dice the parsnips into 1cm cubes. Heat a large, non-stick frying pan and add the butter. Once hot, add the parsnips, season and cook over a low heat, stirring occasionally, until golden, caramelised and tender. Don't rush this stage – the parsnips need to caramelise slowly to achieve the perfect flavour. Use as big a frying pan as possible, so the parsnips cook in one even layer.

Once caramelised and tender, remove the parsnips from the heat and drizzle with truffle oil. Gently crush about one third with a potato masher or a fork and season as necessary.

For the thyme-roasted parsnips, preheat the oven to 200°C/gas mark 6. Peel the parsnips and cut in half lengthways. Cut each half in half again or into thirds, depending on the size of the parsnips and cut out the woody cores. Place in a roasting tin, drizzle with olive oil, season with sea salt and pepper and sprinkle with thyme. Roast in the oven for about 10 minutes, until golden and tender.

Now for the purée. Peel, halve and core the parsnips and slice into 2cm pieces. Place in a saucepan add the milk, a pinch of salt and simmer until soft. Drain the parsnips, reserving the cooking liquor and whizz while hot in a blender, adding the lemon juice and olive oil until smooth but thick. Add a little of the parsnip liquor to thin, if necessary. Season if needed.

Warm the roasted parsnips and the purée; the truffled parsnips should be warm or served at room temperature. Spread a slick of purée on to each plate, top with truffled parsnips followed by the roasted ones.

Toss the watercress leaves with the vinegar and oil and place on top of the parsnips. Sprinkle with the shaved cheese of your choice and serve immediately.

VARIATIONS

- Try serving the truffled parsnips with roasted chicken, guinea fowl or pheasant.

FOR THE TRUFFLED PARSNIPS
2 large parsnips
100g unsalted butter
sea salt and black pepper
4 tbsp truffle oil

FOR THE THYME-ROASTED PARSNIPS
2 large parsnips
50ml olive oil
sea salt and black pepper
2 tsp thyme leaves

FOR THE PARSNIP PURÉE
2 parsnips
250ml milk
pinch of sea salt
1 tbsp lemon juice
1 tbsp olive oil

TO SERVE
1 bunch watercress, picked into small sprigs
2 tbsp Cabernet Sauvignon vinegar (if unavailable, use red wine vinegar)
2 tbsp truffle oil
75g shaved hard sheep's milk cheese, such as Berkswell or pecorino

129

#61

An idea that literally popped into my head one day; adding some spark to flapjacks. This is a great way of introducing fruit and vegetables to a sweet snack!

< MAKES ABOUT 24 FLAPJACKS >

CARROT AND APPLE FLAPJACKS

125g unsalted butter
2 tbsp golden syrup or honey
85g light muscovado sugar
½ tsp baking powder
pinch of sea salt
2 tsp ground cinnamon
1 carrot, grated
1 green apple, grated
325g porridge oats

Preheat the oven to 180°C/gas mark 4. Line a 30 x 20cm baking tray with baking parchment.

Gently melt the butter in a saucepan. Add the golden syrup, sugar, baking powder, salt and cinnamon.

Remove from the heat and stir in the carrot, apple and porridge oats until just combined.

Spoon the mixture into the prepared baking tray and smooth with the back of a spoon. Cook in the oven for 20–25 minutes until golden and fairly firm to touch.

Remove from the oven and cut flapjacks while hot. Leave to cool, before transferring to a wire rack.

VARIATIONS

- Try adding 20g chopped skin-on almonds for a touch of texture.
- Add the zest of 1 orange.
- Experiment with different fruit and vegetable combinations.

Celeriac is not one of the prettiest of vegetables, but its taste makes up for its looks! A member of the parsley family, it tastes a little like celery. You'll need to cut away the skin before using. < SERVES 4 >

#62

CELERIAC AND BUTTER BEAN SOUP SWIRLED WITH SAGE BURNT BUTTER

Warm the butter in a large pan, add the onion, celery and garlic and cook until softened. Add the celeriac and cook for a further 5 minutes. Add the butter beans and milk or stock and cook over a low heat until the celeriac has softened (about 30–40 minutes).

Add the cream and warm through, then whizz in a blender until silky smooth. Add a dash of water if a little too thick.

Transfer the soup back to the pan, reheat gently and season with sea salt and black pepper.

To make the sage burnt butter, place the butter in a saucepan and heat until it begins to foam. Add the sage and cook until the butter has browned, then squeeze in the lemon juice. Spoon the sage burnt butter over the soup or cool and gently reheat when ready to use.

50g unsalted butter

1 onion, finely chopped

1 celery stick, finely chopped

2 garlic cloves, finely chopped

1 medium celeriac (about 600g), roughly chopped into 2cm pieces

1 x 400g can butter beans, drained and rinsed

750ml milk or chicken stock

250ml double cream

sea salt and black pepper

FOR THE SAGE BURNT BUTTER

100g butter

10 sage leaves

1 tbsp lemon juice

131

Baklava is usually sweet, but this recipe is anything but 'usual'! Roasted carrots are combined here with sour feta, crunchy almonds and aromatic dill to create a delicious vegetarian dinner sensation. < SERVES 6–8 >

CARROT, DILL, ALMOND AND FETA BAKLAVA

3 tbsp olive oil

1 large onion, halved and thinly sliced

1 garlic clove, finely chopped

1kg carrots, peeled, halved and thinly sliced

1 bunch fresh dill, finely chopped, including roots (or 3 tsp dried)

3 tsp ground cinnamon

finely grated zest of 1 lemon

juice of ½ lemon

sea salt

1 packet filo pastry (9 sheets)

100g butter, melted

90g whole almonds, blanched and blitzed to a coarse breadcrumb consistency

250g feta cheese, crumbled

4 tbsp clear honey

Preheat the oven to 180°C/gas mark 4.

Heat the olive oil in a large saucepan. Gently fry the onion over a low heat until caramelised (about 15 minutes); don't rush this bit – you want the onion to be nice and sticky, so use the time to prepare the other ingredients while it's cooking.

Stir in the garlic, carrots, dill, cinnamon, lemon zest and juice and heat for a further 2 minutes. Season with salt and add 500ml water. Cook over a medium heat until most of the liquid has been absorbed and the carrots are tender, stirring frequently and adding more liquid if necessary. This will take about 25 minutes.

Remove from the heat and, using a hand blender, whizz about one third of the carrot mixture, then mix with the remaining carrots.

Unfold the filo pastry and cut in half lengthways. Keep it covered with a damp cloth while you work to prevent it from drying out. Brush a 30 x 20cm baking tray with a little melted butter. Brush one sheet of filo with butter, top with another, brush again and top with another. Line the baking tray with this three-sheet layer.(Filo pastry brands differ, so cut according to your tin size.)

Spread half the carrot mixture over the pastry, and sprinkle with half the almonds and feta. Sandwich another three sheets of filo together as before with melted butter and place on top of the carrot mixture. Cover with the remaining carrot mixture, almonds and feta and a final three-sheet layer of filo.

Lightly score the top with a knife, cutting into 6–8 diagonals or squares. Brush with butter and sprinkle with a little water.

Place in the oven and bake for 30–35 minutes until golden. Remove from the oven and leave to cool a little before drizzling with honey.

The baklava is delicious with Carrot and Herb Salad (recipe #59).

add earthy red lentils

Yum – imagine with lamb!

also a memb

tomatoes add acidity

finish with punchy pomegranate molasses

top with creamy yogurt + sprinkle with sumac to give a lemony twist

garam masala

and...

make a soup!

warming spices

ginger

chilli

garlic

tahini, garlic, cumin, lemon juice

BLEND WITH

134

Baba Ghanoush

chargrilled over an open flame – smoky aubergines

Aubergines and halloumi are two of my favourite ingredients, the former because of their versatility and the latter because it reminds me of my childhood! Great as a side with slow roasted lamb. < SERVES 8 >

AUBERGINE WRAPPED HALLOUMI WITH POMEGRANATE LABNEH

Brush each aubergine slice with the olive oil and season with sea salt and pepper.

Preheat a griddle pan or barbecue and cook the slices in batches over a medium heat until golden and tender. Set aside to cool.

Place a piece of the halloumi at the end of each aubergine slice. Squeeze over the lemon juice and sprinkle with a little dried oregano.

Roll each aubergine slice up to enclose the halloumi and place on a baking tray. Heat the parcels under a hot grill or in the oven until the cheese begins to soften. Alternatively, wrap them in foil and heat on a barbecue.

To make the pomegranate molasses dressing, whisk all of the ingredients together with 1 tablespoon water until emulsified.

Serve the halloumi with some rocket leaves dressed with pomegranate dressing. Scatter with pomegranate seeds and serve with the labneh on the side.

VARIATIONS

- I like to serve this dish scattered with a few crushed blanched almonds to add a little texture.
- If you can't get hold of pomegranate molasses, try making your own, using 700ml pomegranate juice, 120ml lemon juice and 100g sugar. (Use less sugar if your juice already has added sugar.) Combine all the ingredients, heat and reduce to a simmer until thickened to a syrup.

2 aubergines, cut lengthways in ½–1cm slices (you'll need 8 slices in all)

good glug of olive oil

sea salt and black pepper

2 x 250g packets of halloumi, each sliced into four lengthways

juice of ½ lemon

large pinch of dried oregano

Pomegranate and Mint Labneh (optional) – recipe #105

handful of rocket leaves

pomegranate seeds

FOR THE POMEGRANATE MOLASSES DRESSING

1 garlic clove, crushed

5 tablespoons extra virgin olive oil

2 tablespoons pomegranate molasses

dash of red wine vinegar

1 tablespoon honey

sea salt and black pepper

This to me would be a perfect campside soup. Smoky aubergines, winter warming spices with a touch of tartness from the pomegranate molasses. A soup with depth of flavour just waiting to be cooked. < SERVES 4 >

SMOKED AUBERGINE, TOMATO AND RED LENTIL SOUP

1 aubergine
1 tbsp olive oil
1 onion, finely chopped
2 garlic cloves, finely chopped
40g fresh ginger, finely chopped
1 red chilli, deseeded and finely chopped
2 tsp garam masala
8 vine-ripe tomatoes, peeled and finely chopped, juices reserved
200g red lentils
sea salt and black pepper
4 tbsp Greek yogurt
2 tbsp pomegranate molasses
2 tsp sumac
1 tbsp roughly chopped flatleaf parsley

Pierce the aubergine with a fork and place directly on an open flame or on a preheated griddle pan. Cook until charred all over and softened. Place in a colander and leave to cool.

Heat the oil in a large saucepan. Add the onion and cook until softened and lightly browned. Add the garlic and ginger, cook for a further 2 minutes. Then add the chilli and garam masala and cook for a further minute before adding the tomatoes. Reduce the heat to a simmer and cook for 10 minutes.

Meanwhile, peel the aubergine and finely chop the flesh. Place in a colander to drain off the bitter juices.

Add 500ml hot water to the tomato mixture and cook for a further 10 minutes. Add the aubergine flesh, then purée two thirds of the soup in batches. Return the puréed soup to the pan with 200ml water and heat.

Rinse the red lentils in a fine sieve until the water runs clear, then add to the soup. Cook over a low heat until the lentils are tender (about 15–20 minutes). If the soup is a little too thick, add a dash of hot water. Once the lentils are tender, season with sea salt and pepper.

Ladle the soup into bowls and top with a swirl of yogurt, pomegranate molasses and a sprinkling of sumac and parsley. Serve hot.

Charred, smoky aubergines, blended with tahini, garlic and lemon juice make a dip bursting with flavour. Perfect as an accompaniment to Middle Eastern Kebab (recipe #5) or Aubergine Wrapped Halloumi (#64). < SERVES 4 >

BABA GHANOUSH

Prick the aubergines all over with a fork; this will stop them from bursting. Place aubergines directly over a gas flame or on a barbecue and cook until the skin is blackened and the flesh soft, turning frequently. (If you have an electric hob, you can place under a hot grill instead – unfortunately, you won't end up with such a smoky flavour though.)

Place the aubergines in a colander until cool enough to handle. Holding on to the stalk, peel away and discard the blackened skins. Place the aubergine flesh in a colander to drain off the bitter juices.

Place the aubergine flesh in a blender and pulse to break up. Add the tahini (best to stir it in the jar before using), garlic, cumin, sea salt and a little lemon juice. Pulse to mix, retaining a little texture. Add more lemon juice and extra salt if required. (If you prefer a smoother texture, blitz until smooth and slowly blend in the olive oil while the motor is running.)

Serve with warm pitta bread for dipping.

2 large aubergines
3 heaped tbsp tahini
2 garlic cloves, finely chopped
pinch of ground cumin
sea salt
juice of 1 lemon
100ml olive oil

139

#67

I promise you, cooking the aubergines to a dark brown colour really does make all the difference. Thank you Neil and Angela at Rockpool in Sydney for the inspiration for this recipe. < SERVES 4 AS A SIDE DISH>

AUBERGINE MULL

300ml olive oil

1 large aubergine, cut in half lengthways, then into 5mm slices

2 garlic cloves, finely chopped

pinch of cayenne pepper

1 tsp paprika

½ tsp ground cumin

4 plum vine tomatoes, peeled and cut into quarters

sea salt

juice of ½ lemon

¼ bunch coriander, picked

¼ bunch flatleaf parsley, picked

Heat two thirds of the oil in a large frying pan, add half the aubergine slices and cook until well browned. Remove and drain on kitchen paper.

Heat the remaining oil gently, add the garlic and swirl around the pan off the heat to infuse. Add the spices and tomatoes and return to a low heat. Cook for 5 minutes to soften the tomatoes before adding the aubergines. Cook over a low heat for a further 5 minutes. Season with sea salt.

Remove from the heat, add the lemon juice and leave to cool to room temperature before stirring in the coriander and parsley.

VARIATIONS

- Serve with fish or meat or by itself with flatbread and labneh or Tahini Yogurt Sauce (recipe #103).
- Try adding some chopped preserved lemons or some chopped dates for extra sweetness.

add some goat's cheese

natural affinity with vanilla – slightly peppery

or serve raw shaved into wafer-thin slices

tender and bursting with flavour – stronger than green beans

my favourite green bean!

RUNNER BEANS

grow on wigwams – beautiful red flowers

complement with a little chilli, add some acidity with sweet cherry tomatoes and season with salty anchovies

142

mix with breadcrumbs + Parmesan too – roll into keftedes and fry

toss together with spaghetti + top with Parmesan for a speedy supper Yummy!

OR

toss through pasta

Don't let the title put you off – 'Courgette Fritters' just didn't do the recipe justice. This is a vegetarian version of a Greek classic usually made with lamb. Perfect for a picnic or light lunch. **< SERVES 4–6 >**

#68

COURGETTE KEFTEDES

Blanch the courgettes in boiling water for 2 minutes then drain and squeeze dry in a cloth.

Heat a little oil in a pan and fry the onions until soft. Place in a bowl and combine with the courgettes, cheeses, herbs, eggs and half the breadcrumbs. Season with salt and pepper. If the mixture is too wet, add a few more breadcrumbs. Chill in the fridge for about 1 hour to allow the mix to set.

Taste for seasoning before shaping into walnut-sized balls. Season the flour with salt and coat the balls in flour.

Heat a little oil and fry the balls in batches until golden on all sides (about 2–3 minutes). Remove and drain on kitchen paper.

Serve with a squeeze of lemon and tzatziki .

VARIATIONS

- Serve with Spiced Carrot Purée (recipe #58) or with griddled halloumi. Also delicious with Dill and Lemon Marinated Lamb (recipe #18) or pan-fried fish, prawns or squid.

450g courgettes, trimmed and grated

vegetable oil, for frying

2 tbsp grated onion

150g feta cheese, crumbled

75g grated Parmesan

2 tbsp chopped parsley

2 tbsp chopped mint

2 eggs, beaten

6–8 tbsp fresh breadcrumbs

sea salt and black pepper

plain flour, for dusting

1 lemon, to serve

tzatziki, to serve

145

Spinach, raisin and pine nuts have a natural affinity to one another. Use as an accompaniment to fish or lamb, and take your spinach to new heights by adjusting the recipe using the variations below. < SERVES 4 AS A SIDE DISH >

SPINACH WITH GARLIC, RAISINS AND PINE NUTS

2 tbsp olive oil
500g spinach, stems removed
2 garlic cloves, finely chopped
2 tbsp pine nuts, lightly roasted
2 tbsp raisins, soaked in hot water for 15 minutes and drained
sea salt

Gently heat half the olive oil in a large frying pan, add the spinach and cook until it starts to wilt. Remove from the heat and drain the spinach in a colander.

Return the pan to the heat, add the remaining olive oil, then fry the garlic until softened, but not browned. Add the spinach, pine nuts and raisins. Season with sea salt and cook for a further minute.

VARIATIONS

- Add some diced potatoes to the spinach to make a more substantial side dish.
- Try adding some capers – they are go brilliantly with raisins.
- Soak the raisins in sherry vinegar to create a little punch. You could also add a some chopped red chilli to the garlic.

Another recipe oozing with Greek flavours – lemon and dill add punch to the broad beans. Best made the day before – and it is well worth the effort to double pod the beans.   < SERVES 4 AS A SIDE DISH >

LEMON AND DILL BRAISED BROAD BEANS

Shell the broad beans and remove their outer coats. If using fresh, the easiest way to do this is to blanch them for 1 minute in boiling water, then refresh in cold water. If using frozen, defrost in water, then pop the beans out of their shells.

Heat the oil in a large pan and gently fry the onion until softened without colour. Add the garlic, sugar and sea salt, and cook for a further 2 minutes. Add the beans and stock and simmer over a low heat for about 20 minutes until the beans are tender and most of the liquid has evaporated.

Remove from the heat, stir in the lemon juice and dill and season to taste. Leave to stand for 1 hour before serving or, preferably, overnight.

Serve at room temperature, sprinkled with a little feta, if desired.

1kg fresh broad beans in their shells (or 375g frozen)

70ml extra virgin olive oil

1 onion, *finely chopped*

1 garlic clove, *finely chopped*

pinch of sugar

pinch of sea salt

300ml chicken stock or water

juice of 1 lemon

small bunch dill, *finely chopped*

feta cheese, to serve (optional)

VARIATION

- Try adding 2 globe artichokes to the ingredients above – you will need to prepare these ahead of time. Place the artichokes in a large pot of acidulated water with a pinch of salt. Cover with paper and weigh down with a plate or small lid. Cook for about 20 minutes until tender and the tough outer leaves can be easily removed (the timing will depend on the size of the artichokes). Remove all the tough outer leaves and trim the stalks, cut in half, remove the fuzzy choke and cut each half into thirds. Place in acidulated water until required, to prevent discolouration. Add the artichokes to the recipe when frying the onion, then continue as above, adding a little extra stock if required.

Fantastic, tangy sorrel leaves, bursting with flavour are available from farmers' markets, along with dandelion leaves. Sorrel has a natural affinity with eggs and oily fish. < SERVES 4 >

ROAST TENDERSTEM BROCCOLI SALAD WITH SOFT-BOILED EGG AND SORREL DRESSING

800g tenderstem broccoli, trimmed to florets of equal size

50ml olive oil

sea salt and black pepper

4 eggs, at room temperature

40g Berkswell, pecorino or Parmesan cheese, freshly shaved

1 head dandelion leaves, washed and cut into 5cm lengths

2 handfuls of mixed baby leaves, such as ruby chard, baby spinach, mizuna and mustard

FOR THE DRESSING

25g shallots, finely chopped

¼ tsp garlic, finely chopped

75ml extra virgin olive oil

75ml olive oil

50ml Chardonnay vinegar (if unavailable, use white wine vinegar)

½ tbsp wholegrain mustard

3 sorrel leaves, finely chopped

Preheat the oven to 190°C/gas mark 5.

Place the broccoli in a bowl, drizzle with olive oil, season with salt and pepper and toss well. Scatter into a roasting tin and roast in the oven for 3–5 minutes or until the broccoli is tender. Remove from the oven and leave to cool.

Place the eggs in boiling water and cook for 4–5 minutes (depending on how soft you like the yolks), then remove from the pan, plunge into cold water and peel carefully.

Next, make the dressing. Whisk all of the ingredients together and refrigerate until required.

Place the broccoli, cheese and leaves in a large bowl, toss with dressing to coat, gently season and serve, garnished with torn soft-boiled eggs.

VARIATIONS

- This recipe would be equally delicious made with cauliflower in place of the broccoli.
- Substitute the soft-boiled hen's eggs for duck's eggs if you can get them; allow a little longer for cooking though.
- If sorrel is unavailable, substitute with parsley, dill, tarragon or chervil.

The asparagus season doesn't last too long, so I always try to embrace this wonderful unique flavour when the opportunity is there. Best to start the oil a day ahead to allow the flavour to infuse. < SERVES 4 >

SHAVED ASPARAGUS, GOAT'S CURD AND VANILLA CROSTINI

FOR THE VANILLA OIL
1 vanilla pod
150ml light olive oil

FOR THE GOAT'S CURD
150g goat's cheese
3 tbsp crème fraîche
8 large asparagus spears
sea salt
2 tbsp lemon juice
1 tbsp chopped chervil (optional)

FOR THE CROSTINI
4 slices crusty bread (I like to use ciabatta)
olive oil, for drizzling

To make the oil, halve the vanilla pods lengthways and scrape out the seeds, mixing all but a pinch with the oil. Add the pods and leave to infuse at room temperature, covered, for a minimum of 1 day.

To make the curd, trim away any rind from the cheese and cut into small pieces. Place in a blender and add the reserved vanilla seeds. Pulse to break down before adding the crème fraîche. Pulse again until smooth, taking care not to overblend causing the curd to split. (If you don't have a blender, use a potato masher to break the cheese down.) If preparing ahead, chill in the refrigerator and remove 20 minutes before serving.

Using a mandolin set over a large bowl (or a vegetable peeler), shave the asparagus lengthways into wafer-thin strips. Season with sea salt, add the lemon juice and chervil, if using. Stir the vanilla oil well and pour half of it over the asparagus; toss and set aside while preparing the crostini.

Preheat a griddle pan. Drizzle the bread slices with olive oil, place on the hot griddle pan and cook until crisp and golden.

Remove the crostini from the heat, spread the curd over the bread and top with the shaved asparagus. Drizzle with the remaining vanilla oil and serve.

VARIATIONS

- To simplify the recipe, top the crostini with a young goat's cheese and omit the curd altogether (you will need 225g in total).
- Omit the goat's cheese and blend a little white crabmeat with a spoonful of crème fraîche or mayonnaise, season, mix with chopped chervil and serve with the crostini and shaved asparagus.

I love the process of making gnocchi, and green olives
add a new dimension. Fresh seasonal greens including
asparagus and peas add an abundance of flavour to
an otherwise everyday Italian staple. < SERVES 4 >

GREEN OLIVE GNOCCHI WITH WILTED GREENS

Preheat the oven to 200°C/gas mark 6.

To make the gnocchi, place the potatoes on a non-stick baking tray and cook until tender, about 1–1½ hours. While still hot, halve and scoop out the flesh, then pass through a fine sieve, potato ricer or mouli into a bowl.

Turn the potatoes out on to a clean work surface dusted with flour. Mix with the olives, sea salt, pepper and nutmeg. Make a well in the centre, pour in the egg and gradually work in two thirds of the flour. Bring the mixture together with your hands to form a smooth, soft dough, adding more flour if necessary.

I always like to test a little of the dough by cooking a small piece in boiling salted water. Cook until the gnocchi floats; if it falls apart, add a little more flour. Check for seasoning and adjust as necessary.

Cut the dough into four, then roll each piece into a sausage 1cm thick. Cut each sausage into 1.5cm pieces and place on a tray lined with baking parchment and sprinkled lightly with flour. You can make the gnocchi ahead of time and refrigerate until required.

Bring a large saucepan of salted water to the boil. Cook the gnocchi in batches (use the baking parchment as a chute to help you transfer them to the pan) until they come to the surface (about 1–2 minutes). Count to 10, then remove with a slotted spoon or sieve, to a bowl of iced water. Drain, drizzle with olive oil and set aside.

Bring a clean saucepan of salted water to the boil. Blanch the peas and asparagus until tender, remove and refresh in iced water, then drain and set aside. Add the chard leaves and blanch until tender; refresh in iced water, drain, roughly chop and set aside.

Heat the oil in a large non-stick frying pan over a high heat. Add the butter and, once foaming, add the gnocchi. Cook until just starting to colour. Add the asparagus, peas, chard leaves and broccoli, tossing gently to combine. Add the spinach, lemon zest and juice and cook until just wilted. Warm through, season to taste and serve immediately, drizzled with oil and scattered with pecorino.

FOR THE GNOCCHI

450g large floury potatoes (such as King Edward, Marfona or Maris Piper)

50g pitted green olives, roughly chopped

sea salt and black pepper

pinch of freshly grated nutmeg

1 egg, beaten

125–150g '00' flour, plus extra for dusting

125g podded peas (that's about 325g unpodded, or 125g frozen petit pois)

1 bunch asparagus, trimmed and cut into 3cm pieces

½ bunch Swiss chard, leaves only (about 200g) or substitute with kale

good glug of olive oil

25g unsalted butter, diced

250g broccoli, cut into miniature florets

200g baby spinach

finely grated zest and juice of ½ lemon

100g pecorino, shaved or grated

I so look forward to runner bean season. What could be better than freshly picked beans, cooked and tossed in salted butter? Well, apart from this recipe, of course – a quick, easy and very yummy supper! < SERVES 4 >

RUNNER BEAN, ANCHOVY AND TOMATO SPAGHETTI

Heat the olive oil in a large frying pan or wok. Once hot, remove from the heat and add the garlic, chilli flakes and anchovies. Gently swirl the pan to infuse the oil; if the oil is too hot, the garlic will burn and the sauce will taste bitter. If the oil is too hot, add some of the tomatoes – they will immediately lower the temperature.

Add the cherry tomatoes (hopefully you didn't have the oil too hot!), sea salt and tomato purée and simmer over a low heat for about 5 minutes until the tomatoes have softened.

Meanwhile, cook the spaghetti in a large pan of boiling, salted water according to the packet instructions. Four minutes before the end of its cooking time, add the runner beans. Before draining the pasta, add about 2 tablespoons of the cooking water to the tomato sauce to loosen it a little.

Drain the pasta and quickly mix with the tomato sauce, flavour with some pepper, a glug of good olive oil and a little salt if necessary.

Toss with the basil leaves and serve immediately, topped with Parmesan. Italians will be cursing me – they think it's sacrilege to serve Parmesan with fish and pasta, but I love it!

2 tbsp olive oil
2 garlic cloves, finely chopped
pinch of chilli flakes (optional)
12 salted anchovy fillets, roughly chopped
300g cherry tomatoes, halved
pinch of sea salt
2 tbsp tomato purée
350g spaghetti
100g runner beans, trimmed
freshly ground black pepper
glug of olive oil
sea salt
handful of basil leaves (optional), torn
50g Parmesan, grated or shaved

VARIATIONS

- Use green beans cut into thirds, or replace runner beans with juliennes (thin strips) of courgettes.
- Replace the anchovies with cooked crabmeat or prawns; just toss through at the end with the pasta.
- Vegetarians can omit the anchovies and mix through with some crumbled feta and maybe a sprinkling of fresh mint leaves and a little lemon zest.
- Fold through some rocket leaves – they add a hint of peppery spice!
- If you have any leftover roast or braised lamb, shred it and add to the tomato sauce, with or without the anchovies.

153

scent with aromatic fig leaves

mix goat's milk with yogurt for a panna cotta

love it sprinkled over peas with a little dill + lemon

made from ewe's + goat's milk

FETA CHEESE

feta must be produced in Greece + has legal designation. By law feta is cured for at least 3 months in brine

salty + sour

sweeten with icing sugar

= a sensational summer salad - serve with bbq lamb

sweeten with pomegranate molasses

flavour with orange flower water or rosewater

154

mix with crunchy watermelon

toss with almonds

MASALA CHAI RICE PUDDING

FOR THE CHAI
4 green cardamom pods
4 cloves
1 cinnamon stick, lightly crushed
3cm piece of fresh ginger, sliced
4 black peppercorns
4 tbsp black tea leaves
50g palm sugar, jaggery or caster sugar
250ml milk

FOR THE RICE PUDDING
200g pudding rice
25g butter, diced
20g cornflour
250ml milk
50g palm sugar, jaggery or caster sugar (optional)

To make the chai, lightly crush the cardamom pods, cloves and cinnamon with a pestle and mortar.

Put 750ml water in a saucepan and add the crushed spices, ginger and black peppercorns. Bring to the boil, then reduce to a simmer for a few minutes. Remove from the heat, add the tea and leave to infuse for 5–10 minutes.

Add the sugar and milk to the pan, return to the heat and bring almost to a boil. Remove from the heat and leave to steep for 4–5 minutes, before straining.

To make the pudding, place the rice, chai and butter in a medium-sized saucepan and bring to the boil. Once boiling, reduce the heat to a simmer, stir and cover. Cook over a low heat for about 25 minutes, stirring occasionally, until the rice is tender.

Mix together the cornflour and milk to form a smooth paste. Once the rice is cooked, stir in the cornflour mixture, bring back to the boil and cook for a further 5 minutes, stirring continuously. For a sweeter rice pudding, stir in the optional sugar of your choice until dissolved. Serve immediately.

VARIATIONS

- Experiment with different flavour teas such as jasmine, Earl Grey or ginger, for example.

A refreshing summer salad. Serve alone for breakfast, for lunch with grilled prawns or for dinner with some barbecued lamb. It's best made just before serving, so the watermelon doesn't emit too many juices. < SERVES 4 >

FETA AND WATERMELON SALAD

500g watermelon, chilled
2 tbsp pomegranate molasses
2 tbsp extra virgin olive oil
2 tsp rosewater
200g feta cheese
small handful of mint leaves
50g flaked almonds, toasted

Cut the watermelon flesh into large cubes, removing as many seeds as possible. Place in a large bowl and drizzle with the pomegranate molasses, olive oil and rosewater.

Roughly dice the feta, tear the mint leaves and add together with the almonds. Toss with the watermelon. Serve immediately.

DAIRY

In my 'Modern Vegetarian' book I made a gorgeous cake with oranges, almonds and semolina. I decided to replace the orange with rhubarb and see what happened. All good, and this recipe was the result! < SERVES 8 >

YOGURT, RHUBARB AND ALMOND SYRUP CAKE

Preheat the oven to 180°C/gas mark 4.

First roast the rhubarb. Combine the rhubarb, sugar, orange zest and orange flower water in a baking dish, cover with foil and roast in the oven for 10 minutes or until tender. Leave to cool and drain off the cooking juices for the syrup.

Reduce the oven temperature to 160°C/gas mark 3. Grease and line the base of a 25cm springform cake tin.

Cream the butter with the sugar until pale. Beat in the egg yolks one at a time, then sift in the flour, baking powder, semolina and almonds. Add the yogurt and the roasted rhubarb, stirring gently until just combined.

Pour the mixture into the prepared tin and bake for about 1 hour until a skewer inserted into the centre of the cake comes out clean. Check after 45 minutes and cover with foil, if necessary, to prevent the cake from becoming too brown.

Meanwhile, make the syrup. Put the reserved cooking juices into a pan with the honey and 100ml water. Slowly bring to the boil over a low heat. Reduce the heat and simmer until syrupy (about 10 minutes).

Remove the cake from the oven and pierce all over with a skewer. Pour the syrup over the warm cake and leave to cool in the tin.

Serve the cake at room temperature with some crème fraîche.

VARIATIONS

- This cake would be delicious served with a zingy fruit sorbet such as blood orange and pomegranate.

200g rhubarb, trimmed and cut into 4cm lengths
35g caster sugar
finely grated zest of 1 orange
2 tbsp orange flower water
170g butter
110g caster sugar
3 egg yolks
35g plain flour
1½ tsp baking powder
225g semolina
100g ground almonds
70g Greek yogurt
3 tbsp honey
crème fraîche, to serve

159

A quick and easy trifle - layers of soft, spiced ginger cake, sweetened with rhubarb and topped with decadent rose-scented cream. Definitely a trifle to take on a flavour journey! < SERVES 8 >

#78

RHUBARB, ROSEWATER AND GINGER TRIFLE

Heat 400ml water and the sugar together in a medium saucepan until the sugar has dissolved. Add the rhubarb and cook over a medium heat for 5 minutes, or until the rhubarb has softened. Strain the mixture, setting aside the cooking liquor and leave to cool. Stir the Grand Marnier into the cooking liquor, if using.

Whisk the mascarpone, Greek yogurt, rosewater and icing sugar together in a bowl until thickened. Set aside.

Place a slice of ginger cake in the bottom of each of four wine glasses or tumblers and drizzle with enough cooking liquor to moisten without drenching the sponge. Place a spoonful of the cooled rhubarb into each glass, and continue layering in this way until you have used up the cake and the rhubarb. Divide the mascarpone mixture between the glasses, sprinkling each with almonds (if using) and stem ginger, then serve.

150g caster sugar

4–6 sticks rhubarb, trimmed, peeled and chopped into 2cm pieces

2 tbsp Grand Marnier (optional)

250g mascarpone

120g Greek yogurt

2 tsp rosewater

50g icing sugar

½ Jamaican ginger cake, sliced into 8 pieces

10g flaked almonds, toasted (optional)

2 pieces preserved stem ginger, finely chopped

VARIATIONS

- Substitute sponge fingers or an orange and almond cake for the ginger cake.
- Use ginger wine instead of Grand Marnier.
- Add a layer of strawberry slices, marinated in a splash of rosewater and a sprinkling of sugar.
- Take your trifle to new heights by making a rose-scented rhubarb jelly. Soak 2 gelatine leaves in cold water. Place 400g rhubarb in a saucepan with a piece of grated ginger, 150g caster sugar and 100ml water. Cover and simmer over a medium heat until the rhubarb is soft enough to mash (about 10 minutes). Strain and push through a fine sieve into a bowl. Squeeze the gelatine of its water and stir into the warm rhubarb syrup until dissolved. Leave to cool, then stir in 2 tsp rosewater. When the jelly has just begun to set, pour over the second layer of rhubarb and place in the refrigerator until completely set (about 2 hours). Top with rose-scented cream, as above.

161

This recipe is inspired by the awesome Brett Graham – chef at The Ledbury, London. Please don't be put off by the fig leaves. I live in the midst of London and still managed to find a tree! < SERVES 4 >

DRIED FIG LEAF AND GOAT'S MILK PANNA COTTA

4 fig leaves, washed and dried
300ml double cream
2 leaves of gelatine
75ml goat's milk
40g icing sugar
300ml natural yogurt
1 fresh fig, sliced
Dried Fig and Polenta Biscuits, to serve (optional – recipe #109)

Wash the fig leaves thoroughly, pat with kitchen paper and leave to dry in an airing cupboard or other warm place for about 1 week. In the summer, leave them outside – they'll take no time. If you have a food-processor, strip the dried leaves from their cores and blitz to a powder; if not, pound with a pestle and mortar to crush a little.

Pour the cream into a saucepan. Bring to the boil over a low heat until reduced to 125ml. Remove from the heat, add the powdered fig leaves, cover with clingfilm and leave to infuse for 1 hour.

Soak the gelatine leaves in cold water.

Pour the goat's milk into a saucepan and heat to just under boiling point. Remove from the heat, squeeze the gelatine leaves of water and add to the milk. Stir to dissolve.

Pass the fig-leaf-infused cream through a fine sieve into a large bowl and mix with the goat's milk. Discard the fig leaves.

Gently whisk the icing sugar and yogurt into the cream and milk mixture and pour into coffee cups or moulds. Leave to cool a little, then cover and refrigerate until set (about 3–4 hours).

When ready to serve, dip the moulds briefly in hot water, run a round-edged knife around each panna cotta, gently shake and tip on to plates.

Serve with slices of fresh figs and the biscuits.

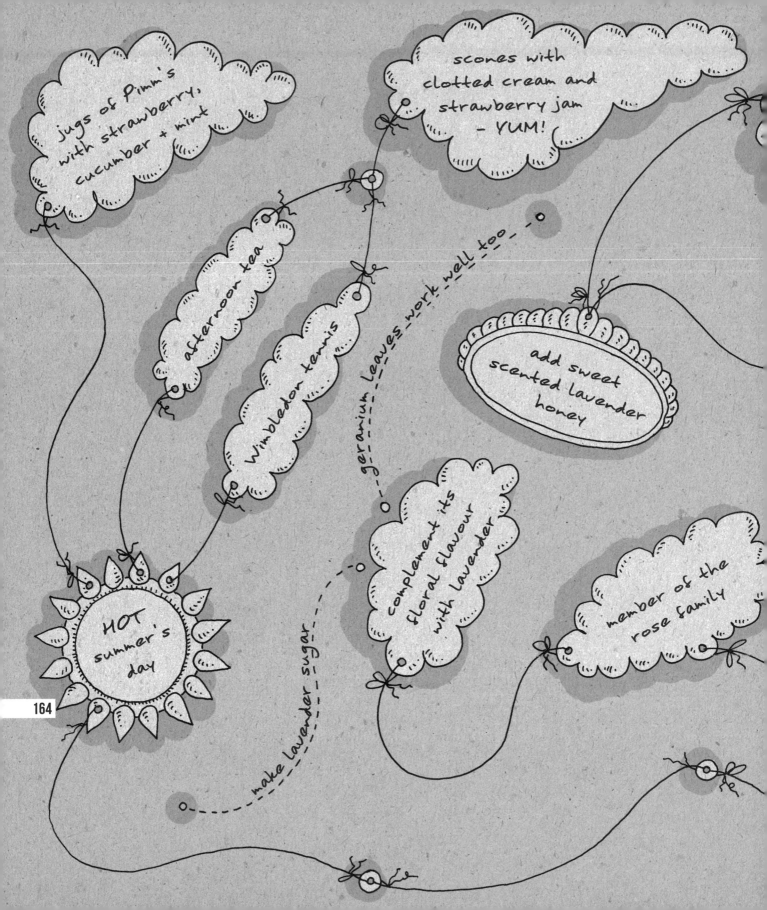

cranberries

raspberries

blueberries

...ulance with sour yogurt mixed
...h softly whipped double cream
— a decadent dessert

fields forever

their sweetness
works in harmony
with buttery
honey dough

BERRIES

STRAWBERRIES

Blueberries are are popular for breakfast — coffee
too. So one day I got to thinking, why not combine the
two ingredients in a muffin? The coffee flavour is really
subtle and works surprisingly well. **< MAKES 6—8 >**

#80

BLUEBERRY AND COFFEE MUFFINS

Preheat the oven to 200°C/gas mark 6. Line six dariole moulds or cups with six 10 x 10cm squares of parchment paper.

Sift the flour and baking powder together in a bowl, then stir in the sugar.

In another bowl, whisk together the eggs, coffee, milk and oil. Pour the liquid ingredients into the flour mixture, add the blueberries and stir until just combined. (Overmixing will result in heavy muffins.)

Spoon the mixture into the prepared moulds, place on a baking tray and cook in the oven for 25 minutes or until golden, and cooked through. Test by inserting the point of a knife to see if it comes out clean.

Leave to cool for 5 minutes in the moulds before turning out on to a wire rack to cool completely. Serve the muffins in their paper 'jackets'.

300g plain flour

1 tbsp baking powder

110g sugar

2 eggs, lightly beaten

4 tsp instant coffee, dissolved in 1 tbsp boiling water

250ml milk

160ml light olive oil

175g blueberries, fresh or frozen

167

BERRIES

#81

Grab gooseberries while you can – their season is pretty short. Turn them into a jelly and use as an accompaniment to sweet or savoury dishes. Great with oily fish such as mackerel, as well as goat's cheese and pork.

GOOSEBERRY JELLY

1.5kg gooseberries
450g sugar per 600ml
gooseberry juice

You will need sterilised jam jars to store your gooseberry jelly, so warm some clean jars in the oven at 100°C/gas mark for 30 minutes.

Wash the gooseberries and sort through them, discarding any that are damaged. Place in a heavy-bottomed saucepan and cover with water. Bring to the boil, then reduce to a simmer and cook until the gooseberries are soft and pulpy (about 30 minutes).

Crush the fruit a little with a potato masher then pour into a jelly bag or a sieve lined with muslin and strain overnight. Place a small plate or saucer in the freezer for later.

Measure the gooseberry juice and heat in a pan with sugar. Add 450g sugar to every 600ml juice. Discard the gooseberries. Heat the juice and sugar in a saucepan, stirring until the sugar is completely dissolved. Bring to the boil and cook rapidly, removing any scum, until the jelly sets when tested. (Test by pouring a little on to your chilled plate or saucer; leave for 30 seconds or so, push the jelly a little and see if it's set. If not, cook for a little longer and test again frequently.)

Pour the jelly into the warmed sterilised jars, cover with a circle of parchment paper and seal when cool. Store in a cool place away from direct sunlight.

VARIATIONS

- Mix a little jelly with some shredded mint and toasted pine nuts and serve with pan-fried mackerel (see recipe #35). Serve with buttered new potatoes and a green leaf salad for a delicious lunch or light dinner after a hard day's fishing!
- Why not use the discarded gooseberry skins to infuse a bottle of vodka? Strain and use in a cocktail with mint and elderflower cordial.

168

I used to dislike rosewater as a kid, but I've since learned to love its delicate perfumed flavour. I think the sourness of the mascarpone and yogurt complements the sweetness of the meringues better than whipped cream. < SERVES 4 >

MIDDLE EASTERN INSPIRED ETON MESS

Whisk together the mascarpone, Greek yogurt, icing sugar and rosewater. Set aside in the refrigerator if using later.

Put the strawberries in a bowl and gently crush about one third of them with the end of a rolling pin. Add the meringues, Turkish delight, almonds and mint. Fold in the mascarpone cream and serve in individual glasses or bowls.

VARIATIONS

- Try replacing the rosewater with orange flower water and use ripe chopped apricots instead of the strawberries.
- Use a different flavoured Turkish delight anothe kind of the nut. For example you could try orange flower Turkish delight with pistachios.

200g mascarpone

100g Greek yogurt

50g icing sugar, sifted

1 tbsp rosewater

200g ripe strawberries, hulled

2 large meringues, broken into rough pieces

4 cubes rose-flavoured Turkish delight, diced

50g skin-on almonds, chopped

8 mint leaves, shredded

#83 Don't worry if you can't find lavender or lavender honey; it'll be just as delicious without! You can prepare the dough two days in advance. Then either fry to order or reheat the cooked dough in the oven. < SERVES 4 >

LAVENDER HONEY DOUGH
WITH CRUSHED STRAWBERRIES, YOGURT AND CREAM

FOR THE DOUGH
1 whole egg plus 3 yolks
50g Lavender Sugar
(recipe #110) or 2 tbsp gently
warmed lavender honey
25g unsalted butter, melted
4 tbsp honey or lavender
honey
225g plain flour
¼ tsp bicarbonate soda
½ tsp baking powder

280ml double cream
280ml Greek yogurt
450g strawberries, hulled and
quartered
50g Lavender Sugar (or just
use caster sugar)
vegetable or grapeseed oil,
for frying

To make the dough, whisk together the whole egg, egg yolks and the lavender sugar, if using, until pale. Whisk in the butter and honey, if using. Sift in the flour, bicarbonate of soda, baking powder and mix until the dough comes together. Turn out on to a lightly floured surface and knead to form a smooth and elastic dough. (If you have a food-processor, use the dough hook for this.) Wrap the dough in clingfilm and leave to rest in a cool place for 30 minutes.

Lightly flour a work surface, roll out the dough to about 2mm thick and cut into twelve 8cm diamonds or rectangles. Place on a lightly flour-dusted sheet of baking parchment and refrigerate until ready to use.

Whisk the cream to form soft peaks, then fold in the yogurt. Refrigerate until required.

Place the strawberries in a bowl and lightly crush with a fork. Sprinkle with the lavender sugar and leave to macerate.

To cook the honey dough, pour the oil into a frying pan until it's 2–3cm deep and heat to 180°C or until a square of bread turns golden in 30 seconds. Fry the honey dough in batches for 1–2 minutes on either side or until golden and puffed. Remove with a slotted spoon and drain on kitchen paper.

To assemble, pile the cream and strawberries on top of the honey dough, drizzle with honey and repeat with another layer. Alternatively, serve separately and allow your guests to assemble their own.

VARIATIONS

- Use any seasonal berry and use the mascarpone yogurt cream recipe that goes with the Eton Mess (recipe #82).
- Omit the fruit and scatter the dough with roasted nuts and sprinkle with honey of your choice.

A retro classic with a twist. I am on a mission to reinvent the arctic roll and take it to new heights! By the way, you'll need to make the ice cream in advance with the aid of an ice cream maker. < SERVES 4 >

RASPBERRY, AMARETTI AND GREEK YOGURT ICE CREAM ARCTIC ROLL

To make the ice cream, whisk the cream, milk, milk powder and sugar together and pour into a saucepan. Bring to the boil, then remove from the heat and leave to cool. Whisk in the yogurt and churn in an ice-cream maker. After 10 minutes, add the raspberries and amaretti biscuits and continue to churn until frozen. Spoon the ice cream on to a sheet of baking parchment, then roll up and mould into a 5 x 30cm sausage and freeze until solid.

Preheat the oven to 190°C/gas mark 5 and line a 23 x 33cm Swiss roll tin with baking parchment.

To make the sponge, whisk together the eggs and sugar until pale and thickened. Sift the flour over the mixture and fold in. Pour into the prepared tin, smooth with a spatula and cook for 10–12 minutes or until just firm to the touch.

Place a sheet of baking parchment that's slightly bigger than the tray on to a work surface and dust with caster sugar. Turn the sponge out and peel away the parchment. Set aside to cool slightly.

To assemble, spread the raspberry jam over the sponge, leaving a 2cm gap around the edge. Remove the baking parchment from the ice-cream sausage and place the ice cream along the long side of the sponge. Using the parchment paper to help you, roll up the sponge so the ice cream is encased. To serve, cut into slices and garnish with fresh raspberries.

FOR THE ICE CREAM
110ml double cream
110ml milk
30g skimmed milk powder
150g caster sugar
350g Greek yogurt
100g raspberries, fresh or frozen
10 amaretti biscuits, coarsely crushed

FOR THE SPONGE
3 eggs
75g caster sugar
75g self-raising flour
5 tbsp raspberry jam, (St Dalfour is good)

16 fresh raspberries, to serve

VARIATIONS

- Stir Turkish delight through the ice cream or swirl through raspberry purée.
- Try serving with a rich chocolate sauce. Substitute raspberries for diced mango or peaches for a twist on peach melba.
- Substitute 50g flour for ground almonds for a nuttier flavour.

173

silky soft and smooth

Provence

combine with lavender

one of the first signs of summer

creamy + floral

good with cardamom

APRICOTS

roast with Earl Grey tea

or cook in dessert wine (Riesling) and serve with blue cheese

the stone tastes similar to almonds

frangipane is a creamy filling made from almonds

but don't eat too many - they contain cyanide!

chocolate pastry, frangipane and fresh cherries - combined in a tart

affinity for dairy - cream, ice cream, goat's cheese, blue cheese

serve with coriander couscous

harmonious with fatty, flavour loaded duck

PEACHES

vanilla

STONE FRUIT

the bark and stems of wild cherries have a scent of almonds

LOLA!

cherry cola

plums

earrings

CHERRIES

Cherry Ripe = tralian chocolate - with cherries + coconut

cherries dipped in chocolate - bliss!

good with sour goat's cheese

Soft, ripe spiced peaches, sticky cardamom-scented braised duck, aromatic couscous and peppery watercress provide a feast for the season. Perfect for a lazy late summer supper. < SERVES 4 >

SLOW-BRAISED DUCK WITH COUSCOUS AND CUMIN ROASTED PEACHES

FOR THE DUCK
1 onion, peeled and sliced
1 red chilli, roughly chopped
2 carrots, roughly chopped
2 celery sticks, roughly chopped
2 litres chicken stock
2 cinnamon sticks
15 cardamom pods
pinch of saffron
4 star anise
4 garlic cloves
100ml clear honey
4 small duck legs

FOR THE COUSCOUS
300g instant couscous
50g butter, diced
2 tbsp raisins
2 tbsp pine nuts, toasted
sea salt and black pepper

FOR THE CUMIN ROASTED PEACHES
2 peaches, quartered
2 tbsp demerara sugar
1 tbsp cumin seeds
1 tbsp ground cumin
25g butter

Place the onion, chilli, carrots, celery and stock in a large pan. Add the cinnamon sticks, cardamom pods, saffron, star anise, garlic and honey. Bring to a simmer.

Add the duck legs to the stock. Cover with a circle of greaseproof paper, carefully pressing it down on to the surface of the liquid, then top with plate that just fits inside the pan. This helps the duck to cook evenly. Simmer gently for about 1½–2 hours or until the duck legs are tender.

Remove the duck legs and set aside. Strain the cooking liquor through a sieve and skim the fat from the surface or, if preparing in advance, leave to cool then refrigerate the liquor overnight with the duck legs. The next day, remove the hard fat that has settled on the surface.

Preheat the oven to 220°C/gas mark 7.

Heat the cooking liquor until boiling. Ladle 300ml of the hot liquor into a jug to use for the couscous, then continue boiling the remaining liquor until it has reduced by half and thickened to a sauce.

Place the couscous in a large heatproof bowl with the butter and raisins; heat the 350ml cooking liquor set aside and pour over the couscous. Cover the bowl immediately with clingfilm and leave for 3 minutes. Remove the clingfilm, fluff up the grains with a fork, then add the pine nuts, season with salt and pepper and set aside.

To prepare the peaches, toss them with the sugar and both types of cumin. Place a frying pan over a high heat and when it is hot add the butter and peaches. Cook until the peaches are soft and caramelised, shaking the pan occasionally.

Reheat the duck legs on a baking tray in the hot oven. Just before serving, place them under a hot grill to caramelise the skin. Serve the duck legs in deep bowls with the peaches and sauce, with the couscous on the side.

176

A simple, easily adapted recipe for roasting apricots. I first thought about using tea bags after my good friend Carrie Anne told me she'd used a mint tea bag to flavour her risotto as she'd forgotten to buy fresh. < SERVES 4 >

EARL GREY ROASTED APRICOTS

110g sugar
1 Earl Grey tea bag
8 apricots, unpeeled, halved and pitted

Preheat the oven to 180°C/gas mark 4.

Place the sugar and 120ml water in a small saucepan and bring to the boil. Add the tea bag and simmer for about 5 minutes until syrupy.

Place the apricots cut-side down in a small roasting tin or ovenproof pan. Remove the tea bag from the syrup, pour the syrup over the apricots and roast for about 10 minutes. Turn the apricots over and baste with the syrup, then roast for a further 5 minutes or until tender.

Serve hot or cold for breakfast, with Masala Chai Rice Pudding (recipe #75). Also delicious with anything chocolatey, goats cheese or meringues.

VARIATIONS

- Take this recipe on a flavour journey by changing the flavour of the tea bags – ginger and lemon tea bags would work equally well, as would various herbal flavours. You could even add a vanilla pod or omit the tea altogether.

There's nothing better than a simple fruit fool. Here's the basic recipe, but you can adapt it as you wish (see variations below). Plums are excellent partnered with ginger, cardamom and cinnamon. < SERVES 4 >

PLUM FOOL

Cut the plums in half and remove the stones, then cut into quarters and place in a pan with 2 tablespoons water and the sugar. Cook over a low heat until the plums have broken down and are meltingly soft (about 10–20 minutes, depending on how ripe the plums are). Discard any skins that have separated.

Place in a blender and whizz to a smooth purée. Leave to cool, then refrigerate until you're ready to make the fool.

Place the cream and vanilla seeds in a bowl and whisk to form soft peaks. Fold in a third of the cooled plums, followed by the remainder. Pour into bowls or glasses and chill for 20 minutes before serving.

500g plums or greengages

80g caster sugar, plus extra to taste

190ml double cream

1 vanilla pod, halved and scraped of seeds

VARIATIONS

- Stem ginger folded through this fool is delicious.
- Try folding in crumbled amaretti biscuits.
- For a lighter dessert, use half the cream and make up the balance with Greek yogurt, folded in.
- I love marzipan, especially those chocolate-covered bars you sometimes find. Try chopping those up and adding to your plum fool – delicious!
- Replace the figs in the Dried Fig and Polenta Biscuits (recipe #109) with chopped prunes for a perfect accompaniment.

Inspired by the Australian chocolate bar, 'Cherry Ripe', this crisp, dark chocolate pastry case is filled with a light coconut frangipane and studded with morello cherries. Serve with a cup of tea, or with ice cream. < SERVES 8–12 >

CHERRY RIPE TART

Place the butter, flour, sugar, cocoa and salt in a food-processor and whizz until the mixture resembles breadcrumbs. With the motor still running, add the egg yolks and milk until the mixture comes together, adding a little more milk if necessary. Wrap the dough in clingfilm and refrigerate for 1 hour or overnight.

Sprinkle a work surface with flour and roll the pastry out into a circle a few centimetres larger than a 24cm tart tin. Line the tin with the pastry, trim off any excess and refrigerate for at least 15 minutes.

To make the coconut frangipane, cream the butter and icing sugar together, then gradually whisk in the eggs. Fold in the almonds, the coconut and the flour.

Preheat the oven to 180°C/gas mark 4.

Line the pastry case with baking parchment and baking beans and bake blind for 15 minutes. Remove the paper and the beans and bake for a further 5 minutes. Remove from the oven, spoon the jam over the pastry base, top with the coconut frangipane, then stud the tart with the whole pitted cherries. Bake for 30–40 minutes until the frangipane has set and is golden. Leave to cool a little before serving.

VARIATIONS

- Serve the tart with cherry compote and chocolate sauce if liked. Garnish with whole cherries.

FOR THE CHOCOLATE PASTRY

175g cold unsalted butter, cut into small cubes

225g plain flour, sifted, plus extra for dusting

75g caster sugar

50g unsweetened cocoa powder

pinch of sea salt

2 egg yolks

40ml milk

FOR THE COCONUT FRANGIPANE

125g unsalted butter, diced

125g icing sugar

3 eggs

70g ground almonds

75g desiccated coconut, unsweetened

30g plain flour

3 tbsp morello cherry jam (St Dalfour is good)

650g fresh cherries, pitted (leave a few with stalks) or 1 x can morello cherries, well drained

181

healthy breakfast with apples, oats, yogurt, nuts + seeds

use to cook puy lentils, mustard + herbs – finish with crème fraîche

juice – cider

Bircher muesli – my favourite way to start the day!

bake in a cheesecake

cooking apples

add texture with raisins – stem ginger gives pizazz!

balance with some classic spice – cinnamon adds warmth

add golden caster sugar + caramelise

Comice are gr... with blue chees...

one of the most gorgeous smells on earth

coat in chocolate

ripen from the inside out

Poires Belle Hélène with a Greek twist

use mixture to stuff the pears

#89

A great brunch recipe: plump juicy scallops wrapped in smoky pancetta, drizzled with maple syrup, sitting on delicate apple pancakes. You will need eight toothpicks for this. < SERVES 4 >

APPLE BUCKWHEAT PANCAKES WITH SCALLOPS, PANCETTA AND CRÈME FRAÎCHE

FOR THE PANCAKES
200g plain flour
100g buckwheat flour
pinch of sea salt
2 tsp baking powder
2 eggs, beaten
330ml apple juice
100ml clear honey
1 tbsp olive oil
1 apple, peeled, cored and coarsely grated
25g butter

FOR THE APPLES
1 apple, peeled, cored and cut into eighths
10g caster sugar

FOR THE SCALLOPS
4 slices smoked pancetta
8 scallops, roe removed
sea salt and black pepper
1 tbsp olive oil
4 tbsp maple syrup

TO SERVE
handful of baby spinach leaves
4 tbsp crème fraîche

Sift the flours, salt and baking powder into a bowl. Beat the eggs with the apple juice, honey and oil. Using an electric whisk, add the liquid ingredients to the flour mixture and blend until smooth. Stir in the apple.

Heat a little butter in a non-stick frying pan. Spoon 1 heaped tablespoon of the pancake mix into the pan and cook over a medium heat for about 2 minutes or until golden on each side. Remove and repeat with the remaining batter. Leave in a warm place.

Next, prepare the apple mixture. Toss the apple pieces in the sugar. Preheat a frying pan over a medium heat, add the apple and allow the sugar to caramelise and the apples to soften (about 2 minutes). Transfer to a plate or tray and leave to cool.

Next, cut the pancetta in half widthways. Season the scallops with sea salt and pepper and wrap in pancetta, securing each with a toothpick.

Heat the olive oil in the frying pan. Once hot, add the scallops and cook over a medium heat for 2 minutes, until the pancetta is crisp. Drizzle with maple syrup and heat through. Alternatively, you can place the scallops under a preheated grill and cook for 2–3 minutes on each side.

To serve, place the pancakes on a plate, top each one with a little baby spinach, a blob of crème fraîche, some apple mixture and two scallops. Drizzle with the pan juices and maple syrup and serve immediately, topped with freshly ground black pepper.

VARIATIONS

- Try using banana in place of the scallops!

184

An alternative to everyone's favourite - apple pie. Sour bramley apples combine with sweet woody cinnamon and ginger. All brought together with creamy mascarpone cheese - absolutely gorgeous! < SERVES 8–10 >

#90

BAKED BRAMLEY APPLE CHEESECAKE

You will need a non-stick springform cake tin, about 24cm in diameter and lined with baking parchment.

Heat a large frying pan. Toss the apple pieces with the caster sugar and cinnamon, then pour into the frying pan. The sugar will caramelise as soon as it hits the hot pan. Shake the pan a little to stop the apples from burning, and cook over a high heat until caramelised, for no more than 2 minutes. Remove from the heat and transfer the apples on to a plate or tray to cool.

Preheat the oven to 190°C/gas mark 5.

Place the gingernuts in a food-processor and blitz to make crumbs. Slowly add the melted butter and mix until combined. Pour into the base of the cake tin and press down with the back of a spoon until even. Top the biscuit base with the apples and scatter with raisins.

Whisk the eggs and sugar together until pale, add the cream cheese, mascarpone and stem ginger and gently whisk, taking care not to overmix or it will separate. Pour the mixture over the apples, place the tin on a baking tray and cook in the oven for about 45–50 minutes until the cheesecake wobbles a little. Turn off the heat and leave the oven door ajar for 20 minutes; the cake will continue to cook and this will prevent the top from cracking.

Remove the cake from the oven, leave to cool, then refrigerate until required. Remove from the fridge 20 minutes before serving.

For the apple chips, preheat the oven to 110°C/gas mark ¼. Using a mandolin, slice the apple vertically as thinly as possible, place in a single layer on a baking tray lined with parchment paper. Sprinkle with sugar and bake for 1½–2 hours until crisp. Loosen the chips with a palate knife and leave to cool. Store in an airtight container until required (these can be ade a few days ahead if you like).

Garnish the cheesecake with the apple chips. This is wonderful served with a spoonful of Calvados crème fraîche!

FOR THE APPLES

2 Bramley apples, peeled, cored and cut into 1cm pieces

50g caster sugar

1 heaped tsp cinnamon

FOR THE CHEESECAKE

1 packet gingernut biscuits

50g butter, melted

10g raisins, soaked in hot water and drained

5 eggs

140g caster sugar

400g cream cheese

400g mascarpone

2 knobs of stem ginger, finely chopped

FOR THE APPLE CHIP GARNISH

1 Bramley apple

50g caster sugar

A recipe inspired by Paul A. Young. When I met him he was cooking a poached pear, which he then dipped in a chocolate and Stilton ganache. I was intrigued! Paul's passion for chocolate is totally inspirational. < SERVES 4 >

CHOCOLATE-DIPPED POACHED PEARS, STUFFED WITH STICKY NUTS

FOR THE STICKY NUTS
2 tbsp honey
½ cinnamon stick
25g walnut halves, toasted
25g blanched
almonds, toasted

FOR THE PEAR POACHING LIQUOR
zest and juice of 1 orange
1 cinnamon stick
250g sugar
750ml red wine
4 firm pears, Williams are ideal

FOR THE GANACHE
100g dark chocolate (70 per cent cocoa solids)
150ml double cream
pinch of ground cinnamon

To make the sticky nuts, place the honey, 50ml water and the cinnamon stick in a small saucepan and bring to the boil. Reduce the heat and simmer until thickened. Leave to cool and discard the cinnamon stick.

Pulse the nuts in a food-processor or crush to a coarse breadcrumb texture and mix with the syrup.

To make the poached pears, place the orange zest and juice, the cinnamon stick, sugar and red wine in a saucepan just big enough to hold the pears. Place over a medium heat and bring to the boil.

Peel the pears and, using an apple corer or melon baller, remove enough of the core from the base end to create a cavity for the nuts. Leave the stalks intact and place in the hot poaching liquor. Cover with a piece of baking parchment and simmer for about 15–20 minutes or until the pears are tender, but holding their shape.

Preheat the oven to 200°C/gas mark 6.

Remove the pears from the poaching liquor and set aside to cool. Reduce the liquor to a syrup, then leave to cool at room temperature.

Pat the pears dry with kitchen paper, then stuff each one with the sticky nuts, levelling the base with a knife so the pears stand upright. Place on a non-stick baking tray and bake in the oven for 10 minutes. Remove from the oven and leave to rest for 5 minutes.

To make the ganache, place the chocolate, cream and cinnamon in a small heatproof bowl set over a pan of simmering water. Once melted, set aside and leave to cool a little before dipping and rolling each pear in the ganache to coat it halfway up. Place on baking parchment, cool and refrigerate until required.

Serve with a little of the poaching liquor and a blob of Greek yogurt or crème fraîche.

I once worked with Jen Beer, a quirky young Australian chef with a huge heart. Jen used to lovingly prepare us all Bircher muesli and it soon became a kitchen favourite. A wonderful healthy way to start the day. < SERVES 4 >

BIRCHER MUESLI WITH GRATED APPLE

Mix together all the ingredients, cover and refrigerate for 2 hours or, preferably, overnight. Serve chilled, drizzled with honey or agave nectar.

VARIATIONS

- You can really experiment with Bircher muesli. Whichever journey you choose to take your muesli on I'm sure you'll agree it's a fabulous breakfast and it will happily sit in the fridge for three days.

- Vary the dried fruits used here and substitute with dried cranberries, cherries or blueberries.

- Use a mix of seeds such as linseed, sunflower and pumpkin.

- Grated pear and pear juice make a great alternative to apple and both provide a natural sweetness, so no need to add any extra.

- Top with fresh berries if in season or serve swirled with rhubarb compote.

100g porridge oats

125ml good-quality apple juice

20g sultanas

20g dried apricots, chopped

1 Granny Smith apple, unpeeled, coarsely grated

180g Greek yogurt

30g pumpkin seeds

30g toasted flaked almonds, roughly chopped

pinch of freshly ground nutmeg

½ tsp ground cinnamon

Posh pear fritters! Robust pears are just 'pearfect' with rosemary scented sugar — make this in advance if you can, you will find all sorts of uses for it. A little lager in the batter really does improve the taste. < SERVES 4–6 >

PEAR BEIGNETS WITH ROSEMARY SUGAR AND PEAR CRÈME ANGLAISE

FOR THE POACHED PEARS
200g caster sugar
1 bay leaf
1 vanilla pod, seeds scraped
1 whole unwaxed lemon
4 pears, peeled and cored

FOR THE BATTER
150g plain flour
3 tbsp sugar
pinch of sea salt
1 large egg
250ml lager or ale
vegetable oil, for frying
icing sugar

FOR THE PEAR CRÈME ANGLAISE
120ml milk
100ml single cream
2 egg yolks
10g caster sugar

FOR THE ROSEMARY SUGAR
2 sprigs of rosemary, dried, leaves stripped
75g caster sugar

Prepare the poaching liquid before preparing the pears as they discolour. Place the sugar, 150ml water, bay leaf, vanilla seeds and pod, bay leaf and the juice and the lemon in a saucepan over a low heat and bring to the boil for 2 minutes.

Cut each pear into 3–4 vertical slices about 1cm thick and add to the cooking liquor. Place a circle of greaseproof paper (a cartouche) on the top and poach until just tender (about 5–7 minutes). Remove the pears from the liquor and leave to cool and drain on a rack or cloth.

In a medium bowl, combine the flour, sugar, a pinch of salt and the egg. Whisk together and gradually add the lager or ale. Whisk until the batter is smooth. Leave to rest for 10 minutes.

To make the rosemary sugar, blitz the rosemary and sugar together in a blender. Store in an airtight container until required.

Heat the oil to 175°C. Working in batches, dip a few slices of poached pear into the batter, then carefully drop them into the oil. Fry until golden on both sides (about 4 minutes).

Drain the pear beignets on absorbent paper and dust with rosemary sugar.

To make the pear crème Anglaise, place the poaching syrup from the pears, the milk and the cream in a saucepan and gently bring to the boil.

In a separate bowl, whisk the egg yolks and sugar until pale. Pour a little of the hot milk mixture into the egg mixture, then gradually pour this back into the hot milk. Cook over a low heat, stirring continuously until the custard thickens. Do not boil or the custard will curdle. Once thickened, pass the custard through a fine sieve and serve with the pears.

Pomelos look like huge grapefruits. Their thick skin and membrane can be ripped away to reveal a segmented fruit with a dense texture, sometimes sweet, a little dry, tart and fruity. < SERVES 4 AS A SIDE SALAD >

POMELO AND LIME LEAF SALAD WITH NAM JIM DRESSING

Break the pomelo into segments and tear each one in half into a bowl. Add the remaining ingredients, then chill in the fridge until required.

To make the dressing, pound the garlic and coriander roots in a pestle and mortar until well crushed, but not to a paste. Add the chillies and crush lightly, then mix in the palm sugar, followed by the fish sauce and lime juice.

Balance the flavours: if a little too salty, add a bit more lime; if too sour, add a splash more fish sauce. Fifty per cent fish sauce to lime juice should give you the perfect balance.

Just before serving, toss the salad with the nam jim and serve immediately.

VARIATIONS

- For a delicious main course, fry or griddle some peeled tiger or king prawns and toss into the salad.
- If watermelons are in season, add a few chunks, some mint leaves, a few roasted peanuts and some sliced spring onions. Dress and serve straight away.
- Alternatively, griddle some rib-eye steak until rare, leave to rest, then slice and toss with the pomelo salad ingredients and any of the ingredients from the prawn suggestion above. To give it some bulk, add some cooked glass or rice noodles.
- Try with some shredded chicken or crabmeat or griddled or barbecued squid. Or use the dressing spooned over freshly shucked oysters.
- If you can get hold of some green papaya, peel and thinly shred it, then mix with the nam jim dressing, some dried prawns, halved cherry tomatoes, roasted peanuts, shredded ginger, spring onions and a handful of coriander, mint and Thai basil leaves – a salad I used to eat every day for lunch in Thailand.

2 pomelos
2 lime leaves, stems removed, finely shredded
handful of coriander, roughly chopped
1 red chilli, deseeded and finely sliced
2cm piece of fresh ginger or galangal, peeled and finely chopped or julienned
few Thai basil leaves (optional), torn

FOR THE NAM JIM DRESSING
2 garlic cloves
4 coriander roots, washed and roughly chopped
1–2 red chillies (depending on their heat), deseeded and roughly chopped
30g palm sugar
2 tbsp Thai fish sauce
60ml fresh lime juice

195

#95 A fantastic, simple summer salad — other than the jelly and dressing, it's more an assembly job than anything else. The zingy jelly cuts through the rich cheese (it also goes very well in a sandwich with cold roast pork). < SERVES 4 >

BLUE CHEESE, PEAR, COPPA, LEMON AND GINGER JELLY AND BITTER LEAF SALAD

FOR THE JELLY

30g fresh ginger, peeled and finely grated

zest of 1 lemon

50ml fresh lemon juice

30g caster sugar

½ tsp agar agar

FOR THE WHITE WINE DRESSING

10ml olive oil

10ml extra virgin olive oil

10ml Chardonnay vinegar (if unavailable, use white wine vinegar)

FOR THE SALAD

20g mizuna or other mixed bitter leaves

1 head dandelion, leaves picked in 5cm lengths and washed

80g blue cheese (I like Barkham Blue), thinly sliced

1 pear, cored, quartered and thinly sliced

12 slices coppa (optional)

freshly ground black pepper

First make the jelly. Put the ginger, lemon zest and juice and sugar in a saucepan, add 200ml water and bring to the boil over a low heat. The moment it starts boiling, lower the heat, whisk in the agar agar and cook for 1 minute. Tip into a shallow container and leave to cool before covering and refrigerating. You can make the jelly up to 3 days in advance. (These quantities make more than you need, but it will keep quite happily in the fridge for up to a week.)

Next make the dressing, by lightly whisking together the oils and vinegar.

To assemble, scatter the leaves in a narrow line on four plates, top with slices of cheese and pear followed by slivers of jelly. Top with coppa, drizzle with dressing, grind over a little black pepper and serve.

196

You could make just the ice cream or the madeleines if you prefer, but if you really want to go to town with lemon verbena, make both! Glazed madeleines are best left uncovered and eaten the day they're made. < SERVES 4 >

LEMON VERBENA ICE CREAM WITH GLAZED MADELEINES

Place the lemon verbena leaves in a heavy-based saucepan with the milk and cream and gently bring to just below boiling point. Remove from the heat, cover and leave to infuse for 2 hours or overnight.

To make the ice cream, gently reheat the infused milk mixture to boiling point again. Meanwhile, whisk the sugar and egg yolks until pale. Once the milk is hot, slowly pour it over the yolks and sugar, whisking continuously. Pour the mixture back into the saucepan and cook, stirring all the time, over a low heat until the custard coats the back of the spoon. (If you are using a thermometer, it should read 80–84°C). Immediately strain the custard through a sieve into a large bowl, pushing down on the verbena leaves to extract as much flavour as possible. Leave to cool, then freeze in an ice-cream maker, according to the manufacturer's instructions.

For the madeleines, melt the butter in a saucepan over a low heat, remove from heat and add the verbena leaves. Leave to infuse for 10 minutes. Sift the flour, baking powder and salt into a medium-sized bowl. Using an electric mixer, beat the eggs and sugar together until thick, light and fluffy. Add the honey and lemon zest and beat for a further minute. Gently fold in the dry ingredients by hand, followed by the verbena-flavoured butter. Press clingfilm directly on to the surface of the batter and chill for at least 3 hours or overnight.

Preheat the oven to 200°C/gas mark 6. Thoroughly grease a madeleine tin with 12 indentations. Dust with flour and tap out the excess. Or use a silicone Madeleine tray. Place the tin on a baking tray. Drop a large tablespoon of batter into each mould (don't smooth out, as it will spread during baking). Place on the middle shelf of the oven and bake until golden (about 10 minutes) or until a skewer inserted into the centre comes out clean. If using a tin, tap on a work surface to loosen the cakes before turning them on to a wire rack to cool slightly before glazing.

To make the glaze, stir all the ingredients together in a small mixing bowl until smooth. The moment the madeleines are cool enough to handle, dip each one in the glaze and rest on the cooking rack until the glaze has set.

Serve the madeleines with the ice cream.

FOR THE ICE CREAM

15g fresh lemon verbena leaves or 2 lemon verbena tea bags

350ml milk

200ml double cream

150g sugar

4 egg yolks

FOR THE MADELEINES

70g unsalted butter, plus extra for greasing

4 tbsp fresh, finely chopped lemon verbena or 2 tbsp dried leaves or lemon verbena tea

100g plain flour, plus extra for dusting

½ tsp baking powder

pinch of sea salt

2 large eggs

70g sugar

2 tbsp honey

½ tsp grated lemon zest

FOR THE LEMON VERBENA GLAZE

150g icing sugar

1 tbsp freshly squeezed lemon juice

3 tbsp finely chopped lemon verbena or 1 tbsp dried

2 tbsp water

A little bit of Italy frozen and encased in a meringue coat – this is a classic dessert, spruced up for the 21st Century. The explosion of cool and refreshing lemon really wakes up the taste buds. < SERVES 6–8 >

LIMONCELLO BAKED ALASKA

FOR THE LEMON AND LIME CAKE
225g unsalted butter
225g caster sugar
4 eggs, beaten
225g self-raising flour
zest of 2 lemons, finely grated
juice of 1 lemon
good glug of limoncello

FOR THE ICE CREAM
8 scoops (about 300g) vanilla ice cream
8 tbsp lemon curd

FOR THE MERINGUE
6 egg whites
250g caster sugar
24 fresh lychees, peeled (or 1 can)
4 lime leaves, finely chopped (optional)

Preheat the oven to 180°C/gas mark 4. Grease and line a 21 x 11cm loaf tin.

Cream together the butter and sugar until pale and creamy. Gradually whisk in the eggs. Sift in the flour, add the lemon zest and fold to combine. Add the lemon juice and pour the batter into the prepared tin. Bake in the oven for 45–50 minutes or until a skewer inserted in the centre comes out clean. Leave to cool a little before turning out on to a wire rack.

Once cool, cut the cake horizontally into three slices.

Grease then line the loaf tin with clingfilm, so it overhangs. Place a layer of cake in the base and drizzle with a good glug of limoncello.

Soften the ice cream a little and beat in the lemon curd. Spread half of the ice cream over the cake. Top with another layer of cake, again dousing in limoncello, followed by the remaining ice cream. Smooth the surface before topping with the remaining cake layer, again dousing in limoncello. Freeze until rock hard. (Note: you can make this step up to a week ahead, then cover with clingfilm until required.)

Preheat the oven to 200°C/gas mark 6.

Place the egg whites in a clean, grease-free bowl. Whisk to form soft peaks, then gradually whisk in the sugar until the meringue is stiff and shiny. (You can make this ahead of time and leave it in the fridge for a couple of hours).

Remove the cake from the tin, using the clingfilm to help. Turn on to an ovenproof serving dish. Top the cake with a thick layer of meringue, forming peaks and swirls as you go. Make sure the cake is entirely covered. Bake for 3–4 minutes, or until meringue is slightly toasted.

Serve immediately with lychees and finely chopped lime leaves for a refreshing accompaniment.

A refreshing sorbet to serve after dinner. Use the zests to make a Pink Grapefruit Vodka (see below) which in turn can be poured over the sorbet.

< SERVES 4–6 >

#98

PINK GRAPEFRUIT AND TARRAGON SORBET

Put the sugar, 200ml water and tarragon stalks in a small saucepan over a low heat and heat gently until the sugar has dissolved. Remove from the heat and leave to infuse for 1 hour.

Strain the liquid, then add the grapefruit juice. Finely chop the tarragon leaves and stir in. Pour into an ice-cream machine and follow the manufacturer's instructions.

For best results, allow the sorbet to soften slightly before serving by placing in the fridge for 20 minutes beforehand.

150g sugar

5 sprigs of tarragon, leaves picked, stalks reserved

800ml freshly squeezed pink grapefruit juice (about 4–5 grapefruits)

I love inventing cocktails. This is one of my favourites!

PINK GRAPEFRUIT VODKA

Before making the sorbet, scrub the grapefruits, then remove the zest in strips using a potato peeler, cutting away any bitter pith. Empty the vodka into a jug, push the grapefruit zest into the now empty bottle and pour over the vodka, there will be a little left (oh dear).

Leave to infuse in a cool place for up to 2 weeks. Serve drizzled over Pink Grapefruit and Tarragon Sorbet (see above) or use as a base for a cocktail: mix with fresh basil, gomme or another sweet syrup and pink grapefruit juice; top up with soda and serve over ice.

zest of 4–5 grapefruits
1-litre bottle vodka

Orange and rosemary complement one another beautifully. I've chosen to use blood oranges here, but if they're out of season, don't worry. Try serving with Orange and Rosemary Biscotti (recipe #108) < SERVES 4—6 >

BLOOD ORANGE AND ROSEMARY CRÈME CARAMEL

FOR THE CARAMEL
110g caster sugar
125ml water

FOR THE CUSTARD
500ml double cream
2 sprigs of rosemary
zest of 2 blood oranges
1 vanilla pod, split
125g caster sugar
2 whole eggs
2 egg yolks

1 blood orange, segmented, to serve

Preheat the oven to 180°C/gas mark 4.

To make the caramel, put the sugar and water in a small pan and heat over a medium heat until melted. Increase the heat and cook until the sugar turns dark amber. Pour the caramel into six ramekins and leave to cool.

To make the custard, heat the cream, rosemary, orange zest and vanilla until simmering. Remove from the heat and leave to infuse for about 30 minutes. Then strain the cream into a pan and heat gently until warm.

Whisk the sugar, eggs and yolks together. Gently whisk a little cream into the eggs, then whisk in the remaining cream. Skim the surface to remove any air bubbles.

Fill each ramekin with custard and place in a baking tin lined with a tea-towel (this will stop the ramekins from moving around). Pour enough boiling water into the tin to come two thirds of the way up the sides of the ramekins. Cook for about 1 hour or until the custards are almost set. Remove from the oven and leave to cool in the water. Chill for at least 1 hour, but preferably overnight, before serving.

To serve, dip the base of each ramekin in boiling or hot water for a few seconds. Turn the custards out on to plates and garnish with a few blood orange segments.

VARIATIONS

• Vary the citrus and herbs to create your own favourite flavours.

202

Pedro Ximénez sherry is sweet and intense, packed with rich, toasty fig and raisin undertones. It's like fruit cake in a glass and makes a perfect accompaniment to a gooey chocolate cake. < SERVES 6 >

CINNAMON CHOCOLATE CAKES WITH SHERRY-SOAKED RAISINS AND SHERRY-SPIKED CRÈME FRAÎCHE

Preheat the oven to 180°C/gas mark 4. Grease 4-6 dariole moulds or tea cups and dust them with cocoa powder.

Whisk all the ingredients for the PX crème fraîche together until smooth and refrigerate for 1 hour before using.

To make the cakes, place the butter and chocolate in a heatproof bowl above a pan of hot water, making sure the bowl doesn't touch the water. Once melted, remove from the heat and leave to cool a little.

Whisk the eggs and sugar together until pale and fluffy, then whisk in the cooled chocolate. Sift the cinnamon, flour, cocoa powder and salt over the chocolate mixture and fold in.

Spoon the mixture into the prepared moulds and place on a baking tray in the oven for 10–12 minutes only. They should be a little soggy, so a skewer inserted in the centre will not come out clean; you should have a lovely fudge-like centre instead.

Leave the cakes to cool a little before gently turning out.

To make the PX sherry-soaked raisins, warm the sherry until almost boiling, add the raisins, then turn off the heat and leave to cool. The raisins will become plump and absorb the sherry. Serve at room temperature.

Serve the cakes topped with sherry-soaked raisins and sherry-spiked crème fraîche. If making ahead of time, heat for 10 seconds only in the microwave, any longer and the gooey insides will harden.

VARIATIONS

- Try serving the PX crème fraîche with the Baked Bramley Apple Cheesecake (recipe #90).

FOR THE PX SHERRY-SPIKED CRÈME FRAÎCHE
300g crème fraîche
15ml Pedro Ximénez sherry
20g light soft brown sugar

FOR THE CHOCOLATE CAKES
150g unsalted butter, plus a little more for greasing
150g dark bitter chocolate (75 per cent cocoa solids)
3 eggs
210g caster sugar
2 tsp ground cinnamon
70g plain flour
30g bitter cocoa powder, plus extra for dusting
pinch of sea salt

FOR THE PX SHERRY-SOAKED RAISINS
125ml Pedro Ximénez sherry
100g raisins

207

A decadent adult trifle, perfect for a dinner party. Make it in individual glasses or fill up a funky retro trifle bowl. You'll need to start this a day ahead, as the jelly will take about 3 hours to set. **< MAKES 6—8 >**

PLUM, PORT AND CHOCOLATE TRIFLES WITH WHITE CHOCOLATE CRÈME FRAÎCHE

BITTER CHOCOLATE AND PORT JELLY
150g caster sugar
300ml port
300g dark chocolate (70 per cent cocoa solids), broken into small pieces
2 leaves gelatine, softened in cold water

FOR THE CREAMY CUSTARD
50g Bird's custard powder
50g caster sugar
250ml milk
250ml double cream
1 vanilla pod, split and scraped

15 sponge fingers
150ml port

FOR THE CARAMELISED PLUMS
8 plums, halved, stones removed, then cut into thirds
75g demerara or caster sugar
50ml port

FOR THE WHITE CHOCOLATE CRÈME FRAÎCHE
150g white chocolate, broken into small pieces
100g crème fraîche
150ml double cream
cocoa powder, for dusting

To make the jelly, combine the sugar, port and 200ml water in a saucepan and bring to the boil over a medium heat. Add the chocolate and stir until smooth. Remove from the heat, squeeze any excess water from the gelatine and add to the port and chocolate mixture. Stir to dissolve. Leave to cool a little, then refrigerate until almost set (this will take a few hours) before spooning over the plums.

While your jelly is setting, prepare the custard. Mix the custard powder and sugar with a little of the milk to form a smooth paste. Heat the cream with the remaining milk and vanilla seeds in a saucepan until almost at boiling point. Reduce the heat and slowly add the custard mix, whisking continuously until thickened. Remove from the heat and cover the surface with clingfilm to prevent a skin from forming. Leave to cool a little while you prepare the sponge fingers and the plums.

Break the sponge fingers into small pieces and divide between individual glasses or place in the base of a large bowl. Drizzle with port and top evenly with the slightly cooled custard.

While the custard cools a little more prepare the plums. Heat a large frying pan and toss plums with the sugar of your choice. Add the plums to the pan and sear over a medium heat for 5 minutes until softened and caramelised. Add a splash of port, then spoon the plums over the custard.

Once the custard and plums are cool, refrigerate until the jelly is almost set. Then spoon the jelly evenly over the plums and refrigerate again until set completely.

Meanwhile, prepare the white chocolate crème fraîche. Place the white chocolate and crème fraîche in a heatproof bowl and place over simmering water, making sure the bowl doesn't touch the water. Stir occasionally, until melted and smooth, then remove from the heat and leave to cool. Whisk the double cream until soft peaks form, then fold into the chocolate and crème fraîche. Spoon over the jelly and refrigerate for 20 minutes. Serve chilled, dusted with a little cocoa.

White chocolate has natural lemon notes. I like to accentuate these by adding some tropical flavours. The good news here is that you don't need an ice-cream machine to make a parfait. < SERVES 4—6 >

WHITE CHOCOLATE PARFAITS

Melt the chocolate in a bowl set over a pan of simmering water and leave to cool.

Whisk the egg yolks until pale.

Place the sugar and 50ml water in a pan and heat gently until dissolved. Increase the heat until the sugar boils and reaches a temperature of 120°C.

Gradually pour the hot syrup down the side of the bowl while the egg yolks are whisking. Continue to whisk until pale and thick and the mixture leaves a trail for 3 seconds. Whisk in the cooled melted chocolate.

Whisk the cream to form soft peaks then fold into the chocolate mixture with the lime zest and juice, ginger and lime leaves.

Pour into a terrine mould lined with clingfilm, stud with the lychees and place in the freezer.

To serve, turn out of the mould and slice. Serve with passion fruit squeezed over the top or served on the side.

175g white chocolate
5 egg yolks
100g caster sugar
400ml cream
zest of 2 limes, finely grated
juice of 1 lime
2cm piece of fresh ginger, peeled and finely grated
2 lime leaves, finely chopped
12 lychees, chopped
2 passion fruits

VARIATIONS

• You could also freeze this parfait in individual moulds.

EXTRAS

#103 TAHINI YOGURT SAUCE

1 garlic clove, crushed
1 tsp sea salt
60ml tahini
pinch ground cumin
2 tbsp lemon juice
200ml Greek yogurt

Crush the garlic in a pestle and mortar with a little salt to form a paste, transfer to a bowl and whisk in tahini, 3 tablespoons water, cumin, lemon juice and yogurt. Refrigerate until required.

#104 WARM CHICKPEA PURÉE

Essentially, this is hummus served warm, but is equally as delicious served cold the next day. You will need to start this recipe the day before.

200g dried chickpeas
1 tsp bicarbonate of soda
200ml tahini
3 garlic cloves, crushed
sea salt
juice of 1–2 lemons, to taste
paprika and extra virgin olive oil, to serve

Soak the chickpeas in plenty of cold water overnight.

The next day, drain and rinse the chickpeas, place in a large saucepan, add the bicarbonate of soda and enough water to cover and bring to a boil. Simmer gently for about 2 hours, or until very tender, skimming the surface regularly.

Drain the chickpeas, reserving the cooking liquor and a few chickpeas for garnishing. Transfer the chickpeas to a food-processor and whizz to a smooth purée, adding a little of the cooking liquor (about 2 tablespoons for now).

Transfer the purée to a bowl and stir in the tahini, garlic, salt and lemon juice, to taste. Mix until smooth, adding some of the cooking liquid if the purée is too thick – it should be soft and creamy, but not runny.

Pour into a shallow bowl and spread the purée across it, raising it slightly up the sides. Top with the reserved chickpeas, drizzle with olive oil, sprinkle with a little paprika and serve.

#105 POMEGRANATE LABNEH

Labneh is strained yogurt that has a firmer cheese-like texture. You'll need to make it the day before you want to serve it.

450ml Greek yogurt
2 garlic cloves, crushed
1 tbsp sea salt
1 tsp roasted cumin and coriander seeds, crushed
1 green chilli, deseeded, finely chopped
pinch sugar
seeds from ½ pomegranate
small bunch coriander or mint, finely chopped

Mix the yogurt with the garlic and salt. Line a small sieve with a piece of cheesecloth or clean J-cloth and set over a bowl. Put the yogurt into the cloth and fold over the sides, top with a couple of saucers and refrigerate. Alternatively you can tie the cloth and suspend from a shelf in your fridge, remember to put a bowl underneath! The yogurt will lose excess moisture and will be left with a firmer consistency.

Put the labneh in a bowl. Gently mix with the cumin, coriander, chilli, sugar and pomegranate seeds.

Sprinkle a plate with the chopped herbs. Shape the labneh into walnut sized balls and roll in the chopped herbs to coat. Refrigerate until required.

#106 PICKLED ENOKI MUSHROOMS

Make a batch of enoki mushrooms and store in your refrigerator. Toss through basmati or jasmine rice, or put in a Californian roll with some avocado. Serve with grilled fish or toss through a Thai chicken or duck noodle salad.

100g enoki – golden or white
2 tbsp grapeseed, groundnut or sunflower oil
½ red chilli, finely sliced
2 tbsp Shoaxing
1 tbsp caster sugar
1½ tbsp soy sauce
1½ tbsp rice wine vinegar
2 tbsp sesame oil

Cut the stems off the enoki and separate a little. Heat the oil in a large frying pan and fry the enoki and chilli over a medium heat until the enoki have softened.

Transfer to a non-metallic bowl and set aside to cool.

Add the remaining ingredients to a small saucepan, and warm over a low heat until combined. Pour over the mushrooms and leave to infuse for 20 minutes or preferably overnight.

Once cooled, store covered in the refrigerator and serve at room temperature.

VARIATIONS

- Crush some coriander seeds and toss through the enoki while cooking, or sauté some julienne of fresh ginger and add to the mix.
- I like to serve these with rice and red braised mushrooms.

#107 PORCINI SALT

Use this salt to season white fish, scallops, prawns, or meat.

25g dried porcini mushrooms
50g coarse sea salt

Grind the porcini in a coffee grinder or blender until powdered. Add the salt and grind until well combined. Store in an airtight container.

VARIATIONS

- This is fabulous tossed through cooked pasta with a little Parmesan.
- Sprinkle on to braised buttered cabbage, new potatoes, corn on the cob, cooked white beans, omelettes or soft-boiled, poached or fried eggs.

213

#108 ORANGE AND ROSEMARY BISCOTTI

This recipe is kindly donated by Danny Boy - my extremely talented Head Chef and kitchen soul mate! Thank you so much for sharing this with all of us; it complements the Blood Orange and Rosemary Crème Caramel (recipe #99) beautifully. Makes about 40.

150g plain flour
30g butter
75g caster sugar
½ tsp baking powder
1 sprig of rosemary, finely chopped
zest of 2 oranges
1 egg, beaten

Preheat the oven to 180°C/gas mark 4.

Mix the flour and butter to form a breadcrumb consistency. Add the sugar, baking powder, rosemary and orange zest. Mix to combine. Make a well in the centre of the dry mix and add the egg, mixing to form a dough. Roll the dough into a log shape, about 30cm long and place on a lined baking tray. Bake in the oven for 30 minutes. Remove from the oven and leave to cool.

Reduce the oven temperature to 120°C/gas mark ½.

Using a sharp bread knife, cut the log into slices of your desired thickness. Place the sliced biscotti back on to the baking tray and return to the oven to dry out for 30–45 minutes.

214

#109 DRIED FIG & POLENTA BISCUITS

To go with panna cotta (recipe #79).

75g dried figs, soaked in hot water until softened
100g unsalted butter, at room temperature
70g caster sugar, and extra for baking
2 tsp orange zest, finely grated
2 egg yolks
pinch of sea salt
150g plain flour
75g polenta

Preheat the oven to 200°C/gas mark 6 and line a baking tray with parchment paper. Drain the figs and cut into small pieces. Cream the butter, sugar and orange zest until pale and fluffy. Add the yolks one at a time. Sift salt and flour over the creamed butter mix, add the polenta and figs and beat until combined. Knead lightly for a couple of minutes then roll into a cylinder about 3cm in diameter, wrap in clingfilm and refrigerate for about 30 minutes or until firm.

Unroll the dough on to a sugared or floured surface and cut into cut into 5mm thick slices. Place on a baking tray, sprinkle with a little sugar and bake for 10–12 minutes or until lightly golden. Cool on wire racks and sprinkle with a little more sugar. Store in an airtight container until required. You could soak the figs in orange flower water, PX sherry or port to add an extra flavour hit!

#110 LAVENDER SUGAR

Make a batch of lavender sugar and use for shortbreads, meringues, ice cream, jelly, mojitos etc!

4 tbsp fresh dry lavender flowers or 2 tbsp dried
175g caster sugar

Mix the flowers with the sugar or place the lavender and sugar in a food processor to finely chop up the flowers into the sugar. Place in an airtight container. Leave to infuse for a week in a cool dark place to allow the flavours to develop.

#111 FLATBREADS

Flatbreads are quick and easy to prepare. Here's the basic recipe for you to adapt by adding different herbs and spices. You can even add things like finely chopped olives or sun-blush tomatoes.

¾ tbsp active dried yeast
½ tbsp caster sugar
250ml lukewarm water
400g plain flour
3 tsp sea salt
1 tbsp olive oil

Combine the yeast, sugar and water in a bowl and leave in a warm place to ferment for about 10 minutes. Sift the flour into a mixing bowl and add the salt, along with any flavour of your choice, if using. Pour in the yeast mix and olive oil and mix with the end of a wooden spoon to bring the dough together. (If you own a food-processor with a dough hook, use this to mix it.)

Turn the dough out on to a lightly floured surface and knead until smooth and elastic. A little oil on your hands will stop the dough from sticking to them. Place the dough in an oiled bowl, cover and leave in a warm place until it has doubled in size (about 1–1½ hours).

Turn the dough out on to a lightly floured surface and knock it back. Divide into 8 balls, roll out each one to about 5mm thickness and arrange on a tray lined with baking parchment.

Preheat a griddle pan. Brush the flatbreads with a little oil and cook for about 1 minute or until golden on either side.

You can make the dough in advance and keep in the fridge for two days. If you cook the flatbread in advance, warm it through in the oven before serving.

TAKE IT FURTHER

GET CREATIVE

This section is all about YOU!

This is your chance to create and develop your own recipes from mine. Be inspired to experiment with them. The examples on the following pages should get you out of the starting blocks. Here are some basic guidelines for you:

* Consider whether the ingredients are in season. If not, adapt with a suitable alternative.
* Take the recipe on a flavour journey. i.e. from a Greek influence to an Asian one.
* Lighten up the recipe. i.e. change lamb to fish. Or do the opposite to add depth.
* Simplify - use only part of the recipe.
* Vary cooking methods - e.g. bbe rather than roast.
* Consider the textures when substituting i.e. change like for like.

Be confident! ADAPT - CREATE - TASTE and let the recipes evolve into your own style as you scribble away in the blank pages of this chapter. Make this book your very own.

BIRDS #6

Slow-roasted Paprika Chicken with Butternut Squash, Smashed Butter Beans and Tomatoes

replace with boneless leg of lamb as in recipe #19

try alternative marinade i.e. garlic, dill, lemon as in recipe #19

use peas instead

replace with baby potatoes

PORK #14

Porchetta with Rosemary Roasted Potatoes

try alternative stuffing i.e. chicken liver stuffing from recipe #28

replace the pork with a leg of lamb

try roasting with sage instead of rosemary

serve with roasted apples

accompany with squash as in recipe #6

or replace the potatoes with barley

My experiments:

TAKE IT FURTHER

LAMB #21

Braised Scrag End of Lamb with Runner Beans and Tomatoes

marinate the lamb with Moroccan spice paste as in recipe #13

replace or add cooked chickpeas

flavour with honey and orange zest

replace potatoes with sweet potatoes, or omit and serve with couscous

BEEF #22

Veal Chop Topped with Melted Manchego and Quince, with Creamy Sage and Onion Polenta

replace with pork chop

flavour polenta with thyme + Parmesan

replace topping with Dolcelatte, thyme + apple slices

220

My experiments:

GAME #31

Pomegranate Marinated Quail, Griddled Radicchio and Bitter Leaf Salad

replace with Middle Eastern chicken marinade (recipe #5)

use lamb instead of quail and serve with the same ingredients

replace with spiced carrot purée + dukkah (recipe #58)

complement with carrot, herb salad (recipe #59)

or serve with aubergine mull, recipe #67

OILY FISH #35

Mackerel with Gooseberry Jelly, Pine Nuts and Mint

replace with duck breast or leg

exchange with plum and ginger jelly

use this jelly, pine nuts + mint with Veal Chop (recipe #22)

My experiments:

WHITE FISH #38

Pan-fried Sea Bream with

Cauliflower, Pistachio and Mint Couscous and Cauliflower Purée

- replace with lamb neck

- marinade as in recipe #19 + griddle

- serve with cauliflower couscous and purée but...

- replace pistachios with almonds

- and add chopped dates to the couscous

SEAFOOD #42

Baked Clams with Rosemary, White Beans and Tomatoes

- use raw prawns instead

- replace with finely chopped ginger, lemongrass, red chilli, garlic and coriander root

- replace with roasted diced squash or pumpkin

My experiments:

GRAINS & PULSES #52

Moroccan Spiced Lentils with

Pan-fried Salmon and Avocado Cream

Go Greek!
Use cinnamon, lemon, dill, mint and garlic, and add a splash of red wine vinegar

replace with griddled leg of lamb as in recipe #19

serve with avocado cream

sprinkle with dukkah – recipe #58

ROOTS #57

Jerusalem Artichoke and Chestnut Soup

with Chorizo and Apple

replace with parsnips

use blanched almonds instead

omit chorizo

replace with roasted pears and shaved pecorino

My experiments:

AUBERGINES #64

Aubergine Wrapped Halloumi with Pomegranate Labneh

replace with feta cheese

flavour with lemon zest + mint

replace pomegranate seeds with dates + almonds (recipe #105)

GREENS #73

Green Olive Gnocchi with Wilted Greens

replace with chopped cooked beetroot

exchange with beetroot leaves, chard leaves + baby spinach

top with shaved Parmesan + truffle oil

serve with shredded pheasant (recipe #30)

My experiments:

DAIRY #78

Rhubarb, Rosewater + Ginger Trifle

replace with roasted or fresh peaches

exchange for orange flavoured water

replace ginger cake with Madeira cake

BERRIES #84

Raspberry, Amaretti + Greek Yogurt Ice Cream Arctic Roll

replace with bananas

use crumbled honeycomb instead

add or replace with vanilla or chocolate ice cream

roll with cocoa

TAKE IT FURTHER

My experiments:

TAKE IT FURTHER

STONE FRUIT #87

Plum Fool

- make with rhubarb instead
- replace half the double cream with Greek yogurt
- flavour with chopped stem ginger
- sprinkle with toasted flaked almonds

APPLES & PEARS #93

Pear Beignets with Rosemary Sugar and Pear Crème Anglaise

- use quince instead
- replace with bay leaves
- use bay leaf and quince to infuse the poaching liquid instead of pears

My experiments:

CITRUS FRUIT #99

Blood Orange and Rosemary Crème Caramel

replace orange zest with lemon zest

replace with lemon verbena leaves or lemon thyme

serve with lemon and lemon thyme scented biscotti (a version of recipe #108)

CHOCOLATE #100

Cinnamon Chocolate Cakes with

Sherry-soaked Raisins and Sherry-spiked Crème Fraîche

replace with cardamom

replace with chopped apricots soaked in dessert wine

flavour crème fraîche with cardamom seeds

My experiments:

INDEX

ACKNOWLEDGEMENTS

From the bottom of my socks I would like to thank:

Kyle, for the opportunity and her trust in me to write a second book – it's been quite a journey!

To Jenny, my editor, who's listened to my crazy ideas and tried to decipher my writing for the past year! Thanks for your guidance, patience and for making my dreams a reality and keeping me on the straight and narrow!

To the 'A team' who once again worked on my second book:

Jonathan 'the one and only photographer' Gregson, who has been an integral part of this book, and whose work I trust and respect. His understanding of my style meant he was able to capture the essence of each dish and bring it to life.

Annie and her assistant, Rachel, who interpreted and prepared the recipes with such stylish results. Mungo – your presence was greatly missed!

Liz Belton, who sourced such beautiful props to complement my recipes perfectly.

To Kath, who's been there every step of the way with her endless support and encouragement; never giving up even through the 'tricky bits', and there certainly have been a few. Your help has been invaluable; you took my vision on board and came up with a truly stunning design that exceeded all my expectations, along with your fabulous illustrations! You have made me feel proud.

To Anne Newman and Nikki Sims, who painstakingly edited the recipes.

Last but not least a few personal thanks to the following:

The one and only 'Danny Boy', truly talented chef, for his support and dedication, without which this book would never have happened! Thank you for always holding the fort – your effort is always appreciated and never goes unnoticed.

To Allison, my best friend, who has always been so generous with her advice and encouragement, I am truly grateful.

To all my friends who have given me the space and time to be totally unsociable while I wrote this book, I've always felt humble knowing you've been there.

To Lucy, Becca and Kath, for testing some of the recipes!

To all the chefs who've given me the opportunity to succeed and believed in me throughout my career.

xx

The National Trust
Cookbook

First published in the United Kingdom in 2016 by National Trust Books
1 Gower Street
London WC1E 6HD

An imprint of Pavilion Books Group

ISBN: 9781909881709

A CIP catalogue record for this book is available from the British Library.

10 9 8 7 6 5 4 3 2 1

Reproduction by Mission, Hong Kong
Printed by 1010 Printing International Ltd, China

Project consultant: Sara Lewis
Food photographer: William Shaw
Prop stylist: Lucy Harvey
Senior Commissioning Editor: Peter Taylor
Senior Editor: Lucy Smith
Designer: Lee-May Lim

This book can be ordered direct from the publisher at the website: www.
pavilionbooks.com, or try your local bookshop. Also available at National Trust
shops or www.shop.nationaltrust.org.uk.

**Warning: recipes containing raw eggs are unsuitable for pregnant women
or young children.**

The National Trust
Cookbook

Contents

Introduction

If you're anything like me, no visit to a National Trust property would be complete without stopping by the café or tea-room to rest the feet and recharge the batteries.

Every year, our visitors tuck into over one hundred thousand plates of sausage and mash, almost seven hundred thousand bowls of homemade soup and well over a million scones, all washed down with almost seven million cups of tea and coffee.

You'll find some of these dishes in our cafés all-year-round – after all, when is it not the right time to bite into a slice of flapjack? But one of my favourite things about our places is how each season brings something unique to the gardens, estates and houses. This is reflected in our cafés' changing dishes. After a stroll through a frosty winter garden, I like to warm up with a bowl of our warming rich and creamy roast onion and garlic soup. For fresh spring days, a delicate goat's cheese tartlet with pickled cucumber. In summer, a slice of green vegetable and mozzarella quiche with a crunchy salad enjoyed from a sunny terrace. Or a satisfying Sissinghurst honey, walnut and cobnut tart to fuel a long ramble through a kaleidoscope of autumn leaves.

These dishes were all developed by us and tried and tested by all our National Trust kitchen teams. They are also simple enough to whip up in your own home – no industrial kitchen equipment or hard-to-find ingredients required. For the first time, we're bringing together favourite seasonal recipes, including many vegetarian and gluten-free options, in this cookbook, along with some of the best local recipes from our chefs across the country. So now you can whip up a taste of the National Trust in your own home.

I have visited National Trust properties since childhood. We didn't travel much when I was a kid (my mum and step-dad didn't drive), but we'd often go on family days out to Clumber Park in Nottinghamshire; it was so close to an industrial area, yet walking through its gates felt like stepping into another world. My grandfather took me on trips to National Trust places further afield and I have cherished memories of long sunny days picnicking by the lake or riding my bike through the woods.

My grandparents also fuelled my interest in food and its provenance. My grandmother never bought anything pre-packaged: everything was made from scratch, whether bread, pastry or ice cream for treats. My grandfather was a keen gardener; he worked with his simple patch to grow vegetables and soft fruit. In spring, I'd pick sticks of rhubarbs to dip into a bag of sugar, my lips soon coated with the sticky granules. In winter, I gathered greens with my grandmother, who insisted that sprouts always taste better after a frost.

So I have a fascination with food and how it works: how the sun completely changes the flavour of a tomato; what does pepper taste like on a strawberry? At school, I was always adapting the recipes we were told to cook. I cooked at home for friends and

family and when I left school I went on to catering college. It's this passion for food and its origins from that led me to work at Clumber Park in 2007. I still lived locally and felt that the Trust's ethos around food was fantastic: in the busy world we live in, here was an organisation still using raw ingredients and cooking from scratch in their kitchens. I loved how we didn't just receive a delivery of ingredients that could be from anywhere; if possible food was sourced locally or even from Clumber itself. The property has a huge walled garden growing a vast range of fruit and vegetables, and you could pick food from it in the morning and be serving it by the afternoon – just like my grandparents used to do.

Clumber isn't our only property with a kitchen garden or orchard that supplies food for the café. Others include Attingham Park, in Shropshire, where many of their intriguing crops, such as the long, prickly cucumber, established in the eighteenth century, are used in the Carriage House Café. At Beningborough Hall, in Yorkshire, their home-grown beetroot is made into a moist beetroot cake. Wimpole Estate, Cambridgeshire has a two-hectare (four-and-a-half acre) walled kitchen garden, which grows around fifty types of tomatoes and provides over 450kg of fruit and vegetables for the café each year.

In some cases, our kitchen teams also work with the estate's tenant farmer, who supplies the café with – often award-winning – produce from the surrounding farmland. For anything beyond their capacity to deliver, we work with local and regional farmers and suppliers who not only provide great-quality ingredients but also share our values around sustainability, animal welfare, looking after the land, and nature. There are inevitably commodities and ingredients which aren't grown in this country that we have to bring in from further afield, but we make sure these too are sourced and delivered responsibly.

We couldn't have a National Trust cookbook without including the recipe for our celebrated fruit scone, best served warm from the oven with lashings of strawberry jam and a generous dollop of fresh, clotted cream. Or (to avoid upsetting any Devonians) a thick spread of Devon clotted cream topped with a dollop of strawberry jam! There are also some dishes you might not have come across before. The brioche sausage Wellington, developed by Josh Hopkins at Calke Abbey, is well worth trying and much more interesting than the traditional sausage roll. And you might not expect to see a 'spiced star anise pork stew' on the menu at a National Trust café but it's a delicious, aromatic and warming one-pot combining free-range pork with spices from the far east.

With such a wealth of ingredients and recipes at our fingertips, we wanted our cookbook to celebrate some of the very best recipes from our 200 restaurants and cafés and to tell some of the stories behind them, such as Churchill's stew from Chartwell on page 183, which was always cooked there for Sir Winston on Tuesdays. Or why not try the plum cake made by Beatrix Potter at her Cumbrian home, Hill Top; the recipe on page 155 is the one she inherited from her maternal grandmother. And on page 65 you'll find a variation of Agatha Christie's favourite, crab and lobster bisque, which she enjoyed as a birthday treat at her holiday home, Greenway. We hope that they will inspire you to share a taste of the Trust at home with your friends and family.

PS. I love cooking all the recipes in this book, but if I had to recommend just one for you to try, it's got to be the Victoria sponge (see page 100). The quintessential English cake, it's the perfect balance of everything and yet so simple to make – perhaps that's why it's the bestselling cake across the Trust!

Clive Goudercourt

Development Chef,
National Trust

Spring

Spring is a time of new green shoots, lengthening days and those first few bulbs full of vibrant colour to cheer the soul. Embrace the changing season with lighter meals such as pearl barley, chickpea and goat's cheese salad or super easy chicken Caesar salad. On the days when the weather is a little unpredictable, enjoy a bowl of vibrant green pea, lettuce and mint soup or try macaroni with tomato ragù all cooked together in just one pot. Welcome in the first of the forced pink rhubarb stems and add to a light posset or to a delicious and comforting traybake with custard.

Pearl barley, chickpea and goat's cheese salad

Packed with healthy grains and pulses, this delicious salad will leave you feeling fuller for longer as the body releases the energy more slowly. The creamy goat's cheese, mellow balsamic vinegar and crunchy pumpkin seeds create a taste sensation.

Serves 4
Prep 15 minutes
Cook 30 minutes

200g/7oz pearl barley
4 tsp balsamic vinegar
3 tablespoons extra virgin
  olive oil or rapeseed oil
400g/14oz can chickpeas,
  drained, rinsed with cold
  water and drained again
4 tomatoes, cut into wedges
2 spring onions, thinly sliced
2 tbsp fresh chopped parsley
50g/1¾ oz rocket leaves
Salt and freshly ground black
  pepper
80g pack salad leaves
125g pack goat's cheese,
  diced
40g/1½ oz pumpkin seeds

Add the pearl barley to a medium-sized saucepan of boiling lightly salted water, bring back to the boil then partly cover with a lid and simmer for 30 minutes until the barley is just soft. Drain into a sieve, rinse with cold water and drain again.

Mix the balsamic vinegar and oil in the base of a large bowl. Add the warm barley and drained chickpeas and stir together to mix well in the dressing.

Add the tomatoes, spring onion, parsley and rocket and gently toss the salad together. Add salt and pepper to taste.

Divide the remaining salad leaves between four serving bowls, spoon over the barley mix, sprinkle with the goat's cheese and pumpkin seeds and serve.

COOK'S TIP You could replace the tomato wedges with oven-roasted cherry tomatoes for an extra kick of flavour.

Primrose salad

Hughenden in Buckinghamshire was Benjamin Disraeli's home until his death in 1881. Mrs Hilda Leyel claimed in her 1930s book, *Green Salads and Fruit Salads*, that the primrose salad was Disraeli's favourite as the pretty leaves were mixed with his favourite springtime flower.

Serves 4
Prep 10 minutes

For the salad
40g/1½ oz lamb's lettuce leaves
2 little gem lettuces, leaves separated
2 small chicories, leaves separated
Inside leaves from a head of celery
A few primrose flowers and tiny leaves

For the dressing
A few strands of saffron or pinch of saffron powder
1 tsp hot water
2 tsp cider vinegar
4 tbsp light olive oil
Salt and freshly ground black pepper
Little finely chopped chervil or chopped parsley

Rinse the lamb's lettuce, lettuce, chicory and celery leaves with cold water to remove any dirt, drain well and pat dry with a clean teacloth. Arrange in a salad bowl and sprinkle with the primrose flowers and leaves.

To make the dressing, add the saffron to a small bowl, pour over the hot water and leave for a few minutes to soak. Add the vinegar and oil, season with salt and pepper then fork together until well mixed. Stir in the chopped chervil or parsley, drizzle over the salad leaves and serve immediately. Alternatively, put the dressing in a jug and allow your guests to serve themselves.

COOK'S TIP Pansies, tiny viola flowers or torn lavender petals also look pretty. Use lavender sparingly as it is very perfumed. Vibrant coloured nasturtium flowers with a few of their tiny peppery leaves can also be scattered over a salad, or you might like to add a few tiny chive flowers with a little chopped chive stems or delicate thyme flowers.

Goat's cheese and spinach quiche

The filling of potato, apple and creamy goat's cheese in this quiche means that it is packed with flavour.

Cuts into 8
Prep 30 minutes, plus chilling
Cook 50-55 minutes

Pastry
225g/8oz plain flour
Pinch salt
½ tsp dried mixed herbs
115g/4oz butter, diced
50g/1¾ oz cheddar cheese,
   grated
1 egg, beaten
1–2 tbsp milk

Filling
200g/7oz potatoes, diced
1 tbsp vegetable oil
140g/5oz onions, thinly sliced
1 garlic clove, finely chopped
85g/3oz frozen spinach,
   defrosted
2 tbsp fresh chopped parsley
1 tbsp fresh chopped sage
1 tsp balsamic vinegar
½ Granny Smith or ½ small
   Bramley apple, peeled, cored
   and diced
125g pack goat's cheese,
   diced
125ml/4fl oz double cream
100ml/3½ fl oz milk
4 eggs
Salt and freshly ground black
   pepper

COOK'S TIP Defrost the frozen spinach before use either at room temperature or for 1½–2 minutes in the microwave on full power. Make sure to drain well.

To make the pastry case, add the flour, salt, herbs and butter to a bowl or electric mixer and rub in until the mixture looks like fine crumbs. Stir in the cheese then mix in the egg and enough milk to make a smooth, soft dough.

Lightly knead the pastry then roll out on a lightly floured surface until a little larger than a 23cm/9in buttered loose-bottomed fluted tart tin. Lift the pastry over a rolling pin and press into the tin. Trim the top of the pastry a little above the top of the tin, to allow for shrinkage, prick the base with a fork then chill for 30 minutes.

Preheat the oven to 190°C/375°F/gas mark 5. Line the tart case with a circle of non-stick baking paper and baking beans then bake for 10 minutes. Remove the paper and beans and cook for 5 more minutes until the base is crisp and dry. Set aside for now.

Meanwhile, make the filling. Add the potatoes to a saucepan of boiling water and cook for 4–5 minutes until just tender; drain. Heat the oil in a frying pan, add the onion and garlic and fry over a medium heat for 5–10 minutes until softened and lightly coloured.

Add the spinach to a sieve and press out the water with the back of a spoon. Stir into the onions then mix in the parsley, sage and balsamic vinegar. Fry gently until the mix starts to dry then take off the heat. Spoon half the spinach mix into the base of the tart case. Scatter the potatoes, apple and remaining spinach mix into the tart then top with the goat's cheese.

Whisk the cream, milk, eggs and a little salt and pepper together in a jug then pour into the tart. Bake at 180°C/350°F/gas mark 4 for 35–40 minutes until the top is golden brown and the filling is set. Leave to stand for 5–10 minutes before removing from the tart tin and slicing. Serve with mixed spring vegetables or salad.

Chicken Caesar salad

This super-easy salad is light, crunchy and fresh-tasting, and can be enjoyed with a chilled glass of white wine or sparkling water.

Serves 4
Prep 15 minutes
Cook 8-10 minutes

4 slices of day old bread or 1 pan rustic, torn into bite-sized pieces or cubed if preferred
4 tbsp extra virgin rapeseed or olive oil
Sea salt flakes and coarsely crushed black pepper
300g/10½ oz or 2 chicken breasts, halved crossways and opened out
2 romaine lettuce hearts, shredded
125ml/4fl oz or 8 tbsp ready-made Caesar dressing
6 anchovy fillets from a 50g/1¾ oz can, drained and chopped
40g/1½ oz piece parmesan cheese, shaved into pieces with a vegetable peeler

Preheat the oven to 200°C/400°F/gas mark 6. Arrange the pieces of bread in a single layer in a roasting tin, drizzle with 3 tbsp of the oil and sprinkle with salt and pepper. Bake for 8–10 minutes until golden.

Meanwhile, rub the remaining oil over the chicken breasts and sprinkle with salt and pepper. Preheat a dry non-stick frying pan for 1 minute then add the chicken breasts and cook for 4–5 minutes each side until golden brown and cooked through with no hint of pink juices. Take out of the pan and shred into pieces.

Add the lettuce to a large salad bowl and toss with the dressing. Add the warm croutons, chicken breast and anchovies and toss gently together then sprinkle with the parmesan shavings and a little ground black pepper. Spoon into shallow bowls to serve.

COOK'S TIP All the elements of this dish can be prepared in advance and stored separately in the fridge ready to toss together before serving.

Curried carrot and tarragon soup

Lightly spiced with just a hint of curry paste, this easy-to-make soup is then drizzled with a little tarragon-infused oil for a twist of anise. The base of this soup is made with yellow split peas, which do need soaking so add to a bowl the night before you plan to cook this soup and cover with cold water.

Serves 4
Prep 20 minutes,
plus overnight soaking
Cook 1 hour 20 minutes

100g/3½ oz yellow split peas
500g/1lb 2oz carrots, chopped
2 tbsp extra virgin rapeseed or olive oil
85g/3oz onion, finely chopped
1 garlic clove, finely chopped
½ red chilli, deseeded and finely chopped
2 tsp tikka masala curry paste
1.3 litre/2¼ pint vegetable stock
1 tbsp fresh chopped tarragon
Salt and freshly ground black pepper

To finish
2 tbsp extra virgin rapeseed or olive oil
1 tbsp fresh chopped tarragon

Add the yellow split peas to a bowl, cover with cold water and leave to soak overnight.

Preheat the oven to 200°C/400°F/gas mark 6. Add the carrots to a roasting tin, drizzle with 1 tbsp oil and roast for 30 minutes until they have just started to colour and soften.

Add the remaining oil to a medium saucepan, add the onion, garlic, chilli and curry paste and fry gently for 5 minutes, stirring until softened.

Stir in the roasted carrots. Drain and add the split peas then pour in the stock and add the tarragon. Season with a little salt and pepper. Bring to the boil, stirring then cover and simmer for 45 minutes or until the split peas are soft.

Meanwhile, heat the remaining oil in a small frying pan, add the tarragon and heat gently for 1 minute then take off the heat and leave to cool and the tarragon to infuse the oil.

Purée the soup with a stick blender still in the saucepan or transfer to a liquidiser and purée in batches. Taste and adjust the seasoning, if needed. Reheat then ladle into bowls. Drizzle with the tarragon oil and serve with warm crusty bread and butter.

COOK'S TIP Make sure the soup is well blended. If your hand blender or liquidiser isn't very powerful, you may need to pour the soup through a fine sieve before reheating.
You might also like to try adding chopped coriander leaves to the soup instead of tarragon.

Lentil, chickpea and fresh coriander soup

You don't need lots of different spices to make this gently spiced soup, just a few teaspoons of tikka masala curry paste and fragrant fresh coriander leaves and stems.

Serves 4
Prep 15 minutes
Cook 37–38 minutes

20g/¾ oz fresh coriander
1 tbsp vegetable oil
140g/5oz onions, chopped
4 tsp tikka masala paste
200g/7oz red lentils, rinsed with cold water, drained
1.2 litre/2 pints vegetable stock
400g/14oz can chickpeas, drained
Salt and freshly ground black pepper

To finish
2 tbsp extra virgin rapeseed or olive oil
1 tsp ground coriander

Trim the stalks from the coriander, reserve the leaves for later and finely chop the stalks. Heat the oil in a medium saucepan, add the coriander stalks and onion and fry over a medium heat, stirring for 5 minutes or until the onion is softened.

Add the curry paste and cook gently, stirring for 2–3 minutes. Add the lentils then pour in the stock. Bring to the boil then cover and simmer for 30 minutes, stirring from time to time and more frequently towards the end of cooking, until the lentils are soft and have absorbed most of the liquid.

Meanwhile, heat the remaining oil in a small frying pan, add the ground coriander and heat gently until the spice sizzles. Take off the heat and leave to cool and infuse.

Purée the soup with a stick blender still in the saucepan or transfer to a liquidiser and purée in batches. Roughly chop the reserved coriander leaves and stir into the soup with the chickpeas. Add a little extra stock, if needed. Bring to the boil, add salt and pepper to taste then ladle into bowls. Drizzle over the coriander oil and serve with fresh, warm naan bread.

COOK'S TIP Add salt and pepper gradually and season the soup after puréeing to get the right balance of flavours.

Pea, lettuce and mint soup

This light, fresh minty soup is made with frozen peas for ease, but if you would rather use fresh peas when they are growing in the garden, weigh after podding or if the pods are very young and tender, add them in too.

Serves 4
Prep 15 minutes
Cook 27–28 minutes

1 tbsp vegetable oil
140g/5oz onions, chopped
1 garlic clove, chopped
850ml/1½ pint vegetable
   stock
250g/9oz potato, diced
200g/7oz frozen peas
1 romaine lettuce heart
3 tbsp fresh chopped mint
1 tsp caster sugar
Salt and freshly ground black
   pepper

To finish
2 tbsp extra virgin rapeseed
   or olive oil
2 tbsp fresh chopped mint

Heat the oil in a medium saucepan, add the onion and garlic and fry over a medium heat for 5 minutes, stirring from time to time until softened.

Add the stock and potatoes then bring to the boil. Cover and simmer for 15 minutes until the potatoes are just cooked.

Add the peas and cook for 5 minutes. Shred the lettuce finely and separate the paler leaves from the darker leaves. Add the darker leaves to the saucepan with the mint. Cover and simmer for 2–3 minutes until the lettuce has just wilted.

Meanwhile, heat the remaining oil in a small frying pan, add the fresh chopped mint and as soon as it begins to sizzle take off the heat.

Stir the sugar into the pea soup then purée with a stick blender still in the saucepan or transfer to a liquidiser and purée in batches. Add salt and pepper to taste and stir in the remaining lettuce. Reheat, stirring, then ladle into bowls and drizzle with the cooled minty oil. Serve with warm crusty bread and butter.

COOK'S TIP Don't overcook this soup or you will lose the lovely delicate green colour. If you are not a fan of bits, then add all the lettuce before puréeing.

Goat's cheese tarlets with pickled cucumber

Filo pastry is a great timesaver – simply unfold the stack of sheets, brush with a little butter and oil and then fold the edges to make a pleated ridge to hold the creamy goat's cheese and chive filling. Serve with a homegrown asparagus, pea and broad bean salad mixed with baby salad leaves.

Serves 6
Prep 20 minutes
Cook 10 minutes

½ cucumber, thinly sliced
Salt and freshly ground black
   pepper
100ml/3½ fl oz cider vinegar
25g/1oz butter
1 tbsp extra virgin rapeseed or
   olive oil
1 frozen pack of 6 x 45g
   sheets of filo pastry,
   each 46 x 25cm/18 x 10in,
   defrosted
200g/7oz goat's cheese, diced
100ml/3½ fl oz double cream
2 tbsp fresh chopped chives

To serve
12 spears of English
   asparagus, woody ends
   trimmed off
55g/2oz podded broad beans
85g/3oz fresh or frozen peas
70g/2½ oz mixed leaf salad
   with rocket
3 tbsp virgin rapeseed or olive
   oil
1 tsp runny honey

COOK'S TIP Filo pastry dries out very quickly once removed from the pack so don't unwrap until you are ready to shape.

Preheat the oven to 200°C/400°F/gas mark 6. Add the cucumber to a shallow bowl, season with salt and pepper then pour over the vinegar and leave to stand for 15 minutes or longer if time.

Melt the butter in a small saucepan or in the microwave then mix with the oil. Unfold the filo pastry and lift off the top sheet. Brush with the butter and oil then fold in half to make a rectangle 23 x 25cm/9 x 10in. Brush the top with a little extra butter and oil then fold and pleat the edge of the pastry over to make a rough shaped round that is about 13cm/5in in diameter. Transfer to a large baking sheet lined with a sheet of nonstick baking paper.

Repeat with the remaining filo sheets to make six pastry cases. Bake for 3 minutes until just beginning to brown.

Meanwhile, mix the goat's cheese with the cream, chives and a little salt and pepper in a bowl. Spoon the cheese mixture into the tart cases and spread into an even layer. Bake for 3–5 minutes until just beginning to bubble.

Add the asparagus, broad beans and peas to saucepan of boiling water, bring the water back to the boil and cook for 30 seconds. Drain into a colander, rinse with cold water and drain again.

To make the dressing, add the oil, honey and 1 tbsp vinegar from the cucumber to a jam jar, screw on the lid and shake. Adjust seasoning if needed. Add the blanched vegetables and salad leaves to a salad bowl and gently toss with the dressing.

Serve the tarts topped with a little of the drained cucumber and spoonfuls of the salad.

Pearl barley risotto with garden greens

This light, creamy risotto is flavoured with white wine, cream and fresh parmesan for a touch of luxury and generously speckled with a colourful mix of fresh herbs, fresh and frozen vegetables and a crisp, peppery rocket garnish.

Serves 4
Prep 20 minutes
Cook 37-40 minutes

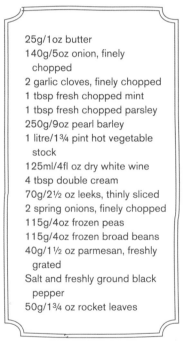

25g/1oz butter
140g/5oz onion, finely chopped
2 garlic cloves, finely chopped
1 tbsp fresh chopped mint
1 tbsp fresh chopped parsley
250g/9oz pearl barley
1 litre/1¾ pint hot vegetable stock
125ml/4fl oz dry white wine
4 tbsp double cream
70g/2½ oz leeks, thinly sliced
2 spring onions, finely chopped
115g/4oz frozen peas
115g/4oz frozen broad beans
40g/1½ oz parmesan, freshly grated
Salt and freshly ground black pepper
50g/1¾ oz rocket leaves

Heat the butter in a large deep frying pan, add the onion, garlic and chopped herbs and cook for 2–3 minutes over a low heat until just beginning to soften but not colour. Stir in the pearl barley to coat in the butter and cook for 2–3 minutes.

Pour in 450ml/¾ pint of the hot stock, increase the heat and bring to the boil, stirring. Reduce the heat, cover and simmer for 30 minutes, stirring from time to time and topping up with extra stock as needed until the barley is tender.

Pour in the wine and stir well. Drizzle over the cream then sprinkle the leeks, spring onion and frozen peas and beans on top. Stir together, cover and simmer for 3–4 minutes until the vegetables are hot and just tender and the barley has absorbed most of the liquid. Stir in half the parmesan and stir well. Adjust the seasoning to taste and stir in a little boiling water if the risotto is very thick.

Spoon into bowls and top with the rocket and the remaining grated parmesan.

COOK'S TIP A risotto is best served as soon as it is made, but if you get a little delayed keep the risotto hot and top up with a little extra hot stock before serving. Just like rice, barley absorbs the liquid and thickens with standing.

Spiced bean patties

Burgers don't need to be made with meat. These chunky burger-style patties are packed with spiced beans and topped with a fiery tomato salsa.

Serves 4
Prep 30 minutes, plus chilling
Cook 27–32 minutes

150g/5½ oz potatoes,
 cut into chunks
115g/4oz frozen broad beans
400g/14oz can five-bean mix,
 drained
400g/14oz can red kidney
 beans, drained
1 tsp ground cumin
2 tsp ground coriander
Small handful fresh coriander
 leaves
Salt and freshly ground black
 pepper
1 slice of bread, torn into
 pieces
3 tbsp vegetable oil
200g/7oz onions, finely
 chopped
½ red chilli, deseeded and
 finely chopped
1 garlic clove, finely chopped
1 tbsp lemon juice
25g/1oz plain flour

Mexican salsa
2 tsp vegetable oil
100g/3½ oz red onion, finely
 chopped
1 tsp mild paprika
1 tsp cayenne pepper
85g/3oz tomato purée
200g/7oz tomatoes, skinned if
 liked, deseeded and diced
½ bunch spring onions, finely
 chopped
2 tbsp fresh chopped parsley
 or coriander

Add the potatoes to a saucepan of boiling water and cook for 5–10 minutes until tender. Steam the broad beans above the potatoes for 5 minutes. Drain and mash the potatoes.

Tip the canned beans into a sieve, rinse with cold water and drain again. Add half the broad beans and half the canned beans to a food processor along with the ground spices, coriander leaves and salt and pepper. Blitz to a coarse paste then spoon into a bowl.

Blitz the bread in the food processor until fine crumbs. Heat 1 tbsp of the oil in a frying pan, add the onion, chilli and garlic and fry gently for 5 minutes until softened. Add the mashed potato, remaining whole beans, breadcrumbs, onion mix and lemon juice to the crushed bean mixture in the bowl. Stir together then divide into eight mounds, shape into balls then flatten into thick rounds.

Sprinkle the flour over a plate then dip the patties into the flour until lightly coated on both sides. Transfer to a tray and chill for 30 minutes.

Meanwhile, make the salsa. Heat the oil in a small frying pan, add the onion and fry for 5 minutes until softened. Stir in the paprika, cayenne and tomato purée and cook for 1 minute then spoon into a bowl and mix in the tomatoes, spring onions and parsley or coriander.

Heat 1 tbsp of the oil in a large non-stick frying pan, fry four patties for 6 minutes, turning once until browned on both sides and hot through. Transfer to a baking sheet and keep hot in the oven while you cook the second batch in the same way with the remaining oil. Transfer to serving plates and serve with spoonfuls of the salsa and salad or seasonal vegetables.

COOK'S TIP The cayenne pepper makes for quite a kick in the salsa so make sure you use mild paprika. If you have smoked paprika double check that it is the mild sweet version rather than the hot one as this is as hot as chilli powder.

Brioche sausage Wellington

This tasty twist on the traditional Wellington recipe was submitted by Josh Hopkins, a chef at Calke Abbey in Derbyshire, to our seasonal recipe contest. The thyme-scented, spiced mushroom and pork mix won us over.

Makes 8
Prep 30 minutes
Rising 1 hour – 1 hour 20 minutes
Cook 24–35 minutes

225ml/8fl oz warm water
2 tsp traditional dried yeast
100g/3½ oz butter, melted
2 eggs
200–225g/7–8oz plain flour
200–225g/7–8oz strong white
   bread flour
½ tsp salt
40g/1½ oz caster sugar

Filling
140g/5oz mushrooms, finely
   chopped
25g/1oz butter
55g/2oz onion, finely chopped
Salt and freshly ground black
   pepper
500g/1lb 2oz pork sausage meat
Few sprigs fresh thyme, leaves
   torn from stems
½ lemon, juice only

To finish
Few thyme leaves and coarse
   salt flakes to garnish, optional

Pour the warm water into a bowl, stir in the yeast. Add the warm butter and one of the eggs and fork together. Set aside for a few minutes until the yeast begins to bubble.

Add 400g/14oz of the flour to the bowl of your electric mixer fitted with a dough hook. Add in the salt and sugar and mix together then pour in the yeast mixture and beat on medium speed for 10 minutes until the dough is soft and elastic. The dough should form a ball and leave the sides of the bowl; if it looks a little sticky, slowly and gradually mix in enough flour until it does.

Add the dough to a lightly oiled bowl, cover with oiled clingfilm and leave in a warm place for 40–50 minutes or until doubled in size.

While the dough proves, add the mushrooms to a dry frying pan and fry over a medium heat for 4–5 minutes, stirring until their natural juices come out and then evaporate. When the mushrooms have shrunk and are dry, mix in the butter, onion and thyme then season with a little salt and pepper and leave to cool.

Preheat the oven to 200°C/400°F/gas mark 6. Line two baking sheets with non-stick baking paper and set aside. Mix the sausage meat with onion, thyme and lemon juice, then season with a little salt and pepper. Shape into eight balls.

Knock the dough back with your fist, scoop out of the bowl and divide into eight equal pieces. Lightly beat the remaining egg in a small bowl. Lightly knead one of the dough pieces into a ball then roll out to a circle 13cm/5in in diameter and about 1cm/½in thick.

Add one eighth of the mushroom mix, and one of the sausage meat balls. Brush the edges of the dough with a little beaten egg and pleat the edges of the dough together so that the filling is completely enclosed. Transfer to the paper-lined baking sheet. Continue until you have eight brioche Wellingtons on the baking sheets.

Cover loosely with oiled clingfilm and leave to rise in a warm place for 20–30 minutes. Remove the clingfilm, brush gently with the remaining beaten egg and a few thyme leaves and add a little coarse salt if liked. Bake for 20–30 minutes until golden brown and the filling is thoroughly cooked through. Check after 15 minutes and cover with foil if they seem to be browning too quickly. Take out of the oven and leave to cool for 10 minutes before serving hot or cold.

COOK'S TIP Knead the brioche dough very lightly after rising or you will find it very difficult to roll out as the gluten will become overworked. Use traditional dried yeast for this recipe, but if you have only have easy-blend dried yeast stir the yeast into the dry flour mix then add the butter, egg and warm water.

Chicken buknade

In the summer of 2015, we ran a competition for our restaurants to provide a recipe for this book. The winning dish came from Speke Hall, a Tudor manor house in Liverpool. They adapted a Tudor chicken dish that would have been served by only very wealthy families, as chicken was regarded as a luxury ingredient at the time. This slow-cooked stew would have been originally flavoured with sage, hyssop, mace and cloves then finished with ginger, saffron, salt and verjuice.

Serves 4
Prep 25 minutes, plus 1 hour or more marinating
Cook 45 minutes

Marinade
30ml/1fl oz vegetable oil
4 garlic cloves, finely chopped
15g/1 tbsp fresh parsley, finely chopped
10g/2 tsp fresh sage, finely chopped
½ tsp ground nutmeg
3tsps ground ginger
20ml/1 tbsp white wine vinegar
Salt and pepper
4 large chicken thighs, on the bone

Vegetable mix
200g/7oz carrots, cut into chunks
200g/7oz onion, roughly chopped
250g/9oz celery, diced
350g/12oz fresh tomatoes, chopped
750ml/1¼ pt chicken stock
15g/1 tbsp fresh parsley, roughly chopped
5g/1 tsp fresh sage, chopped
250g/9oz green cabbage, shredded

Add 2 tbsp of the oil to a shallow china or glass bowl then add the garlic, parsley, sage, nutmeg, ginger and wine vinegar. Season with salt and pepper to taste then mix together. Score the chicken skin several times with a small sharp knife then add the chicken to the marinade and turn several times, massaging the marinade in with your hands. Cover with clingfilm and chill for at least 1 hour.

Preheat the oven to 180°C/350°F/gas mark 4. Add the carrots, onion and celery to a casserole dish then mix in the chopped tomatoes, stock, parsley and sage. Drain the marinade from the chicken into the vegetables then season with salt and pepper. Cover and cook in the oven for 45 minutes or until the vegetables are tender.

Heat the remaining oil in a frying pan, add the chicken and fry skin side down for 2 minutes until the skin is golden then turn over and brown the underside. Lift out of the pan and put into a small roasting tin, cover with foil and bake above the vegetables for 30–40 minutes until the juices run clear, with no hint of pink when one of the pieces is pierced with a small knife.

Steam the cabbage over a saucepan of boiling water for 3–5 minutes until just tender, stir into the cooked vegetables with any chicken juices. Ladle the vegetables into bowls then top each bowl with a piece of chicken. Serve with warm bread rolls and butter.

COOK'S TIP This spiced stew would have been served with a manchet. Manchette or *michette* a small circular bread that was small enough to be held in the hand.

Macaroni with tomato ragù

Rather than cooking the macaroni in a pan of boiling water then adding to a sauce at the end, here it is added to a triple tomato and garlic sauce right at the beginning for an easy supper that is packed full of Mediterranean flavours.

Serves 4
Prep 20 minutes
Cook 20–25 minutes

400g/14oz carton chopped tomatoes
1 tbsp tomato purée
30g/1oz sundried tomatoes, in oil, drained and chopped
225g/8oz fresh tomatoes, chopped
140g/5oz onion, finely chopped
2 garlic cloves, finely chopped
115g/4oz closed cup mushrooms, chopped
1 litre/1¾ pint vegetable stock
1 tsp dried marjoram
½ x 400g/14oz can five-bean salad, drained
200g/7oz dried macaroni
Salt and freshly ground black pepper
50g/2oz mixed pitted black and green olives, halved
3 tbsp double cream
3 tbsp fresh chopped parsley
50g/1¾ oz piece fresh parmesan, grated

Add the carton of tomatoes and tomato purée to a large saucepan. Stir in the sundried tomatoes, fresh tomatoes, onion, garlic and mushrooms.

Pour in the stock then mix in the marjoram and beans. Bring to the boil, then mix in the macaroni and a little salt and pepper. Cover and simmer for 20–25 minutes until the macaroni is tender, stirring from time to time, but more frequently towards the end of cooking as the macaroni absorbs the stock.

Stir in the olives, cream and parsley. Taste and adjust the seasoning if needed. Spoon into bowls and sprinkle with parmesan. Serve with a green salad.

COOK'S TIP If you have some day-old cheese scones, then break into small pieces and sprinkle over the macaroni instead of sprinkling with grated cheese.

Chicken and leek pie

Leeks are a common site in Trust vegetable gardens – though some have more unusual varieties than others. (Porthcothan In Cornwall is home to the nationally rare Babington's variety.) You can use any kind in this comforting and homely pie.

Serves 4
Prep 35 minutes
Cook 49–55 minutes

Filling
1 tbsp vegetable oil
1 sprig of fresh rosemary
140g/5oz onion, chopped
1 clove garlic, finely chopped
600g/1lb 5oz skinless, boneless chicken thigh, diced
115g/4oz carrot, diced
115g/4oz mushrooms, sliced
115g/4oz leek, thinly sliced
350ml/12 fl oz chicken stock
125ml/4fl oz dry white wine
Salt and freshly ground black pepper
1 tbsp butter
1 tbsp plain flour
4 tbsp double cream
3 tbsp fresh chopped parsley

Pastry
225g/8oz plain flour
Pinch salt
½ tsp dried mixed herbs
115g/4oz butter, diced
50g/1¾ oz cheddar cheese, grated
1 egg, beaten, plus extra beaten egg to glaze
1–2 tbsp milk

Heat the oil in a deep frying pan, add the rosemary, onion and garlic and fry over a medium heat for 3–4 minutes until the onion is just beginning to soften. Add the chicken and fry for 5 minutes, stirring until lightly browned. Stir in the carrots, mushrooms and leek then pour in the stock and wine. Season with a little salt and pepper and bring to the boil. Cover and simmer for 20 minutes or until the chicken is cooked through with no hint of pink juices. Drain the meat and vegetables through a sieve, reserving the stock.

Heat the butter in a saucepan, stir in the flour and cook for 1 minute then gradually mix in the reserved stock and bring to the boil until lightly thickened. Stir in the cream and parsley, taste and adjust the seasoning if needed then mix in the chicken and vegetables and cool.

To make the pastry, add the flour, salt, herbs and butter to a bowl or electric mixer and rub in the butter until the mixture resembles fine crumbs. Stir in the cheese, mix in the egg and add enough milk to make a smooth, soft dough.

Spoon the chicken pie filling into the base of four 300ml/½ pint individual pie dishes. Cut the pastry into four pieces, then roll each piece out until a little larger than the top of the pie dish. Moisten the rim of the pie dish, lift the pastry on to the pie dish and press in place. Trim off the excess pastry, crimp the edge and make leaves from the trimmings.

When ready to bake the pies, preheat the oven to 190°C/375°F/gas mark 5. Brush the tops of the pie with a little beaten egg and bake for 20–25 minutes until the pastry is golden and the filling piping hot. Serve with crushed new potatoes and mixed spring vegetables.

COOK'S TIP If you don't have any individual pie dishes then use one large 1.2 litre/ 2 pint pie dish and bake for 35–40 minutes. Or use individual disposable foil freezer dishes.

Honeyed pork casserole

Pork and apples have long been a classic favourite but here they are mixed with a hint of honey and cider vinegar and slow cooked with vegetables and healthy beans for a comforting meal in a bowl.

Serves 4
Prep 20 minutes
Cook 1 hour 10 minutes – 1 hour 25 minutes

1 tbsp vegetable oil
500g/1lb 2oz diced pork
200g/7oz onion, chopped
400g/14oz carrots, cut into chunks
200g/7oz leeks, thickly sliced diagonally
2 sticks celery, cut into chunks
450ml/¾ pint chicken stock
4 tsp clear honey
100ml/3½ fl oz cider
1 tbsp Worcestershire sauce
1 tsp tomato purée
Salt and freshly ground black pepper
400g/14oz can of five-bean mix, drained

Preheat the oven to 180°C/350°F/gas mark 4. Heat the oil in a frying pan, add the pork, a few pieces at a time until all the pieces are in the pan then fry for 5 minutes over a medium to high heat, stirring until browned. Scoop out of the pan with a draining spoon and add to a casserole dish.

Add the onion to the meat juices in the frying pan and fry over a medium heat for a few minutes until just beginning to soften then increase the heat and cook, stirring until the onions are just beginning to caramelise.

Add the carrots, leeks and celery and fry for a few minutes until just beginning to soften. Mix the stock, honey, vinegar, Worcestershire sauce and tomato purée together, pour over the vegetables and bring to the boil, stirring. Season with a little salt and pepper.

Stir the canned beans into the casserole dish then pour over the vegetable mix. Press the pork beneath the surface of the stock then cover and cook in the oven for 1–1¼ hours until the pork is tender. Spoon into bowls and serve with warm crusty bread and butter.

COOK'S TIP The vegetables can be prepped well in advance and kept in the fridge in plastic bags until ready to use.

Chicken and spring vegetables one-pot

Packed full of bright green veggies, this tasty one-pot supper can be started on the hob then transferred to the oven, leaving you free to get on with helping the kids with their homework, take the dog for a quick walk or just have time to relax on the sofa.

Serves 4
Prep 20 minutes
Cook 1 hour

1 tbsp vegetable oil
225g/8oz onion, chopped
2 garlic cloves, finely chopped
1 bay leaf
1 tsp dried mixed herbs
500g/1lb 2oz boneless,
   skinless chicken thighs,
   cubed
175g/6oz carrots, diced
140g/5oz leeks, diced
280g/10oz potatoes, cut into
   chunks
4 tbsp dry white wine
450ml/¾ pint chicken stock
4 tsp cornflour mixed with
   2 tbsp cold water
Salt and freshly ground black
   pepper
2 sticks celery, trimmed and
   diced
85g/3oz mushrooms, sliced
55g/2oz frozen peas
85g/3oz frozen broad beans
85g/3oz fresh baby spinach
   leaves

Preheat the oven to 180°C/350°F/gas mark 4. Heat the oil in a large deep frying pan, add the onion, garlic, bay leaf and dried herbs and fry over a low heat for 10 minutes, stirring until softened and just beginning to turn golden.

Add the chicken pieces, increase the heat slightly and fry for 5 minutes, stirring until the chicken is lightly browned all over.

Stir in the carrots, leeks, and potatoes. Add the wine and stock. Stir in the cornflour with and season with a little salt and pepper. Bring to the boil stirring then transfer to a casserole dish and stir in the celery and mushrooms.

Cover and cook in the oven for 45 minutes until the chicken is cooked through with no hint of pink when a piece is cut in half. Add the frozen peas, broad beans and the fresh spinach, stir well and return to the oven for 10 minutes until the green vegetables are piping hot. Spoon into bowls and serve with crusty bread and butter.

COOK'S TIP If you have a large flameproof casserole use this on the hob when frying off the vegetables and chicken then transfer to the oven to minimise washing up. This stew freezes well in individual portions. Simply defrost in the fridge overnight then microwave to reheat – handy for those nights when you know you will be home late from work.

Steak and kidney one-pot

Kidney isn't cooked so much nowadays, but it adds a richness and depth to the stew. If you can't find it as a mix with ready-diced stewing beef then buy a plain pack of diced beef and two lamb kidneys or 115g/4oz and dice and mix them at home.

Serves 4
Prep 20 minutes
Cook 2 hours 10 minutes–2 hours 40 minutes

1–2 tbsp vegetable oil
350g/12oz onion, chopped
2 bay leaves
500g/1lb 2oz mixed cubed braising steak and kidney mix
350g/12oz carrots, cut into chunks
150g/5½ oz swede, cut into chunks
600–900ml/1–1½ pt beef stock
2 tsp English mustard
Salt and freshly ground black pepper
350g/12oz potatoes, cut into chunks
2 tsp cornflour mixed with 1 tbsp cold water

Heat 1 tbsp of the oil in a large saucepan, add the onion and bay leaves and fry over a medium heat for 5 minutes, stirring from time to time until softened.

Add the remaining oil if needed then gradually add all the pieces of beef and kidney to the pan and fry for about 5 minutes, stirring until evenly browned.

Add the carrots, swede, stock and mustard then season with salt and pepper. Bring to the boil, stirring then cover and simmer gently for 1½–2 hours or until the beef is tender.

Stir in the potatoes and top up with extra stock if needed. Cover and simmer for 30 minutes until the potatoes are just cooked. Mix the cornflour with a little water in a cup until a smooth paste. Stir into the stew, bring back to the boil and stir until thickened. Ladle into bowls and serve with warm crusty bread and butter.

COOK'S TIP The stew can also be cooked in the oven rather than on the hob. Make as above without the potatoes and then cook in a covered casserole dish in an oven preheated to 180°C/350°F/gas mark 4 for 1½–2 hours or until the meat is tender. Stir in the potatoes, (no extra stock) and the cornflour, return to the oven and cook for 30 minutes more.

Steamed rhubarb and ginger sponge puddings

At Clumber Park in Nottinghamshire, the produce from the Walled Garden includes over 130 varieties of rhubarb. These dainty individual steamed puds only require one kind, and are a great way to celebrate the early-season rhubarb.

Serves 4
Prep 20 minutes
Cook 48–49 minutes

200g/7oz trimmed rhubarb, sliced or diced if stems are large
25g/1oz light muscovado sugar
115g/4oz caster sugar
115g/4oz self-raising flour
115g/4oz soft margarine
2 eggs
1 tsp ground ginger

Add the rhubarb and muscovado sugar to a saucepan with 1 tablespoon of water. Cook gently for 3–4 minutes, stirring occasionally until the rhubarb is just beginning to soften. Remove from the heat and divide between the bases of four 250ml/9fl oz greased pudding moulds.

Spoon the caster sugar, flour and margarine into the bowl of your electric mixer. Add the eggs and ginger and beat until light and fluffy.

Divide the sponge mixture between the pudding moulds and level the tops with a round bladed knife. Cover with squares of oiled foil, doming up the top so that there is room for the puddings to rise and pressing the foil against sides of the pudding moulds.

Stand the puddings in the top of a steamer, cover and cook for 45 minutes until the sponges are light and fluffy and when a skewer is inserted into the centre it comes out free from sponge with just a little moisture from the rhubarb. Leave to cool for a few minutes then loosen the sides of the puddings with a knife and turn out into shallow bowls. Serve with hot custard.

COOK'S TIP If you don't have a steamer or your steamer isn't very big add the foil covered pudding moulds to a roasting tin. Pour boiling water into the tin to come halfway up the sides of the moulds. Cover the top of the roasting tin tightly with foil, sealing well around the edges of the tin. Bake in an oven preheated to 180°C/350°F/gas mark 4 for 45 minutes.

Fruit scones

Our champion dish, serve simply with good strawberry jam and generous spoonfuls of clotted cream for the perfect afternoon tea.

Makes 8
Prep 15 minutes
Cook 10-15 minutes

450g/1lb self-raising flour
115g/4oz soft margarine
85g/3oz caster sugar
85g/3oz sultanas
1 egg, beaten
200ml/7fl oz milk

To serve
Strawberry jam and clotted
  cream

Preheat the oven to 200°C/400°F/gas mark 6. Add the flour and margarine to the bowl of an electric mixer and rub in the margarine until the mixture resembles fine crumbs. Stir in the sugar and sultanas.

Add the egg and gradually mix in 150 ml/¼ pint of the milk to make a soft dough. Knead lightly on a floured surface then roll out thickly to a generous 2cm/¾in thickness, or two fingers. Stamp out circles using a 7cm/2¾in fluted biscuit cutter and transfer the scones to a lightly oiled baking sheet. Knead the trimmings and continue rolling and stamping until you have made eight scones.

Brush the top of the scones with a little of the remaining milk then bake for 10–15 minutes until well risen and golden brown. Serve warm, split and topped with jam and clotted cream.

COOK'S TIP Scones are really best baked on the day of serving, but you can rub the margarine into the flour and sugar then stir in the sultanas and keep in the fridge in a plastic box ready to add the egg and milk at the last minute.

Rhubarb and custard traybake

A light sponge base topped with swirls of cheesecake and tart slices of rhubarb., this easy traybake can be served warm from the oven with a scoop of ice cream or enjoyed cold with a cup of tea. Rhubarb has been grown in the magnificient Chirk Castle in the Welsh Marches for an incredible 300 years.

Cuts into 10 slices
Prep 30 minutes
Cook 20–30 minutes

Cheesecake drizzle
140g/5oz full-fat cream cheese
40g/1½ oz caster sugar
1 tsp ground ginger
1 tsp vanilla extract
1 egg

Sponge base
175g/6oz self-raising flour
140g/5oz soft light muscovado
  sugar
140g/5oz soft margarine
2 eggs
2 tablespoons milk
140g/5oz trimmed rhubarb,
  sliced or chopped if stems
  are large
Little icing sugar, sifted to
  decorate, optional

Preheat the oven to 180°C/350°F/gas mark 4. Lightly oil a 20 x 30 x 4cm/8 x 12 x 1½in rectangular cake tin and line the base with a piece of non-stick baking paper.

Add all the cheesecake ingredients to a bowl and whisk together until smooth then set aside.

To make the sponge base, add the flour, sugar and margarine to the bowl of your electric mixer then add the eggs and milk. Beat together for a few minutes until smooth.

Spoon the sponge mixture into the prepared cake tin and spread into an even layer. Spoon the cheesecake mixture over the top in random blobs and drizzles then run a spatula or spoon through the cheesecake and sponge mixture to marble together. Make sure the cheesecake drizzle is pushed into the edges so it bakes more evenly and has a coating around the edge.

Sprinkle the rhubarb over the top and gently press the pieces into the sponge. Bake for 20–30 minutes until the top is golden brown, the rhubarb is cooked and the sponge is firm when gently pressed with a fingertip.

Leave to cool in the tin for 10 minutes then lift out of the tin, peel off the lining paper and cut into slices if serving now or leave to cool completely then slice. Dust lightly with a little sifted icing sugar, if liked.

COOK'S TIP You might also like to try this traybake with different fruits that are in season. Sliced fresh apricots, chopped peaches or stoned fresh cherries would also taste delicious.

Bramley apple and rhubarb crumble

A classic favourite with a gingery, oaty crumble. Delicious served with hot custard or a scoop of good vanilla ice cream.

Serves 4–6
Prep 20 minutes
Cook 20–25 minutes

550g/1¼ lb Bramley apples, quartered, cored, peeled and sliced
350g/12oz trimmed rhubarb, thickly sliced
55g/2oz caster sugar

Topping
175g/6oz plain flour
40g/1½ oz rolled oats
85g/3oz caster sugar
115g/4oz soft margarine
1 tsp ground ginger
1 tbsp soft light muscovado sugar

Preheat the oven to 190°C/375°F/gas mark 5. Add the apple, rhubarb and sugar to a bowl, stir together and spoon into the base of a 1.2litre/2 pint ovenproof dish.

Place the flour, oats, sugar, margarine and ginger into a bowl and rub in the margarine until the mixture resembles fine crumbs. You can use an electric mixer for this, if desired.

Spoon over the fruit and sprinkle with the muscovado sugar. Bake for 20–25 minutes until golden brown and the fruit is soft. Serve scooped into bowls with hot custard.

COOK'S TIP The crumble topping can be multiplied up and packed into single or 4-person portion sized bags. Seal and label the bags and freeze for 2 months. Use straight from the freezer, no need to defrost first.

Toffee fudge gateaux

This cake is a real crowd-pleaser, and gluten free. Dress up with candles or sparklers for a special occasion. The cake can be made and wrapped in clingfilm or foil and kept in the fridge up to 3 days or frozen for up to 3 months and then decorated on the day you need it.

Cuts into 12
Prep 45 minutes
Cook 34–40 minutes

400g/14oz stoned dates
200ml/7fl oz water
1 tsp bicarbonate of soda
2 tbsp golden syrup
200ml/7fl oz vegetable oil
5 eggs
250g/9oz light muscovado sugar
1 tsp vanilla extract
400g/14oz gluten-free self-
  raising flour

To finish
115g/4oz butter
150g/5½ oz icing sugar
115g/4oz caster sugar
2 tbsp water
3 tbsp double cream
100g/3½ oz coarsely grated or
  shaved dark chocolate

Add the dates to a medium saucepan with the water, bicarbonate of soda and syrup. Stir well and bring to the boil, reduce the heat and simmer for 5 minutes until the dates are soft. Purée still in the pan with a stick blender or transfer to a food processor, checking that there aren't any stray stones, and blitz until smooth. Leave to cool.

Preheat the oven to 180°C/350°F/gas mark 4. Grease two 23cm/9in Victoria sandwich tins and line the bases with non-stick baking paper.

Add the oil, eggs, sugar and vanilla to the bowl of your electric mixer fitted with a whisk and beat for 5 minutes until light and frothy.

Spoon in the cooled date mixture and mix briefly until just combined. Add the gluten-free flour and whisk briefly until just combined. Divide evenly between the two tins, spread level and bake for 25–30 minutes until well risen and a skewer inserted into the middle comes out cleanly.

Remove from the oven, leave to cool for 5 minutes then loosen the edge, turn out on to a wire rack and peel off the lining paper. Leave to cool completely.

To make the frosting, beat the butter and icing sugar together in an electric mixer or food processor until light and fluffy. Add the caster sugar and water to a small saucepan, heat gently until the sugar has dissolved, gently tilting the pan to mix. Bring to the boil and cook for 3–4 minutes until just turning a golden caramel colour.

Take the pan off the heat and quickly stir in the cream. Keep stirring until the bubbles subside then gradually beat into the buttercream in a thin trickle to make a smooth spreadable fudge frosting. Use while still warm to sandwich the cakes together and to spread over the top, smoothing with a round bladed knife.

Leave the frosting to cool a little then sprinkle with the grated or shaved chocolate. Chill until ready to serve.

COOK'S TIP Boiled sugar can be a little unpredictable to make so don't try to multi-task. Heat the sugar and water together over a low heat until the sugar has completely dissolved and then boil rapidly. Resist the urge to stir and keep a very close eye on the syrup as it begins to turn colour around the edges. You are aiming for a rich golden colour. If the finished frosting is a little too soft to spread, chill for a few minutes. If the caramel was a bit on the dark side and so very hot you may find the frosting too thick to spread. If so, scoop into the pan with an extra tablespoon of cream and heat, stirring until soft enough to spread.

Orange and rhubarb posset

Creamy possets have to be the easiest desserts to make. Similar in texture to a panna cotta, the creamy topping thickens, as if by magic, with the addition of tangy orange and lemon juice – no need for gelatine in this dessert. It is spooned over poached rhubarb but you might also like to try it with poached apricots or peaches.

Serves 6
Prep 15 minutes
Cook 8-14 minutes
Chill 3-4 hours

250g/9oz trimmed rhubarb, sliced
100ml/3½ fl oz water
55g/2oz caster sugar

Posset
2 medium oranges, finely grated zest and juice
Grated zest of ½ lemon
4 tbsp fresh lemon juice
100g/3½ oz caster sugar
600ml/1 pint whipping cream
200ml/7fl oz milk
Little extra grated orange and lemon zest to decorate, optional

Add the rhubarb, water and sugar to a medium saucepan, cover and gently poach the fruit for 5–10 minutes until the rhubarb is soft. Transfer to a bowl and leave to cool.

Rinse and dry the pan and add the orange zest, orange juice and lemon zest. Add the sugar and heat gently, stirring until the sugar has dissolved. Bring up to the boil, reduce the heat and simmer for 1 minute. Stir in the lemon juice.

Pour the cream and milk into a second saucepan and bring to the boil. Reduce the heat and simmer for 2–3 minutes, stirring. Take the pan off the heat and gradually whisk in the warm orange mix in a thin steady stream. Pour through a fine sieve into a jug and leave to stand for a few minutes.

Add the fruit zest from the sieve to the rhubarb and mix well then spoon into the bases of six individual glass serving dishes with a little of the rhubarb juice. Pour the warm cream mixture over the top then chill the glasses for several hours until set. Decorate with extra grated fruit zest if liked. Store in the fridge up to two days.

COOK'S TIP As the rhubarb is poached you can use slightly tougher or thicker stems in this dessert.

Chocolate brownies

With more and more of our customers requesting gluten-free cakes, these gooey chocolate brownies look the part, and taste just like a good brownie should, but are made with gluten-free flour.

Cuts into 10 bars
Prep 15 minutes
Cook 18-20 minutes

175g/6oz soft margarine
65g/2½ oz cocoa powder
300g/10½ oz caster sugar
3 eggs, beaten
1½ tsp vanilla extract
Pinch of salt
115g/4oz gluten-free, self-raising flour

Preheat the oven to 180°C/350°F/gas mark 4. Line a 20cm/8in shallow square cake tin with a large square of non-stick baking paper, snipping the paper diagonally into the corners of the tin and pressing the paper down so that the base and sides of the tin are lined.

Heat the margarine in a medium-sized saucepan over a low heat, stirring until just melted. Mix in the cocoa and stir until dissolved.

Take the pan off the heat and stir in the sugar. Lightly beat the eggs, vanilla and salt together. Beat half the egg mixture into the cocoa then beat in the remaining mixture until smooth. Mix in the gluten-free flour and beat until smooth.

Pour the brownie mixture into the lined tin, spread into an even layer then bake for 18–20 minutes or until well risen, lightly cracked around the edges and the centre has a slight wobble.

Leave to cool in the tin for 15 minutes then mark into ten bars and leave to cool completely. Lift the brownies out of the tin holding the paper then cut into bars and peel off the paper.

COOK'S TIP Keep an eye on the brownies towards the end of cooking: you want to take them out of the oven when the centre is still a little soft with a slight wobble; they will firm up a little as they cool so by taking out a little before a traditional cake you can keep that yummy gooey texture.

Summer

This is the season to celebrate the great outdoors: seaside feasts with the kids, posh picnics at an open-air concert, relaxed suppers in the garden. Even a snatched coffee and slice of cake can all be enjoyed in the sunshine. Make the most of the plentiful produce with light crumbly quiches packed with green vegetables, garden herbs and mozzarella or smoked trout and watercress. Cook your favourite potato salad with a twist of minty poppy seed dressing. Try lighter one-pan suppers such as spiced star anise pork stew finished with shredded lettuce or barbecue sausage one-pot – the perfect way to use up those extra barbecued sausages.

Spinach, bacon and stilton salad

Crunchy, slightly bitter salad leaves contrast with the creamy smoothness of the stilton dressing, and mixed with bite-sized pieces of potato, crispy bacon and hardboiled egg, this makes a tasty lunch or starter.

Serves 4
Prep 20 minutes
Cook 15 minutes

85g/3oz baby new potatoes
  (or cooked leftover potatoes)
4 eggs
225g/8oz smoked back bacon
1 small radicchio lettuce
50g/1¾ oz baby spinach
  leaves
3 spring onions, thinly sliced
1 small red onion, halved and
  thinly sliced
40g/1 ½ oz stilton cheese,
  rind removed, diced
1 tbsp fresh chopped tarragon
  leaves

Stilton dressing
3 tbsp crème fraîche
1 tablespoon mayonnaise
2 tsp white wine vinegar
1 tsp caster sugar
40g/1 ½ oz stilton cheese, rind
  removed, diced
Little freshly ground black
  pepper
2–3 tsp milk

Add the potatoes to a small saucepan of boiling water and cook for 15 minutes until just tender. Add the eggs to a second small saucepan, bring the water to the boil then simmer for 8 minutes until the eggs are just hard boiled. Grill the bacon for 8–10 minutes, turning once until the fat is golden.

Drain the eggs, crack the shells, rinse with cold water then peel away the shells and reserve.

Cut the stalk from the centre of the radicchio then cut the leaves into bite-sized pieces. Add to a salad bowl with the spinach leaves, spring onions and red onion and gently toss together.

Add all the dressing ingredients to a bowl with just 2 tsp of the milk and blend with a stick blender or add to a liquidiser and blend until smooth. Mix in the remaining milk, if needed. Spoon into a serving dish.

Cut the potatoes into small cubes, the eggs into wedges and the bacon into strips. Sprinkle over the salad leaves with the diced stilton and tarragon leaves. Spoon on to serving plates and drizzle with the dressing to taste.

COOK'S TIP Whole radicchio are most often sold in local farm shops rather than the supermarket, but if you can't find one then substitute with a bag of ready-prepared salad leaves with sliced radicchio or use a little gem lettuce instead.

Potato and summer green salad

Potato salad is one of those timeless favourites, but here it is given a bit of a makeover with a mustard and poppy seed dressing and a colourful speckling of chopped fresh herbs, green beans, peas and radishes.

Serves 4
Prep 15 minutes
Cook 18 minutes

500g/1lb 2oz baby new potatoes, scrubbed
85g/3oz green beans, halved
200g/7oz frozen peas
100ml/3½ fl oz mayonnaise
2 tsp wholegrain mustard
4 tsp extra virgin rapeseed or olive oil
1 tsp poppy seeds
½ bunch spring onions, finely chopped
140g/5oz courgette, quarter lengthways and thinly sliced
100g/3½ oz trimmed radishes, thinly sliced
4 tbsp fresh chopped mint
Salt and freshly ground black pepper
½ small iceberg lettuce, shredded
4 tbsp fresh chopped parsley

Add the potatoes to a medium saucepan of boiling water, cover and simmer for 15 minutes until just tender. Add the green beans and peas to a steamer set over the potato pan, cover and cook for 3 minutes until just tender or al dente (with a little bite). Drain the potatoes and leave all the vegetables to cool.

Whisk the mayonnaise, mustard, oil and poppy seeds together in a large bowl until smooth.

Quarter the potatoes then add to the dressing with the green beans and peas. Sprinkle over the spring onions, courgettes, radishes and mint and gently mix together. Season to taste with salt and pepper.

Arrange the lettuce in the base of a large salad bowl or individual dishes, top with spoonfuls of the potato salad and sprinkle with the remaining parsley.

COOK'S TIP The mayonnaise-dressed salad can be made up in advance and kept in a covered bowl in the fridge. Just add the shredded lettuce and parsley when serving.
Slightly undercook the potatoes and choose smaller ones if you can.

Summer tomato soup

An impressive 102 varieties of heritage tomato are grown at Knightshayes Court in Devon, and they often end up in the restaurant kitchen. This soup is rich and full of flavour, the perfect recipe for homegrown summer tomatoes.

Serves 4
Prep 20 minutes
Cook 25 minutes

2 tbsp vegetable oil
200g/7oz onion, chopped
1 stick celery, chopped
2 garlic cloves, chopped
4 tablespoons tomato purée
400g/14oz fresh tomatoes, chopped
400g/14oz carton chopped tomatoes
1 litre/1¾ pint vegetable stock
1 tsp dried tarragon
1 bay leaf
20–40g/¾–1½ oz caster sugar
Salt and freshly ground black pepper
3 tbsp fresh chopped basil
30g/1oz sundried tomatoes in oil, drained, chopped
3 tbsp olive oil (or use some of the oil from the jar of tomatoes)

Heat the oil in a medium saucepan, add the onion, celery and garlic and fry over a medium heat for 5 minutes, stirring from time to time until the onions are softened.

Stir in the tomato purée and mix well then add the fresh and carton tomatoes, the stock, dried herbs and bay leaf. Stir in half the sugar and a little salt and pepper and bring to the boil. Cover and simmer for 20 minutes.

Discard the bay leaf and purée the soup with a stick blender still in the saucepan or transfer to a liquidiser and purée in batches until smooth. Press through a sieve if needed. Taste and adjust the seasoning, adding the remaining sugar if needed.

Mix the basil, sundried tomatoes and oil together in a small bowl. Reheat the soup, ladle into bowls and sprinkle with the sundried tomato mix. Serve with warm crusty bread and butter.

COOK'S TIP
If you don't have any dried tarragon, dried oregano or mixed herbs could be used instead.

Pesto, pasta and superseed salad

Packed with protein and energy-boosting carbs, this healthy salad will help you power through the afternoon.

Serves 4
Prep 15 minutes
Cook 12–15 minutes

140g/5oz dried pasta bows
115g/4oz pesto
2 tbsp sunflower seeds
3 tbsp pumpkin seeds
30g/1oz walnut pieces
½ small iceberg lettuce, shredded
1 medium carrot, grated
3 tbsp fresh chopped parsley
30g/1oz mange tout, sliced
400g/14oz can five-bean mix, drained, rinsed with cold water and drained again
3 tbsp mayonnaise
Salt and freshly ground black pepper

Add the pasta to a large saucepan of boiling water and cook for 10–12 minutes until just tender. Drain into a colander, rinse with cold water and drain again.

Spoon the pesto into a large bowl, add the pasta and stir into the pesto until evenly coated.

Add the sunflower seeds, pumpkin seeds and walnut pieces to a frying pan and dry fry for 2–3 minutes until lightly toasted. Remove from the heat and add to the pasta while still hot.

Add the lettuce, carrot, parsley and mange tout to the pasta then mix in the beans and mayonnaise. Season to taste with salt and pepper. Spoon into individual bowls to serve.

COOK'S TIP Iceberg lettuce has been suggested here but if you have salad leaves growing in the garden or a bag of mixed salad leaves in the fridge then do use these instead.

Courgette and stilton soup

This is a delicate pale green soup with just a hint of garlic and creamy richness from the stilton. If you have wild garlic growing in the garden then decorate the soup with some of the tiny flower heads along with the chopped garlic.

Serves 4
Prep 20 minutes
Cook 25 minutes

1 tbsp vegetable oil
250g/9oz onion, chopped
2 garlic cloves, chopped
500g/1lb 2oz courgettes, cut into chunks
200g/7oz potatoes, diced
850ml/1½ pints vegetable stock
Salt and freshly ground black pepper
85g/3oz stilton cheese, rind removed, diced
2 tbsp fresh chopped chives

Heat the oil in a medium saucepan, add the onion and garlic and fry over a low heat for 10 minutes, stirring until softened. Add the courgette and potatoes and mix well.

Pour over the stock, add a little salt and pepper and bring to the boil. Cover and simmer for 15 minutes.

Purée the soup with a stick blender still in the saucepan, adding half the stilton until smooth, or transfer to a liquidiser and purée in batches. Taste and adjust the seasoning if needed. Reheat then ladle into bowls, sprinkle with the chopped chives and remaining stilton. Serve with warm crusty bread and butter.

COOK'S TIP You could use leftover jacket potatoes in this recipe, simply scoop out the filling and add to the soup when you add the stilton.

Greenway crab and lobster bisque

Greenway was the beloved holiday home of Agatha Christie, and where she celebrated her 60th, 70th and 80th birthdays. For her 80th birthday, a huge family picnic was held on Dartmoor, followed by a grand dinner in Greenway's dining room, which included her favourite dishes of hot lobster and blackberry ice cream.

Serves 4
Prep 20 minutes
Cook 35 minutes

500g/1lb 2oz frozen part-
  prepared crab, defrosted or
  fresh crab, prepared but not
  dressed with mayonnaise
25g/1oz butter
1 tbsp light rapeseed or olive
  oil
100g/3½ oz onion, finely
  chopped
100g/3½ oz carrot, diced
115g/4oz potatoes, diced
2 tomatoes, diced
5mm/¼ in piece root
  ginger, peeled and chopped
125ml/4 fl oz dry white wine
450ml/¾ pint fish stock
Salt and freshly ground black
  pepper
125ml/4 fl oz semi-skimmed
  milk
125ml/4 fl oz double cream

To finish
1 tsp light rapeseed or olive oil
140g/5oz cooked lobster meat
  or cooked, peeled crayfish
  tails
Paprika

If using the defrosted crab, remove the claws, crack with poultry shears or hit with a rolling pin. Peel away the shell and pick the white meat out with a small knife or skewer. Put half the defrosted or fresh white crab meat back into the fridge.

Heat the butter and oil in a medium saucepan, add the onion and fry gently over a low heat for 5 minutes, stirring until softened but not browned.

Add the carrot, potato, tomatoes and ginger and fry gently for 5 minutes, stirring from time to time. Stir in the wine, stock, brown crab meat and half the white meat. Season lightly with salt and pepper and bring to the boil. Reduce the heat, cover and simmer for about 20 minutes until the potato is soft.

Purée the soup using a stick blender in the saucepan or transfer to a liquidiser. Add the milk and half the cream to the soup and reheat, stirring. Taste and adjust the seasoning.

Heat the remaining oil in a frying pan, add the remaining white crab meat and lobster meat and heat through until piping hot. Ladle the soup into bowls, spoon the rest of the cream in swirls over the top, then scatter with the white crab meat and lobster. Sprinkle with a little paprika and serve immediately.

COOK'S TIP If you have some saffron in the cupboard then add a pinch of the strands to the soup when adding the tomatoes.

Sweetcorn and chilli soup

Frozen vegetables make a great standby and save on prep time too. This golden-yellow soup tastes delicious with a drizzle of chilli oil.

Prep 15 minutes
Cook 20 minutes

1 tbsp vegetable oil
250g/9oz onion, chopped
1 garlic clove, chopped
Few stems fresh thyme
2 sticks celery, chopped
100g/3½ oz potatoes, diced
500g/1lb 2oz frozen sweetcorn
1 litre/1¾ pints vegetable
  stock
Salt and freshly ground black
  pepper

To finish
2 tbsp extra virgin rapeseed or
  olive oil
¼–½ red chilli, deseeded and
  finely chopped

Heat the oil in a medium saucepan, add the onion and garlic and fry over a medium heat for 5 minutes, stirring from time to time until the onions are softened.

Strip the leaves from the thyme stems and add to the saucepan with the celery, potatoes and sweetcorn and stir together. Pour in the stock, season with a little salt and pepper and bring to the boil, stirring. Cover and simmer for about 15 minutes until the potatoes are tender.

Meanwhile, heat the remaining oil in a small frying pan, add the chilli and as soon as it begins to sizzle take off the heat.

Purée the soup with a stick blender still in the saucepan or transfer to a liquidiser and purée in batches until smooth. As sweetcorn can be a little fibrous you may need to pour through a sieve and then reheat. Taste and adjust the seasoning if needed. Ladle into bowls then drizzle a little chilli oil over each portion. Serve with warm crusty bread and butter

COOK'S TIP If you grow your own sweetcorn then take the niblets off the corn cobs with a small sharp knife in long slices and then weigh.

Mottisfont Abbey smoked trout and watercress tart

Mottisfont Abbey was built next to the River Test, a pure, clean chalk stream favoured by a steady population of brown trout. Non-residents needn't miss out – more and more supermarkets now sell packs of ready-to-use smoked trout, perfect for this delicious creamy tart.

Serves 4–6
Prep 30 minute, plus chilling
Cook 40 minutes

Pastry
125g/4½ oz plain wholemeal flour
Pinch salt
70g/2½ oz butter, diced
5–6 tsp cold water

Filling
1 tbsp extra virgin rapeseed or olive oil
100g/3½ oz onion, finely chopped
2 garlic cloves, finely chopped
150g/5½ oz hot smoked trout
30g/1oz watercress
3 eggs
200ml/7fl oz whipping cream
2 tbsp fresh chopped chives
Salt and freshly ground black pepper

To make the pastry case, add the flour, salt and butter to a bowl or electric mixer and rub in until the mixture looks like fine crumbs. Gradually mix in enough water to make a smooth dough.

Lightly knead the pastry then roll out on a lightly floured surface until a little larger than a 20cm/8in buttered loose-bottomed tart tin. Lift the pastry over a rolling pin and press into the tin. Trim the top a little above the top of the tin to allow for shrinkage. Prick the base with a fork then chill for 30 minutes.

Preheat the oven to 190°C/375°F/gas mark 5. Line the tart case with a circle of non-stick baking paper and baking beans then bake for 10 minutes. Remove the paper and beans and cook for 5 more minutes until the base is crisp and dry. Set aside.

Meanwhile, make the filling. Heat the oil in a small frying pan, add the onion and garlic and fry over a medium heat for 5 minutes, stirring until softened but not coloured.

Spread the onion mix in the base of the baked tart case. Flake the trout into pieces, discarding any skin then sprinkle over the onion. Roughly chop the watercress then sprinkle over the trout, reserving a little for garnish. Beat the eggs, cream and chives with a little salt and pepper until smooth. Pour into the tart case then bake at 180°C/350°F/gas mark 4 for about 25 minutes until the filling is set and the top is golden brown.

Leave the tart to cool then remove from the tart tin, garnish with extra watercress, cut into wedges and serve with salad.

Cherry tomato tarts

Light, fresh-tasting summery tarts filled with melting brie with just a hint of chilli in a crisp cheesy pastry. Delicious eaten as a light lunch in the garden or starter for a supper party.

Makes 8 tarts
Prep 30 minutes,
plus 30 minutes chilling
Cook 18–20 minutes

Cheesy pastry
225g/8oz plain flour
115g/4oz butter, diced
50g/1¾ oz cheddar cheese,
  finely grated
½ tsp dried mixed herbs
1 egg, beaten
1–2 tbsp milk

Filling
500g/1lb 2oz small cherry
  tomatoes
2 tbsp extra virgin rapeseed or
  olive oil
Salt flakes and coarsely
  crushed black pepper
1 red chilli, halved, deseeded,
  finely chopped
150g/5oz brie, diced
2 tbsp fresh chopped parsley
30g/1oz drained sundried
  tomatoes in oil, thinly sliced

COOK'S TIP The pastry cases can be made in advance, cooked, cooled and kept in the fridge overnight or even frozen well wrapped in clingfilm up to six weeks. Add the cheesy filling and roasted tomatoes when ready to heat through.

To make the pastry, add the flour and butter to a bowl and rub in with fingertips or an electric mixer until it resembles fine crumbs. Stir in the cheese and herbs then mix in the egg and enough milk to mix to a smooth dough.

Knead the pastry lightly then cut into eight pieces. Roll each piece out until a little larger than a 10cm/4in diameter, 2cm/¾in deep loose-bottomed individual fluted tart tin. Press the pastry into the tin and trim a little above the top of the tin to allow for shrinkage in cooking. Continue until you have made eight tart cases.

Prick the bases with a fork then chill for 30 minutes. Preheat the oven to 190°C/375°F/gas mark 5.

Arrange the tart cases on a baking sheet. Line with squares of non-stick baking paper and half fill with baking beans. Bake for 8 minutes. Carefully remove the paper and beans and cook for 5 minutes until just beginning to turn golden around the tops and the bases are crisp and dry.

Meanwhile, pierce each tomato with a small knife, add to a roasting tin, drizzle with the oil, sprinkle with salt and pepper and roast for 10–15 minutes until just softened and the juices are beginning to run.

Mix the chilli, brie and half the parsley with the sundried tomatoes and a little pepper. Mash roughly with a fork or potato masher to break down the cheese a little more.

Spoon the brie mix into the base of each tart. Top with the roasted tomatoes, drizzle with a little of the cooking juices and bake for 5 minutes to warm through. Sprinkle with the remaining parsley and serve.

Chicken and basil stew

Light and refreshing, this herby chicken stew can be on the table within 40 minutes so it makes for a great after-work supper that is packed with healthy veggies and high fibre chickpeas.

Serves 4
Prep 20 minutes
Cook 35–40 minutes

1 tbsp vegetable oil
140g/5oz onion, chopped
500g/1lb 2oz boneless, skinless chicken thighs, cubed
4 tbsp red wine
250ml/8fl oz chicken stock
½ red or yellow pepper, cored, deseeded and diced
½ orange pepper, cored, deseeded and diced
2 sticks celery, diced
250g/9oz potatoes, cut into chunks
175g/6oz carrots, diced
½ tsp dried mixed herbs
4 tbsp fresh chopped basil
400g/14oz can chickpeas, drained
400g/14oz carton chopped tomatoes
Salt and freshly ground black pepper

Basil dressing
3 tbsp extra virgin rapeseed or olive oil
3 tbsp fresh chopped basil
1 tsp white wine vinegar
1 tsp caster sugar

Heat the oil in a large frying pan, add the onion and fry over a medium heat for 5 minutes, stirring until softened. Add the chicken and fry for 5 more minutes, stirring until the chicken pieces are evenly browned.

Add the red wine and bring to the boil. Stir in the stock then mix in the peppers, celery, potatoes, carrots, dried herbs and fresh basil. Add the chickpeas and canned tomatoes. Season with a little salt and pepper and bring to the boil, stirring.

Cover and simmer for 25–30 minutes until the vegetables are cooked and there is no hint of pink juices when a piece of the chicken is pierced with a knife.

To make the basil dressing, heat the remaining oil in a frying pan, add the remaining basil, vinegar and sugar and heat until the sugar has dissolved. Spoon the stew into bowls, drizzle with the basil dressing and serve with warm crusty bread and butter.

COOK'S TIP If you have fresh herbs growing in the garden then use these instead of dried herbs. If you transplant supermarket pots of basil into a larger pot they will continue to grow for a few weeks.

BBQ sausage and chilli beans

Mellow spiced chilli beans topped with sticky glazed sausages makes this a winner with the whole family.

Serves 4
Prep 20 minutes
Cook 27–40 minutes

400g/14oz or 6 good pork sausages
1 tbsp vegetable oil
250g/9oz onion, chopped
2 garlic cloves, finely chopped
1 tsp ground coriander
½ tsp ground cumin
¼ tsp ground ginger
¼ tsp chilli powder
1 tbsp tomato purée
1 tbsp black treacle
100ml/3½ fl oz red wine
400g/14oz carton chopped tomatoes
400g/14oz can five-bean mix, drained
400g/14oz can red kidney beans, drained
200ml/7fl oz chicken stock
Salt and freshly ground black pepper
4 tbsp fresh chopped coriander leaves

Sausage glaze
2 tsp tomato purée
2 tsp brown sugar
½ tsp English mustard
¼ tsp ground cinnamon
½ tsp dried mixed herbs
2 tsp Worcestershire sauce

Preheat the grill and the oven to 200°C/400°F/gas mark 6. Grill the sausages for 12–15 minutes, turning until evenly browned. Heat the oil in a medium saucepan, add the onion and garlic and fry over a medium heat for 5 minutes, stirring until softened.

Stir the ground spices into the onion and garlic and cook for 1 minute then mix in the tomato paste, treacle and wine and cook gently for 5 minutes, stirring from time to time.

Add the tomatoes, beans and half the stock then bring to the boil, stirring. Cover and simmer for 10–15 minutes until the sauce thickens slightly. Top up with the remaining stock, if needed.

Thickly slice the sausages. Fork all the glaze ingredients together in a mixing bowl, add the sausages and turn to coat evenly. Tip the sausages out on to a large roasting tin and spread into a single layer. Roast for 5–10 minutes until the glaze is sticky and the sausages piping hot.

Spoon the sausages into the chilli beans, season with salt and pepper and sprinkle with the chopped coriander. Serve with warm crusty bread and butter.

COOK'S TIP This recipe also works well with leftover cooked sausages after a barbecue. Just add as many as you have, ideally allowing one per person or more if you have them. Slice and reheat in the oven in the sticky glaze.

Meatballs with tomato sauce

Meatballs are one of those recipes that are popular with everyone and delicious served with pasta or rice. This is a good recipe to prepare ahead: make and shape the meatballs and cook the sauce then chill both in the fridge until ready to finish later that day or the next.

Serves 4
Prep 40 minutes
Cook 40 minutes

25g/1oz bread
225g/8oz onions
2 garlic cloves
Small handful fresh parsley
700g/1lb 9oz minced beef
1 tbsp tomato purée
Salt and freshly ground black
  pepper
2 tbsp vegetable oil

Tomato sauce
1 tbsp vegetable oil
200g/7oz onion, finely
  chopped
2 garlic cloves, finely chopped
115g/4oz or 1 carrot, grated
4 sticks celery, diced
400g/14oz carton chopped
  tomatoes
450ml/¾ pint beef stock
Small bunch of fresh coriander
  or parsley, finely chopped

To make the meatballs, tear the bread into pieces and blitz in a food processor into fine crumbs. Scoop out of the processor bowl then finely chop the onion, garlic and parsley. Add the minced beef and tomato purée, spoon the breadcrumbs back into the food processor and season generously with salt and pepper. Blitz together until just mixed.

Spoon the mince mixture into 24 mounds on a baking sheet then roll into balls with your hands. Cover and chill for 30 minutes, or longer if preferred.

Meanwhile, make the sauce. Heat the oil in a medium saucepan, add the onion and garlic and fry over a medium heat for 5 minutes, stirring until softened. Stir in the grated carrot, celery, tomatoes and stock. Season with salt and pepper and bring to the boil, stirring. Cover and simmer for 15 minutes.

To cook the meatballs, heat the remaining 2 tbsp oil in a large frying pan, add the meatballs and fry for 10 minutes over a medium heat, turning until evenly browned all over. Drain off the excess oil from the pan then pour in the tomato sauce. Cover and cook for 10–15 minutes until the meatballs are cooked through to the centre. Take one of the balls out of the sauce and cut in half to check. Sprinkle with the chopped coriander or parsley and serve with just-cooked tagliatelle.

COOK'S TIP If you don't have a food processor, finely chop the onion, garlic and parsley for the meatballs with a large cook's knife then add to a large mixing bowl with the minced beef, tomato purée and plenty of salt and pepper. Make the bread into breadcrumbs by rubbing over a coarse grater – stale bread is best for this. Add to the minced beef and mix together with a large spoon or clean hands then shape as above.

Summer vegetable and pasta bake

This popular pasta dish is great for using up gluts of beans and tomatoes during the summer months. Walled gardens supplying the kitchens with produce is a long-standing tradition at the Natioanl Trust. The gardens at Chartwell in Kent, even supplied vegetables to 10 Dowing Street during the war years.

Serves 4
Prep 25 minutes
Cook 35 minutes

Ragú sauce
1 tbsp extra virgin rapeseed or olive oil
175g/6oz red onion, finely chopped
2 garlic cloves, finely chopped
1 bay leaf
1 tsp dried marjoram
3 tbsp fresh chopped basil leaves
1 tsp caster sugar
1 tbsp tomato purée
400g/14oz carton chopped tomatoes
4 tbsp red wine or extra stock
250ml/9fl oz vegetable stock
Salt and freshly ground black pepper

To finish
1 large red pepper, halved, cored, deseeded and thinly sliced
225g/8oz courgette, halved lengthways, thinly sliced
1 tbsp extra virgin rapeseed or olive oil
200g/7oz dried pasta twists
55g/2oz frozen sweetcorn
55g/2oz green beans, cut into 2.5cm/1in lengths
3 spring onions, thinly sliced
100g/3½ oz cherry tomatoes, quartered
115g/4oz mature cheddar cheese, grated
Few small basil leaves to garnish

To make the ragú sauce, heat the oil in a medium saucepan, add the onion and garlic and fry over a medium heat for 5 minutes, stirring until softened. Stir in the bay leaf, marjoram, fresh basil, sugar and tomato purée then add the carton of tomatoes, wine and stock. Season with salt and pepper and bring to the boil, stirring. Cover and simmer for 30 minutes, stirring occasionally.

Meanwhile, preheat the oven to 200°C/400°F/gas mark 6. Add the red pepper and courgettes to a roasting tin and drizzle with the oil. Roast for 15 minutes.

Half fill a second saucepan with water, bring to the boil then add the pasta and cook for 5 minutes. Add the sweetcorn and green beans and cook for 3–5 minutes until the pasta is tender. Drain, reserving the cooking water.

Remove the bay leaf from the ragú sauce then purée the sauce with a stick blender still in the pan or transfer to a liquidiser, purée and return to the pan. Alternatively, leave the sauce chunky if preferred.

Stir the drained pasta, sweetcorn and green beans into the ragú sauce then add the roasted vegetables, spring onions and cherry tomatoes. Mix in a ladleful of reserved pasta water, if needed. Spoon into an ovenproof dish, sprinkle with the cheese and cook under a hot grill for about 5 minutes until the cheese is bubbling and golden brown. Garnish with basil leaves and serve with a green salad.

COOK'S TIP Instead of finishing the dish under the grill, simply leave the oven on after roasting the vegetables and pop the bake in for 15–20 minutes.

Green vegetable and mozzarella quiche

Teaming British green vegetables with the Italian trio of basil, mozzarella and tomato, this is fusion cooking at its best.

Cuts into 8
Prep 30 minutes, plus chilling
Cook 55-60 minutes

Pastry
225g/8oz plain four
Pinch of salt
½ tsp dried mixed herbs
115g/4oz butter, diced
50g/1¾ oz cheddar cheese, grated
1 egg, beaten
1–2 tbsp milk

Filling
1 tbsp vegetable oil
115g/4oz leeks, thinly sliced
70g/2½ oz mange tout, sliced
115g/4oz green beans, thickly sliced
125ml/4fl oz double cream
100ml/3½ fl oz milk
4 eggs
3 tbsp fresh chopped basil
1 tsp dried marjoram
Salt and freshly ground black pepper
70g/2½ oz sundried tomatoes in oil, drained and chopped
125g/4½ oz mozzarella, drained and chopped
115g/4oz cherry tomatoes, halved

To make the pastry case, add the flour, salt, herbs and butter to a bowl or electric mixer and rub in until the mixture looks like fine crumbs. Stir in the cheese then mix in the egg and enough milk to make a smooth, soft dough.

Lightly knead the pastry then roll out on a lightly floured surface until a little larger than a 23cm/9in buttered loose-bottomed fluted tart tin. Lift the pastry over a rolling pin and press into the tin. Trim the top of the pastry a little above the top of the tin to allow for shrinkage, prick the base with a fork then chill for 30 minutes.

Preheat the oven to 190°C/375°F/gas mark 5. Line the tart case with a circle of non-stick baking paper and baking beans then bake for 10 minutes. Remove the paper and beans and cook for 5 minutes until the base is crisp and dry. Set aside.

Meanwhile, make the filling. Heat the oil in a frying pan, add the leeks, mange tout and beans and fry over a medium heat, for 5 minutes, stirring until just softened.

Beat the cream, milk and eggs together in a jug. Mix in the basil and dried marjoram and season with salt and pepper.

Spoon the leek mixture into the base of the tart case, sprinkle with the sundried tomatoes and mozzarella then pour over the custard. Arrange the cherry tomatoes on top then bake at 180°C/350°F/gas mark 4 for 35–40 minutes until the top is golden brown and the filling is set. Leave to stand for 5–10 minutes before removing from the tart tin and slicing. Serve with summer salad and new potatoes.

COOK'S TIP If you have two tart tins, why not make up double the quantity of pastry? Make and bake two tart cases then freeze one, empty, for another time, and fill one to use now. It doesn't take much longer, especially if you make the pastry in a mixer.

Beef lasagne

A comforting layered beef and pasta ovenbake that is popular with all ages.

Serves 4
Prep 30 minutes
Cook 1 hour – 1 hour 5 minutes

1 tbsp vegetable oil
115g/4oz onion, chopped
1 carrot, diced
2 sticks celery, diced
250g/9oz minced beef
500g/1lb 2oz jar tomato
 pasta sauce
1 tsp dried mixed herbs
140g/5oz mushrooms,
 roughly chopped
20g/¾ oz butter
20g/¾ oz plain flour
300ml/½ pint milk
85g/3oz cheddar cheese,
 grated
200g/7oz or 9 dried no
 pre-cook lasagne sheets,
 prepared as pack instructions

Preheat the oven to 190°C/375°F/gas mark 5. Heat the oil in a medium saucepan, add the onion, carrot and celery and fry over a medium heat for 5 minutes, stirring until softened. Add the mince and fry for 10 minutes, stirring until browned.

Mix in the tomato sauce, herbs and mushrooms then bring to the boil, stirring.

To make the cheese sauce, heat the butter in a second saucepan, stir in the flour and cook for 1 minute then gradually whisk in the milk and bring to the boil, still whisking until thickened and smooth. Mix in half the cheese and season with salt and pepper.

Spoon one third of the meat sauce over the base of a 20cm/8in square ovenproof dish. Cover with a layer of lasagne sheets then a second layer of meat and continue with a third layer of meat sauce and lasagne. Pour the cheese sauce over the top to cover the lasagne completely. Sprinkle with the remaining cheese.

Cover the dish with foil and bake for 30 minutes. Remove the foil and bake for 15–20 minutes until the topping is golden brown and the pasta is cooked through. Cut into four portions and serve with summer salad, see page 85.

COOK'S TIP For garlic fans, add two finely chopped garlic cloves to the onions when frying and serve the lasagne with hot garlic bread.

Chicken with lemon and tarragon

Fresh tarragon and lemon are a classic combination that really brings out the flavour of chicken for a light, fresh-tasting summer supper.

Serves 4
Prep 20 minutes
Cook 30–35 minutes

1 tbsp vegetable oil
175g/6oz onion, chopped
2 garlic cloves, finely chopped
500g/1lb 2oz chicken breast
  fillets, cut into chunks
350g/12oz potatoes, cut into
  chunks
250g/9oz carrots, diced
1 lemon, grated zest and juice
2 tbsp fresh chopped tarragon
125ml/4 fl oz dry white wine
300ml/½ pint chicken stock
Salt and freshly ground black
  pepper
1 tbsp cornflour mixed with 1
  tbsp cold water

Heat the oil in a medium frying pan, add the onion and garlic and fry over a medium heat for 5 minutes until softened. Add the chicken, a few pieces at a time, until all the pieces are added to the pan then fry for 5 minutes, stirring until lightly browned.

Stir in the potatoes and carrots then add the lemon zest and juice and half the tarragon.

Pour over the white wine and stock and season with a little salt and pepper. Bring to the boil, stirring. Cover and simmer for 20–25 minutes until the vegetables are tender and there is no hint of pink juices when a piece of chicken is pierced with a knife.

Stir in the cornflour and cook for 2 minutes until thickened then mix in the remaining tarragon. Spoon into bowls and serve with warm crusty bread and butter.

COOK'S TIP If you have some double cream in the fridge you might like to stir three tablespoons into the sauce along with the cornflour.

Roast honey-mustard chicken

Rather than roasting a whole chicken, yogurt-marinated chicken thighs are roasted then served on a colourful warm new potato and chickpea salad for a healthy dish, ideal for a midweek lunch.

Serves 4
Prep 20 minutes
Cook 30-40 minutes

2 tsp wholegrain mustard
4 tsp runny honey
1 tsp white wine vinegar
1 tsp light muscovado sugar
2 tbsp natural yogurt
1 garlic clove, finely crushed
  with a little salt
2 tsp vegetable oil
2 tbsp fresh chopped parsley
Salt and freshly ground black
  pepper
4 large chicken thighs, skin on

Summer salad
200g/7oz new potatoes
50g/1¾ oz green breans,
  trimmed
40g/1½ oz broccoli stalk, cut
  into thin batons
1 tbsp vegetable oil
½ red pepper, cored,
  deseeded and cut into strips
115g/4oz courgette, halved,
  cut into batons
70g/2½ oz mange tout
200g/7oz or ½ can of
  chickpeas, drained, rinsed
  and drained again
3 tbsp fresh chopped parsley
2-3 stems fresh thyme, leaves
  pulled from stems

Add the mustard, honey and vinegar to a shallow china dish then add the sugar, yogurt and garlic and whisk together. Add the oil, parsley and a little salt and pepper and whisk again.

Slash the top of the chicken joints two or three times with a small knife then add to the yogurt mix, slashed side downwards then turn over so that they are completely coated in the yogurt mix. Cover with clingfilm and chill in the fridge for 6 hours or overnight. When ready to cook the chicken, preheat the oven to 180°C/350°F/gas mark 4. Remove the clingfilm and transfer the chicken pieces to a small roasting tin lined with non-stick baking paper, spooning any remaining marinade over the top of the chicken pieces. Roast for 30–40 minutes until golden brown and when one of the chicken pieces is pierced with a small sharp knife there is no hint of pink juices.

While the chicken cooks, add the potatoes to a saucepan of boiling water and cook for 15 minutes until just tender. Add the green beans and broccoli to a steamer and set over the potatoes. Cover and cook for 4–5 minutes until just tender.

Heat the oil in a frying pan, add the peppers and courgettes and fry for 2–3 minutes until just tender. Add the mange tout and cook for 1 minute. Drain the potatoes, halve or quarter depending on size then add to the pan with the just-cooked beans and broccoli. Mix in the chickpeas and fresh herbs. Season with salt and pepper.

Spoon the warm salad on to plates, top each with a piece of chicken and drizzle over the pan juices.

COOK'S TIP Always double check that chicken is cooked thoroughly right to the centre before serving, so pierce with a small sharp knife through the thickest part and check that the meat is the same colour throughout with no hint of pink juices or if you have a meat thermometer it should read a minimum of 75°C/167°F.

Spiced soy and star anise pork

Slow-cooked, meltingly soft pork in a rich star anise, ginger and honeyed sauce topped with shredded lettuce. The addition of lettuce might sound a little unusual but adds a really summery touch to the recipe. Delicious served with bread, rice or noodles.

Serves 4
Prep 20 minutes
Cook 1 hour 40 minutes

1 tbsp vegetable oil
250g/9oz onion, roughly chopped
3 garlic cloves, finely chopped
½ red chilli, deseeded and finely chopped
2 star anise
1 tsp ground mixed spice
1 tsp ground coriander
1 tsp ground ginger
700g/1lb 9oz diced pork
4 tsp runny honey
1 tbsp black treacle
2 tbsp soy sauce
5 tbsp white wine
400ml/14 fl oz chicken stock
Salt and freshly ground black pepper
½ romaine or cos lettuce, finely shredded

Preheat the oven to 160°C/320°F/gas mark 3. Heat the oil in a large frying pan, add the onion and garlic and fry over a medium heat for 5 minutes, stirring until softened. Stir in the chilli, star anise and ground spices and cook for 1 minute to release their flavours.

Add the pork a few pieces at a time until all the pieces are in the pan then fry for 5 minutes, stirring until lightly browned.

Stir in the honey, treacle and soy sauce and mix well. Pour in the wine and stock and bring to the boil, stirring.

Transfer to a casserole dish, cover and cook in the oven for 1½ hours or until the pork is tender.

Stir the casserole, taste and adjust the seasoning with salt and pepper if needed. Add the shredded lettuce and allow to stand for a few minutes until the lettuce has just begun to wilt a little then spoon into bowls and serve with warm crusty bread, rice or noodles.

COOK'S TIP Traditionally Chinese dishes would have shredded Chinese leaves added, but lettuce makes a great alternative and it is a good way to use up a glut from the garden when you are a little tired of salad.

Cheese scones

Scones are an essential part of the classic English afternoon tea, traditionally served at 4pm. This savoury version is made with mature cheese and is delicious served warm from the oven with a bowl of soup.

Makes 8 scones
Prep 20 minutes
Cook 12–15 minutes

450g/1lb self-raising flour
115g/4oz soft margarine
140g/5oz mature cheddar cheese, grated
Salt and freshly ground black pepper
1 egg
150ml/¼ pint milk
1 tsp English mustard

Preheat the oven to 200°C/400°F/gas mark 6. Add the flour and margarine to a bowl and rub in with fingertips or an electric mixer until it resembles fine crumbs. Reserve 25g/1oz of the cheese then stir the rest into the flour with a little salt and pepper.

Fork the egg, 125ml/4fl oz milk and the mustard together in a jug then gradually stir into the flour to make a smooth, soft dough.

Lightly knead the dough on a floured work surface then cut in half. Shape each half into a ball, flatten slightly then roll to a circle 15cm/6in in diameter. Cut the circles into four quarters then arrange on a greased baking sheet, leaving space between the quarters so that there is room for them to rise.

Brush the tops with the remaining milk and sprinkle with the cheese. Bake for 12–15 minutes until well risen and golden brown.

COOK'S TIP Scones should really be made on the day you plan to eat them, but you can weigh out and part prepare all the dry ingredients the day before and keep the mix in a plastic bag in the fridge. This will save time if you want to take the scones on a picnic.

Potato, pepper and courgette curry

A seasonal spicy vegetable curry that is a great way of using up homegrown courgettes. Serve in bowls with crusty bread, naan bread or rice.

Serves 4
Prep 20 minutes
Cook 30 minutes

2 tbsp vegetable oil
200g/7oz onion, chopped
2 garlic cloves, finely chopped
½ red chilli, deseeded and finely chopped
½ tsp ground ginger
2 tsp ground coriander
1 tsp medium curry powder
4 tbsp dry white wine
400g/14oz carton chopped tomatoes
450ml/¾ pint vegetable stock
Salt and freshly ground black pepper
350g/12oz potatoes, cut into chunks
2 tbsp natural yogurt
250g/9oz courgettes, cut into chunks
2 large peppers, halved, cored, deseeded and cut into chunks
3 tbsp fresh chopped coriander leaves

Heat the oil in a medium saucepan, add the onion, garlic and chilli then stir in the ground spices. Cover over a low heat for 10 minutes, stirring until the onion is softened.

Stir in the wine and deglaze the pan then add the tomatoes and stock and season with salt and pepper. Bring to the boil and simmer, uncovered, for 15 minutes. Meanwhile, add the potatoes to a second smaller saucepan of boiling water and cook for 8–10 minutes until tender then drain.

Purée the tomato sauce in the saucepan with a stick blender or transfer to a liquidiser, purée then pour back into the pan. Stir in the yogurt then add the potatoes, courgettes and peppers, cook gently for 5 minutes until tender then stir in the chopped coriander. Spoon into bowls and serve with warm bread or rice.

COOK'S TIP Vary the vegetables depending on what you have in the fridge – butternut squash, cauliflower, green beans or spinach also taste delicious added to the curry sauce.
Taste the curry before serving, and if it is a little hotter than you would like, mix in a little extra yogurt or double cream.

Vegetable pizza puff

Quick and easy to make with ready-to-roll puff pastry. These mini pizzas are generously topped with peppers, red onion, sundried tomatoes, olives and mushrooms, golden bubbling cheese and fresh basil. Serve warm from the oven for a light lunch or starter.

Serves 4
Prep 20 minutes
Cook 20 minutes

250g/9oz block chilled puff pastry
Beaten egg for glazing
1 tbsp tomato purée
½ red pepper, cored, deseeded and chopped
½ orange pepper, cored, deseeded and chopped
½ small red onion, thinly sliced
20g/¾ oz drained sundried tomatoes in oil, chopped
8 pitted olives, roughly chopped
40g/1½ oz mushrooms, chopped
4 tsp fresh chopped basil leaves, plus extra tiny leaves to garnish
85g/3oz Cheddar cheese, grated

Preheat the oven to 200°C/400°F/gas mark 6. Roll out the pastry to 5mm/¼in thickness then trim to a 30cm/12in square. Cut into four smaller squares each 15cm/6in.

Score lightly around the edge of each pastry square with a small sharp knife, leaving a 1cm/½in border. Brush lightly with beaten egg and fold the pastry edge over to the marked line, crimping as you go to form a 'crust'.

Lift the pastry squares on to a lightly oiled or non-stick paper lined baking tray, leaving a little space between each square. Prick the base of each with a fork then spread lightly with the tomato purée.

Scatter over two thirds of the peppers, onion, sundried tomatoes, olives, mushrooms and basil. Sprinkle over all the cheese then add the remaining vegetables and chopped basil.

Bake for 20 minutes until the pastry is golden and risen, the base is cooked through and the cheese is bubbling. Serve warm sprinkled with tiny basil leaves.

COOK'S TIP Most packs of puff pastry come in 350g or 500g packs so wrap the leftover pastry in clingfilm, seal, label and freeze for another time.

Summer fruit crumble

Peaches and mixed summer berries add a real feeling of luxury to a much-loved crumble.

Serves 4–6
Prep 20 minutes
Cook 20–25 minutes

2 peaches, halved, stoned and sliced
1 medium, 200g/7oz Bramley apple, quartered, cored, peeled and cut into chunks
300g/10½ oz frozen mixed summer fruits

Crumble topping
140g/5oz plain flour
55g/2oz porridge oats
50g/1¾ oz caster sugar
100g/3½ oz soft margarine
4 tsp demerara sugar

Preheat the oven to 190°C375°F/gas mark 5. Add the peaches, apples and frozen summer fruits to a 1.2litre/2 pint ovenproof dish and mix together.

To make the topping, add the flour, oats, sugar and margarine to a bowl and rub in until the mixture resembles fine crumbs. Alternatively, use an electric mixer.

Sprinkle the crumble over the fruit then scatter with the demerara sugar. Bake for 20–25 minutes until the topping is golden and the fruit softened. Spoon into bowls and serve with a scoop of vanilla ice cream or hot custard.

COOK'S TIP A pack of frozen summer fruit mix makes a great handy standby, but if you would rather use fresh fruit then make up your own mix of quartered strawberries, raspberries and blueberries.

Mrs Greville's strawberry meringue cream

Edwardian society hostess Mrs Ronnie Greville welcomed dinner guests such as Edward VII and the Aga Khan to her home, Polesden Lacey in Surrey. She planned the menus and presentations of her dinners meticulously. If strawberries were served, she would insist they were all of equal size and shape.

Serves 6
Prep 30 minutes
Cook 1-1¼ hours

For the meringues
2 egg whites
115g/4oz caster sugar

To finish
300ml/½ pint whipping cream
300g/10½ oz fromage frais
2 tbsp vanilla sugar, see
    Cook's Tip
450g/1lb strawberries, hulled
    and sliced
2 tbsp flaked almonds, lightly
    toasted

To make the meringues, preheat the oven to 110°C/225°F/gas mark ¼ and line a large baking sheet with nonstick baking paper. Whisk the egg whites in a large, dry, grease-free bowl until thick enough to stand in moist-looking peaks. If you can turn the bowl upside down without the whites moving, they are ready.

Gradually whisk in the sugar a teaspoonful at a time until all the sugar has been added. Continue to whisk for a minute or two more until the meringue is very thick and glossy.

Spoon dessert spoonfuls of the meringue on to the paper-lined baking sheet. Bake for 1–1¼ hours or until the meringues may be lifted easily off the paper and the centre is still slightly soft. Leave to cool.

When ready to serve, whisk the cream in a large bowl until it forms soft swirls. Fold in the fromage frais and vanilla sugar.

Break the meringues into pieces and fold through the cream with the sliced strawberries. Spoon into one large bowl or individual glass dishes if you would rather. Sprinkle with flaked almonds and serve immediately. (Don't be tempted to assemble this in advance or the meringues will lose their wonderful texture.)

COOK'S TIP Vanilla pods are expensive so don't throw away the used pod after you have scraped out the seeds when flavouring custards or syrups. Rinse the pod with cold water, dry with kitchen towel then add to a storage jar with 350g/12oz of caster sugar. Add the lid and shake the sugar and vanilla pod together. Keep in the larder for several weeks before using. The longer you leave it the stronger the vanilla flavour will be. If you have enough you might like to use vanilla sugar in the meringues too.

Fruit tartlets

These dainty glazed fruit tarts just seem to capture the very essence of summer. If you grow your own fruit, you might like to make up your own mix of strawberries, raspberries, redcurrants or cherries.

Makes 8
Prep 40 minutes plus chilling
Cook 13 minutes

Pastry
225g/8oz plain flour
115g/4oz butter, diced
60g/2¼ oz icing sugar
1 egg
2–3 tsp milk

Filling
25g/1oz custard powder
20g/¾ oz caster sugar
450ml/¾ pint milk
100ml/3½ fl oz double cream
150g/5½ oz strawberries,
  hulled and sliced
100g/3½ oz red seedless
  grapes, halved
2 kiwi fruit, peeled and sliced
140g/5oz red plums, halved,
  stoned and sliced
2 tbsp strawberry jam

COOK'S TIP We use custard powder in the restaurant kitchen but you could use a 400g/14oz can of readymade custard and fold in the whipped cream if you would rather.

To make the tart cases, add the flour, butter and sugar to a bowl or electric mixer and rub in the butter until the mixture looks like fine crumbs. Stir in the egg and mix in enough milk to make a smooth, soft dough.

Lightly knead the pastry then cut into eight pieces. Shape each into a ball then roll out until a little larger than a 10cm/4in diameter, 2cm/¾in deep individual loose-bottomed fluted tart tin. Press into the tin and trim a little above the top of the tin to allow for shrinkage during cooking. Continue until you have eight tart cases.

Prick the bases with a fork then chill for 30 minutes. Preheat the oven to 190°C/375°F/gas mark 5. Arrange the tart cases on a baking sheet, line with squares of non-stick baking paper and half fill with baking beans. Bake for 8 minutes. Carefully remove the paper and beans and cook for 5 minutes until just beginning to turn golden around the tops and the bases are crisp and dry.

Meanwhile, make the custard filling, mix the custard powder, sugar and a little of the milk to a smooth paste in a bowl. Heat the remaining milk in a saucepan until just boiling then gradually whisk into the custard powder until smooth. Pour the milk mixture into the pan and bring to the boil, whisking until thickened. Take off the heat, pour into a bowl, sprinkle the top with a little extra sugar to stop a skin forming then cover with clingfilm and chill well.

Whisk the cream in a small bowl until it forms soft swirls then whisk into the cooled custard.

Take the tarts out of the tins, arrange on a serving plate and spoon in the custard filling. Arrange the fruits attractively over the top. Warm the jam in the microwave for 10–20 seconds to soften then brush over the fruit. Chill until ready to serve.

Plum and vanilla slice

This sponge cake is topped with a vanilla cheesecake and fresh juicy plums for a cake that is a little different and very moreish.

Cuts into 10 slices
Prep 25 minutes
Cook 25–30 minutes

140g/5oz self-raising flour
115g/4oz soft light
  muscovado sugar
115g/4oz soft margarine
2 eggs

Topping
115g/4oz cream cheese
40g/1¾ oz caster sugar
1 tsp vanilla extract
1 egg, beaten
140g/5oz ripe red plums,
  halved, stoned and sliced
Little icing sugar, sifted,
  to decorate

Preheat the oven to 180°C/350°F/gas mark 4. Line a 20cm/8in shallow square cake tin with a large square of non-stick baking paper, snipping the paper diagonally into the corners of the tin and pressing the paper down so that the base and sides of the tin are lined.

To make the base, add the flour, sugar, margarine and eggs to the bowl of an electric mixer or food processor and beat until smooth. Spoon into the lined tin and spread level.

To make the topping, beat the cream cheese, sugar and vanilla together in a small bowl then gradually beat in the egg until smooth.

Pour the mixture over the top of the tin and ease into an even layer then swirl together using the handle of a teaspoon.

Arrange the plum slices over the top and press down gently. Bake for 25–30 minutes until well risen, golden brown and the cheesecake topping is just beginning to crack slightly. Test by inserting a skewer into the centre of the cake, it should come out cleanly when ready.

Leave to cool in the tin then lift the cake out and peel away the paper. Dust with a little sifted icing sugar and cut into ten equal slices.

COOK'S TIP This is the same base as used in the apple crumble bake on p146, so why not make up double the base mixture and divide between two tins then finish each cake with a different topping and bake.

Trifle

Here's one of those timeless desserts, popular with our local visitors and those from overseas. We often have cake offcuts or leftover sponge cake in our restaurants, which make an ideal base for this dessert but if you don't, Madeira cake from the supermarket can be used instead.

Serves 4
Prep 25 minutes, plus chilling
Cook 2–3 minutes

55g/2oz sponge cake, cut into small cubes
½ x 13g sachet raspberry or strawberry jelly crystals
150ml/¼ pint boiling water
140g/5oz frozen or fresh berry fruit mix
25g/1oz custard powder
20g/¾ oz caster sugar
450ml/¾ pint milk
250ml/9fl oz double cream
Few toasted flaked almonds to decorate

Divide the sponge evenly between four tumblers or wine glasses and set aside. Add the jelly to a measuring jug, dissolve in the boiling water then make up to 300ml/½ pint with cold water or as the pack directs.

Divide the fruits between the glasses then pour over the warm jelly, (no need to defrost the frozen fruits first as the warm jelly will). Chill until set.

Meanwhile, to make the custard, add the custard powder and sugar to a bowl and mix to a smooth paste with a little of the milk. Pour the remaining milk into a saucepan and bring just to the boil. Gradually whisk into the custard powder until smooth then pour into the saucepan. Bring back to the boil and whisk until thickened. Sprinkle the surface with a little extra sugar to prevent a skin forming then cover with clingfilm and chill well.

Spoon the cooled custard over the set jelly layer. Lightly whisk the cream in a bowl until it forms soft swirls then spoon over the custard layer and sprinkle with the flaked almonds. Chill until ready to serve.

COOK'S TIP This version is alcohol-free, but you can always add a little sweet or dry sherry to the sponge base when you are making up this easy dessert.

Fruit curd ice cream

The fruit curd quantity in this recipe make two jars – keep one to enjoy on your breakfast toast or give as a gift. You could cheat and buy a jar of fruit curd from our shop if you are a little short of time. Delicious scooped into bowls, topped with extra berries and served with some dainty shortbread biscuits or simply scoop into cones for children.

Serves 4 plus 1 jar of fruit curd
Prep 20 minutes
Cook 35 minutes
Freeze 3–6 hours

Raspberry curd
350g/12oz fresh raspberries
225g/8oz cooking apple, quartered, cored, peeled and diced
100g/3½ oz butter, diced
350g/12oz caster sugar
1 lemon, grated zest and juice
4 large eggs, beaten

To finish
500g/1lb 2oz carton Greek-style yogurt

COOK'S TIP If you have been blackberry picking then you might like to try making the fruit curd with blackberries instead of raspberries or use half blackberries and half raspberries along with the apple.

To make the curd, add the raspberries and diced apple to a saucepan and cook uncovered over a low heat for 15 minutes, stirring from time to time until the fruit is soft and pulpy. (There is no need to add water to the fruit as the juices quickly run from the raspberries.) Press the soft fruit through a sieve into a bowl.

Half fill a medium saucepan with water, bring up to a simmer then set a large mixing bowl on top, making sure that the bowl is a little above the water. Add the butter and heat gently until completely melted.

Pour the sugar into the bowl of butter, add the lemon zest and juice and warm sieved fruits. Whisk together until smooth.

Beat the eggs in a bowl then strain into a second bowl. Gradually whisk into the berry mixture until smooth. Cook for about 20 minutes, stirring frequently with a wooden spoon until thick.

Pour into two warmed dry jars, right to the top. Cover with a waxed disc and a cellophane disc secured with an elastic band or screw on lid. Leave to cool completely. Store in the fridge for up to 2 weeks.

To make the ice cream, pour the yogurt into a plastic container then stir in one jar of cooled fruit curd. Cover with the lid and freeze for 3–6 hours until firm.

15 minutes before you are ready to serve, bring the ice cream out of the freezer and leave to soften slightly. Scoop into bowls or into ice cream cones and serve.

Victoria sponge

The secret to a really good Victoria sponge is all about the addition of air and trapping it in the cake mixture. Make sure all the ingredients are at room temperature before you begin, beat the sugar and margarine until very light and fluffy and beat well when adding the eggs. Then fold in the flour gently.

Cuts into 8 slices
Prep 20 minutes
Cook 20 minutes

175g/6oz caster sugar, plus extra to decorate
175g/6oz soft margarine
3 eggs, beaten
175g/6oz self-raising flour
4 tbsp seedless raspberry jam

Preheat the oven to 180°C/350°F/gas mark 4. Grease two 20cm/8in Victoria sandwich tins and line the bases with non-stick baking paper.

Add the sugar and margarine to the bowl of your electric mixer and cream together until light and fluffy.

Gradually beat in the eggs little by little and beat well after each addition. If the mixture looks as if it may curdle, the addition of a little flour will bring it back.

Sift the flour over the cake mixture and gently fold in until smooth. Divide equally between the tins and spread level. Bake for 20 minutes until well risen and the tops spring back when gently pressed with a fingertip.

Allow the cakes to cool in the tins for 5 minutes then loosen the edges and turn out on to a wire rack. Peel off the lining paper and leave to cool completely.

Arrange one of the cakes on a serving plate and, spread with the jam. Top with the second cake and dust with a little extra sugar to decorate. Cut into slices to serve.

COOK'S TIP Traditonal Victoria sponges, as served in National Trust cafés, are sandwiched with a layer of jam. For an indulgent treat, you can lightly whip 150ml/¼ pint double cream and spoon this over the jam before topping with the second cake.

Mrs Beale's coconut creams

Set in the pretty Sussex countryside, Standen, famous for its Arts & Crafts decor, made the perfect holiday getaway for James and Margaret Beale, their children and, later, grandchildren. In *Standen Memories*, Mrs Beale's granddaughter Phyllis writes, 'As children we never ventured beyond the baize door to the kitchen passage, except to greet cook on our arrival and to bid her goodbye on our departure after a four – six week summer holiday, with thank yous for all the scrumptious food, especially the pink creams.'

Makes 16 pieces
Prep 15 minutes
Chill overnight

500g/1lb 2oz icing sugar (no need to sift)
400g/14oz can condensed milk
Few drops raspberry essence
350g/12oz desiccated coconut

Line a 23cm/9in shallow cake tin with nonstick baking paper, snipping diagonally into the corners then pressing the paper into the tin so that the base and sides are lined.

Mix the sugar, condensed milk and raspberry essence together then gradually mix in the coconut, stirring at first with a wooden spoon then kneading with your hands when too stiff to mix. Or if you have a large food processor, mix on the pulse setting.

Press into an even layer in the paper-lined tin, mark into 16 squares then cover with clingfilm and chill in the fridge overnight until set. Lift the coconut creams out of the tin by holding the paper then peel off and cut into squares. Store in a plastic container with layers interleaved with nonstick baking paper or wrap strips of the coconut creams in cellophane, clingfilm or foil. Store in the fridge.

COOK'S TIP Raspberry essence isn't available in all supermarkets. If you can't buy it, stir in a few drops of pink food colouring instead so that the coconut creams or 'pinkies' as the Beale children called them really are pink.

Eton mess

Need a dessert in a hurry? Fold softly whipped cream, chopped mint and crushed berries together with crumbled meringues for a creamy dessert in a glass that captures the very essence of summer.

Serves 4
Prep 10 minutes

250g/9oz mixed raspberries
  and strawberries, hulled
300ml/½ pint double cream
2 tsp elderflower cordial
2 tbsp fresh chopped mint
2 readymade meringue nests
  (or make your own, using the
  recipe on page 94)

Roughly chop then mash the berries with a fork. Lightly whip the cream in a bowl until it forms soft swirls. Be careful not to overwhip.

Add the elderflower cordial, chopped mint and three-quarters of the berries to the whipped cream. Crumble the meringues over the top and gently fold together.

Spoon into glasses, top with the rest of the berries and serve within 20 minutes.

COOK'S TIP For the best taste, use British berries for this dessert, or when out of season use a mix of frozen berry fruits and defrost before adding to the cream.

Lime and coconut cake

For all those fans of lemon drizzle cake this version is a mix of lime zest and juice, desiccated coconut and coconut milk, drizzled with a lime syrup and filled with buttercream, and what's more it's gluten free.

Cuts into 8 slices
Prep 30 minutes
Cook 25 minutes

175g/6oz soft margarine
175g/6oz caster sugar
3 eggs
115g/4oz gluten-free
   self-raising flour
50g/1¾ oz desiccated
   coconut
125ml/4fl oz canned coconut
   milk
1 lime, grated zest and juice
140g/5oz icing sugar, sifted
85g/3oz butter, at room
   temperature, diced
Little extra grated lime zest
   to decorate

COOK'S TIP When preparing foods in a kitchen that also uses wheat or gluten ingredients it is important to wash all the equipment well and wipe down the work surface with a fresh dishcloth before you begin so that there is no possibility of cross-contamination.

Preheat the oven to 180°C/350°F/gas mark 4. Brush two 20cm/8in Victoria sandwich tins with a little oil and line the bases with circles of non-stick baking paper.

Add the margarine and sugar to the bowl of an electric mixer and beat until light and fluffy. Gradually beat in the eggs, one at a time, adding a little of the flour after each addition and mix until smooth.

Add the remaining flour, the desiccated coconut, coconut milk and the lime zest and beat until light and fluffy.

Divide the cake mixture evenly between the two tins and spread into an even layer. Bake for about 25 minutes until golden brown and the tops spring back when gently pressed with a fingertip.

While the cakes cook, mix 55g/2oz of the sifted icing sugar with half the lime juice until smooth.

Leave the cakes to cool for 5 minutes then run a knife around the edge, turn out on to a wire rack and peel off the lining paper. Carefully turn the cakes so that the tops are uppermost. Drizzle with the lime juice mix and leave to cool.

Beat the remaining icing sugar and lime juice together then whisk in the butter until you have a softy creamy frosting. Transfer one of the cakes to a serving plate. Spoon the buttercream over the top and spread into an even layer. Add the second cake and gently press in place.

Decorate the top with extra grated lime zest. Cut into slices to serve.

Salted chocolate caramel shortbread

Buttery shortbread, topped with a rich golden caramel and rich dark vanilla chocolate with just a hint of salt. What's not to love?

Cuts into 16 bars
Prep 25 minutes
Cook 35–42 minutes

Shortbread base
350g/12oz plain flour
115g/4oz butter, diced
115g/4oz soft margarine
115g/4oz caster sugar

Topping
2 tbsp golden syrup
1 x 397g can condensed milk
140g/5oz caster sugar
85g/3oz butter
200g/7oz dark chocolate,
  broken into pieces
1 tsp vanilla extract
Large pinch salt flakes

Preheat the oven to 160°C/320°F/gas mark 3. Add the flour, butter, margarine and sugar to a large bowl and rub in with fingertips or an electric mixer until it resembles fine crumbs. Continue to mix until the crumbs begin to stick together then press into a ball.

Press the dough into the base of a buttered 20 x 30 x 4cm/8 x 12 x 1½in rectangular cake tin. Prick with a fork then bake in the oven for 30–35 minutes or until pale golden. Leave to cool.

Add the golden syrup, condensed milk, caster sugar and butter to a heavy-based saucepan and heat gently, stirring until the sugar has dissolved and the butter melted.

Increase the heat to medium and continue to cook until to golden caramel, stirring all the time and being careful that the mixture doesn't catch on the base of the pan. This should take about 5–7 minutes.

Quickly pour the caramel over the shortbread base and tilt the tin to ease into an even layer. Leave to cool.

Melt the chocolate in a bowl set over a saucepan of gently simmering water. Stir in the vanilla, spoon over the caramel and spread into an even layer with a round bladed knife. Sprinkle with the salt. Leave until just beginning to set then mark into 16 bars. Chill well then cut into bars, lift out of the tin and serve.

COOK'S TIP When making the caramel, if you are not sure it it is ready, err on the slightly underdone and then drop a little on to a chilled plate. Leave for a minute or so until cool enough to handle then roll it with your fingertips – it should form a soft ball that will hold its shape. There is a short amount of time between soft caramel and hard toffee!

Carrot cake

Carrots are available all year round, but are particularly sweet and aromatic in the summer. This cake is moist and moreish with a fluffy cream cheese frosting, making it hard to resist

Cuts into 12 slices
Prep 30 minutes
Cook 25–30 minutes

300g/10½ oz soft dark muscovado sugar
3 eggs
300ml/½ pint vegetable oil
1 tsp vanilla extract
300g/10½ oz plain flour
1 tsp bicarbonate of soda
1 tsp baking powder
1 tsp ground cinnamon
½ tsp salt
300g/10½ oz carrots, finely grated
55g/2oz walnut pieces, roughly chopped

Frosting
300g/10½ oz icing sugar
55g/2oz butter, at room temperature
115g/4oz cream cheese
25g/1oz walnut pieces, roughly chopped

Preheat the oven to 180°C/350°F/gas mark 4. Grease two 23cm/9in Victoria sandwich tins and line the bases with non-stick baking paper.

Add the sugar, eggs, oil and vanilla to the bowl of your electric mixer. Add the flour, bicarbonate of soda, baking powder, cinnamon and salt to a second, smaller bowl and stir together.

Whisk the sugar and egg mixture for a few minutes until light and fluffy. Tip in the flour mix and fold through until almost mixed – don't worry if there are a few lumps. Add the carrots and walnuts and continue to mix until evenly combined.

Divide the cake mixture evenly between the two tins, spread level and bake for 25–30 minutes or until well risen and a deep golden brown and a skewer comes out cleanly when inserted into the centre of one of the cakes. Leave to cool for 5 minutes then loosen the edge, turn out on to a wire rack and peel away the lining paper. Leave to cool completely.

To make the frosting, beat the icing sugar and butter together in an electric mixer or food processor until it resembles crumbs then add the cream cheese in one go and beat for a few minutes until smooth and fluffy.

Put one of the cakes on to a serving plate. Spread half the frosting on top, cover with the second cake then top with swirls of frosting and a sprinkling of walnuts. Cut into slices to serve.

COOK'S TIP
If the carrots seem very wet after grating, put into a sieve, cover with kitchen towel and press down to remove the moisture.

Fell Foot milkshakes

In the picturesque setting of Fell Foot Park in Cumbria, an ice cream van sells frothy milkshakes with flavours such as cookies and cream or summer berry. They are sure to be popular with all the young family members, and big kids too.

Serves 4
Prep 5 minutes

300ml/½ pint vanilla ice cream
250g/9oz mixed frozen summer berries, or all strawberries, if preferred
750ml/1¼ pint full-fat milk

Add the ice cream, frozen berries and milk to a liquidiser goblet then blend together on a low speed until partially mixed. Increase the speed and blend until smooth and frothy. If your liquidiser goblet isn't very big you may need to add half to two thirds of the milk to begin with then add the rest once the ice cream and berries have been blended.

Pour into glasses or small milk bottles and serve immediately with straws.

COOK'S TIP
Supermarket packs of frozen mixed summer berries make a great freezer standby but why not make your own? Spread hulled raspberries, strawberries and blackberries over a large baking sheet so that they are in a single layer, slicing the strawberries if large. Open freeze for several hours until the fruits are firm then pack into a plastic container, seal with a lid and label. Freeze up to 12 months.

Strawberry Swiss roll

Wonderfully retro and nostalgic, this cake is light and fluffy with a summery burst of fresh strawberries and a marbled strawberry buttercream filling.

Cuts into 8 slices
Prep 30 minutes, plus cooling
Cook 10 minutes

6 eggs
140g/5oz caster sugar, plus
  a little extra for dusting
140g/5oz self-raising flour

To finish
100g/3½ oz butter, at room
  temperature
200g/7oz icing sugar
2 tablespoons strawberry jam
140g/5oz strawberries,
  hulled and chopped

Preheat the oven to 190°C/375°F/gas mark 5. Line a large 28 x 43cm/11 x 17in Swiss roll tin with a large piece of non-stick baking paper, snipping diagonally into the corners of the paper then pressing into the tin so that the paper stands a little above the sides of the tin.

Add the eggs and sugar to the bowl of an electric mixer and whisk for about 5 minutes until tripled in volume and the mixture will leave a trail on the surface when the whisk is lifted above the bowl.

Gently sift the flour over the top then fold in with a large spoon, being careful not to knock out the air. Pour into the lined tin, gently ease into an even layer then bake for about 10 minutes until the sponge is golden brown, can be gently pressed with a fingertip and has begun to shrink slightly from the sides of the tin.

Leave to sit for a couple of minutes while you arrange a clean tea cloth on the work surface with the short edges facing you, top with a second piece of non-stick baking paper and dust with a little caster sugar. Tip the sponge out on to the sugared paper. Peel off the lining paper then cover with a third piece of paper. Gently and loosely roll up starting from the shortest edge nearest you and leave to cool for at least an hour on a wire rack loosely covered with paper.

To make the filling, beat the butter and icing sugar together until light and fluffy. Stir in the jam until partly mixed and marbled together. Leave at room temperature.

Gently unroll the Swiss roll and spread with the buttercream. Sprinkle with the chopped strawberries then roll up again, starting from the shortest side and rolling more tightly this time. Use a teacloth to help create a tight spiral. Remove the paper and transfer to a serving plate with the join downwards. Dust with a little extra sugar, if liked. Cut a thin slice off each end to neaten then thickly slice to serve.

Autumn

Autumn is a time of harvest – of orchard fruits gathered in, blackberries picked on family walks then made into delicious crumbles, and colourful squashes and pumpkins for warming soups and stews, or adding depth to nutty pearl barley risotto. Enjoy walks through amber woodlands and take in the rich colours of the autumn, shuffle through the fallen leaves and tuck into an easy one-pot supper of mellow spiced vegetable tagine, chicken and mustard one-pot or potato-topped Cragside hodgepodge pie. Or you could curl up in front of a fire with a cuppa and slice of Sissinghurst honey, walnut and cobnut tart or Hidcote spiced apple Bakewell.

Butternut squash, red pepper and chilli soup

This soup is an autumnal winner – literally. This recipe was submitted for our seasonal recipe contest by Rachel, the cook at the eighteenth-century manor house, Kedleston Hall in Derbyshire.

Serves 4
Prep 20 minutes
Cook 50 minutes

500g/1lb 2oz butternut squash, peeled, deseeded and cut into chunks
2 red peppers, halved and deseeded
1 tbsp vegetable oil
1 small onion, chopped
1 garlic clove, chopped
Large pinch dried crushed chillies
750ml/1¼ pints vegetable stock
Salt and freshly ground black pepper
2 tbsp pumpkin seeds to garnish

Preheat the oven to 180°C/350°F/gas mark 4. Add the butternut squash and peppers, with the skins uppermost on a large baking sheet and bake in the oven for about 30 minutes until tender.

Heat the oil in a medium saucepan, add the onion, garlic and chilli and fry over a medium heat for 5 minutes until softened.

Peel the skins from the pepper, roughly chop the flesh then add to the onions with the butternut squash. Pour in the stock, season with a little salt and pepper and bring to the boil, stirring. Cover and simmer for 15 minutes.

Purée the soup in the pan with a stick blender or transfer to a liquidiser and purée in batches. Taste and adjust the seasoning if needed. Reheat then ladle into bowls, garnish with pumpkin seeds and serve with warm crusty bread and butter.

COOK'S TIP The flavour of this soup seems to improve if made the day before. It also freezes successfully, either in individual portions for an easy microwave lunch or in one big batch.

Parsnip and apple soup

Velvety smooth with the perfect balance of sweet parsnips and slightly sharp appley flavours.

Serves 4
Prep 20 minutes
Cook 30 minutes

1 tbsp vegetable oil
115g/4oz onion, chopped
2 garlic cloves, chopped
¼ tsp grated nutmeg
400g/14oz parsnips, chopped
1 Granny Smith apple or small Bramley apple, peeled, cored and sliced
1 litre/1¾ pints vegetable stock
Salt and freshly ground black pepper

To finish
2 tbsp extra virgin rapeseed or olive oil
2 tbsp fresh chopped sage

Heat the oil in a medium saucepan, add the onion, garlic and nutmeg and fry over a medium heat for 5 minutes, stirring from time to time until softened. Stir in the parsnips and apple and fry over a low heat for 5 minutes.

Pour in the stock, season with a little salt and pepper and bring to the boil. Cover and simmer for 20 minutes or until the parsnips are soft.

Meanwhile, heat the oil for the infusion in a small frying pan, add the sage and heat until just sizzling. Take off the heat and leave to cool.

Remove the soup from the heat and purée with a stick blender still in the saucepan or transfer to a liquidiser and purée in batches until smooth. Taste and adjust the seasoning then add a little more stock if needed.

Reheat the soup, ladle into bowls and drizzle with a little of the sage oil. Serve with warm crusty bread and butter.

COOK'S TIP This soup tastes better if made the day before. It does thicken once cooled so you may find that you need to add a little extra stock when reheating.

Honey-roasted swede soup

Gone are the days of tasteless boiled swede. Roasting this root vegetable brings out fantastic flavours. This wonderfully golden coloured soup, with just a hint of honey, is drizzled with spiced oil.

Serves 4
Prep 20 minutes
Cook 35–40 minutes

500g/1lb 2oz swede, cut into chunks
140g/5oz carrots, cut into chunks
175g/6oz onion, roughly chopped
2 garlic cloves, roughly chopped
1 tbsp vegetable oil
2 tsp runny honey
1.2 litre/2 pints vegetable stock
Salt and freshly ground black pepper

To finish
2 tbsp extra virgin rapeseed or olive oil
¼ tsp grated nutmeg
Large pinch ground turmeric
1 tsp runny honey
2 tbsp fresh chopped chives

Preheat the oven to 200°C/400°F/gas mark 6. Add the swede, carrots, onion and garlic to a roasting tin and spread into a single layer. Drizzle with the oil and roast for 25–30 minutes until golden brown around the edges.

Add the honey to a medium saucepan and warm through. Add the roasted vegetables, toss in the honey then pour in the stock. Season with a little salt and pepper. Bring to the boil then simmer, uncovered for 10 minutes.

Meanwhile, add the oil, nutmeg, turmeric and honey for the spiced oil to a small frying pan and warm the ingredients together then take off the heat and leave to stand.

Purée the soup with a stick blender still in the saucepan or transfer to a liquidiser and purée in batches. Taste and adjust the seasoning, if needed. Reheat then ladle into bowls. Drizzle with the oil and sprinkle with the chopped chives. Serve with warm crusty bread and butter.

COOK'S TIP Check the sweetness of the soup before adding the honey to the oil for the finishing drizzle. If it is sweet enough then reduce the amount of honey that you add to the oil.

Autumn chestnut salad

Sweet chesnuts were probably brought to England by the Romans, who planted them on their campaigns. Now sadly underused, they actually work really well in salads as here, adding protein and sweetness.

Serves 4
Prep 15 minutes
Cook 20 minutes

115g/4oz puy lentils, rinsed
3 tbsp pumpkin seeds
2 tbsp sunflower seeds
2 tbsp vegetable oil
140g/5oz cauliflower, cut into small florets
140g/5oz courgettes, thinly sliced
115g/4oz ready-prepared chestnuts from a vacuum pack
115g/4oz baby spinach leaves
85g/3oz trimmed radishes, thinly sliced
3 tbsp fresh chopped parsley

Dressing
3 tbsp extra virgin rapeseed or olive oil
3 tsp white wine vinegar
4 tsp runny honey
Salt and freshly ground black pepper

Add the lentils to a saucepan of boiling water, cover and simmer for about 20 minutes until tender. Drain into a sieve, rinse with cold water and drain again.

Meanwhile, add the pumpkin and sunflower seeds to a dry frying pan and cook over a medium heat for a few minutes until lightly toasted then scoop out of the pan on to a plate and reserve.

Heat the oil in the frying pan, add the cauliflower and fry over a medium heat, stirring for 3–4 minutes until lightly coloured all over. Add the courgette slices and cook for 3–4 minutes until lightly coloured.

To make the dressing, add all the ingredients to a jam jar, screw on the lid and shake well. Tip the just-cooked and drained lentils into a salad bowl and toss with the dressing. Make sure to mix with the dressing while the lentils are hot so that they absorb more of the flavour. Stir in the cauliflower, courgette and chestnuts then leave to cool.

Add the spinach, radishes, toasted seeds and chopped parsley to the lentil salad and toss gently together then spoon into serving bowls. Serve with warm crusty bread and butter.

COOK'S TIP We use vaccum-pack chesnuts for speed, but if you would like o use fresh ones, make a cross cut in the top of each one then roast in a medium over for 10–15 minutes, leave until cool enough to handle then peel off the skins.

Roasted squash, bean and tomato salad

Packed with flavour, this crunchy salad is a mix of sweet roasted squash, sundried tomatoes, earthy hazelnuts and crunchy pumpkin seeds tossed with fresh crisp salad leaves and peppery cress.

Serves 4
Prep 20 minutes
Cook 20 minutes

350g/12oz butternut squash, peeled, deseeded and cut into small dice
1½ tbsp vegetable oil
40g/1½ oz hazelnuts, roughly chopped
40g/1½ oz pumpkin seeds
85g/3oz leek, white part only, thinly sliced
4 spring onions, thinly sliced
3 tbsp fresh chopped parsley
400g/14oz can five-bean mix, drained
55g/2oz drained sundried tomatoes in oil, chopped
40g/1½ oz sultanas
100g/3½ oz mixed baby salad leaves
1 punnet mustard and cress, leaves snipped from base

Vinaigrette dressing
4 tbsp extra virgin rapeseed or olive oil
1 tbsp white wine vinegar
1 tsp Dijon mustard
1 tsp caster sugar
1 tbsp tomato ketchup
Salt and freshly ground black pepper

Preheat the oven to 180°C/350°F/gas mark 4. Sprinkle the butternut squash over the base of a small roasting tin and drizzle with the oil. Roast for 15 minutes or until softened and just beginning to colour. Add the chopped nuts and pumpkin seeds, stir together and roast for 5 minutes.

Add the leeks, spring onions and chopped parsley to a salad bowl. Sprinkle over the drained beans, sundried tomatoes and sultanas then add the warm squash, nuts and seeds.

To make the dressing, add all the ingredients to a jam jar, screw on the lid and shake until well mixed. Pour over the salad and toss gently together.

Add the salad leaves and mustard and cress at the very last minute and gently toss with the other salad ingredients. Spoon on to plates and serve with warm bread and butter.

COOK'S TIP If you would like to make this salad a little in advance, add the dressing but do not add the salad leaves and mustard and cress until just before serving so that the leaves stay crisp.

Vegetable stuffed peppers

While we all know the healthy eating mantra of eating five portions of fruit and veg a day, there are just some days when it doesn't quite happen. This colourful supper dish is an easy and great way to boost our range of veggies and to get back on track.

Serves 4
Prep 20 minutes
Cook 30–40 minutes

4 red or orange peppers with green stalks, halved lengthways, cored and deseeded
85g/3oz long grain white rice
1 tbsp sunflower oil
1 onion, chopped
2 garlic cloves, finely chopped
115g/4oz carrots, grated
½ x 400g/14oz can five-bean mix, drained
85g/3oz frozen sweetcorn
1 tsp ground cumin
1½ tsp ground coriander
2 tomatoes, chopped
4 tsp tomato purée
4 tbsp fresh chopped parsley, plus a little extra to garnish
Salt and freshly ground black pepper

Preheat the oven to 180°C/350°F/gas mark 4. Arrange the peppers on a baking sheet, skin side uppermost, then bake for 15–20 minutes until just softened.

Meanwhile, add the rice to a saucepan of boiling water and simmer for 8–10 minutes until just tender. Drain into a sieve, rinse with cold water and drain again.

Heat the oil in a frying pan, add the onion and garlic and fry over a medium heat for 5 minutes until softened and lightly coloured.

Add the rice, carrots, five-bean mix and sweetcorn then stir in the ground cumin, coriander, chopped tomatoes, tomato purée and parsley. Season with salt and pepper and mix well.

Turn the peppers over then spoon in the filling and pack down well. Cover with foil and return to the oven for 15–20 minutes until the filling is piping hot. Remove the foil, sprinkle with a little extra parsley and serve with roasted vegetables and mashed potato.

COOK'S TIP Choose peppers that are a similar size with the green stalk still intact as this help to hold the pepper together when stuffed.

Caramelised onion, leek and tomato quiche

A delicious deep-filled quiche made with slowly fried onions, leek, sundried tomatoes, diced potato and parsley bathed in a creamy cheese custard. Serve warm from the oven with roasted vegetables and root vegetable mash.

Cuts into 8 slices
Prep 30 minutes, plus chilling
Cook 30–35 minutes

Pastry
225g/8oz plain flour
Pinch salt
½ tsp dried mixed herbs
115g/4oz butter, diced
50g/1¾ oz cheddar cheese, grated
1 egg, beaten
1–2 tbsp milk

Filling
4 tsp olive oil, or oil from the jar of sundried tomatoes
200g/7oz onion, chopped
140g/5oz leek, thinly sliced
250g/9oz potatoes, diced
65g/2½ oz sundried tomatoes
4 eggs
300ml/½ pint single cream
3 tbsp fresh chopped parsley
85g/3oz mature cheddar cheese, grated
Salt and freshly ground black pepper

COOK'S TIP The onions really boost the flavour of the quiche, so fry them until they are really soft and just tinged golden to bring out their natural sweetness. This quiche freezes well – chill well then wrap in foil. Defrost in the fridge then reheat before serving.

To make the pastry case, add the flour, salt, herbs and butter to a bowl or electric mixer and rub in until the mixture looks like fine crumbs. Stir in the cheese then mix in the egg and enough milk to mix to a smooth, soft dough.

Lightly knead the pastry then roll out on a lightly floured surface until a little larger than a 23cm/9in buttered deep loose-bottomed fluted tart tin. Lift the pastry over a rolling pin and press into the tin. Trim the top of the pastry a little above the top of the tin to allow for shrinkage. Prick the base with a fork then chill for 30 minutes.

Preheat the oven to 190°C/375°F/gas mark 5. Line the tart case with a circle of non-stick baking paper and baking beans then bake for 10 minutes. Remove the paper and beans and cook for 5 more minutes until the base is crisp and dry. Leave to cool.

To make the filling, heat the oil in a large frying pan, add the onion and fry over a medium heat for 5 minutes until softened. Add the leeks and fry for 3 minutes until just beginning to soften. Blanch the potatoes in a saucepan of boiling water for 3 minutes, drain then add to the leeks with the sundried tomatoes and fry for 5 minutes.

Whisk the eggs, cream and parsley together in a large bowl. Add the onion and leek mix and then the cheese and season well with salt and pepper. Mix together then spoon into the pastry case.

Reduce the oven to 180°C/350°F/gas mark 4 and bake the tart for 30 minutes until golden with a slight wobble to the centre. Leave to stand for 5–10 minutes before removing the tart tin and slicing. Serve with autumn vegetables and root veg mash.

Wensleydale, black pudding and walnut salad

Forget about a simple bowl of salad leaves, this generous main course salad is anything but. It is packed with warm crispy bacon, morerish black pudding, crunchy croutons and toasted walnuts that complement the creaminess of the Wensleydale cheese and salad leaves for a gourmet feast.

Serves 4
Prep 15 minutes
Cook 15–18 minutes

4 eggs
70g/2½ oz walnut pieces
225g/8oz smoked streaky bacon
115g/4oz leek, thinly sliced
2–3 tbsp vegetable oil
225g/8oz black pudding, diced
100g/3½ oz sliced bread, crusts trimming off, cut into squares
55g/2oz rocket leaves
55g/2oz mixed leaf salad
140g/5oz Wensleydale cheese, crumbled

Vinaigrette dressing
4 tbsp extra virgin rapeseed or olive oil
1 tbsp white wine vinegar
1 tsp Dijon mustard
½ tsp caster sugar
Salt and freshly ground black pepper

Add the eggs to a saucepan of cold water, bring to the boil and simmer for 8 minutes. Drain, crack the shells, cool quickly in cold water, peel and set aside.

Dry roast the walnuts in a large frying pan for 2–3 minutes then transfer to a plate. Wipe the pan with kitchen paper, add the bacon and heat gently until the fat begins to run then increase the heat and cook until golden. Add the leek slices and cook for 1 minute to soften. Lift out of the pan with a slotted spoon, drain well and chop the bacon.

Add 1 tbsp of the oil and the black pudding to the pan and fry for 2–3 minutes, turning until browned. Lift out of the pan and reserve.

Heat a little extra oil in the frying pan then fry the bread for 3–4 minutes until crisp and golden, stirring and adding extra oil if needed. Scoop out with a draining spoon on to a plate lined with kitchen towel.

Add the salad leaves to a large salad bowl. Add the dressing ingredients to a jam jar, screw on the top then shake well. Pour over the salad leaves and toss gently together.

Sprinkle the cheese, walnuts, bacon, leeks and black pudding over the salad. Quarter the eggs, arrange on top and sprinkle with the croutons.

COOK'S TIP Black pudding is rather like Marmite, you either love it or hate it. For those who are not fans, simply leave it out.

Chicken and mustard one-pot

National Trust properties grow autumnal root vegetables in abundance, and some, like Attingham Park in Shropshire, even have a Harvest Fair. This simple dinner recipe makes the most of this fantastic British produce.

Serves 4
Prep 20 minutes
Cook 1 hour

1 tbsp vegetable oil
500g/1lb 2oz boneless, skinless chicken thighs, diced
200g/7oz onion, chopped
450ml/¾ pint chicken stock
2 tsp wholegrain mustard
1 tsp English mustard
2 tsp runny honey
Salt and freshly ground black pepper
200g/7oz parsnips, cut into chunks
250g/9oz carrots, cut into chunks
350g/12oz potatoes, cut into chunks
1 tsp dried thyme
100g/3½ oz green cabbage, finely shredded
2 tbsp chopped fresh parsley

Preheat the oven to 180°C/350°F/gas mark 4. Heat the oil in a large frying pan, add the chicken to the pan, a few pieces at a time, until they are all in the pan, then fry, stirring for 5 minutes over a medium to high heat until evenly browned. Scoop out of the pan with a draining spoon and add to a casserole dish.

Add the onions to the meat juices in the frying pan and fry gently for 10 minutes until softened and just beginning to turn golden around the edges.

Mix the stock with the mustards, honey and a little salt and pepper. Pour into the frying pan and bring to the boil.

Add the parsnips, carrot and potatoes to the chicken then sprinkle with the thyme. Pour over the onion and stock mix then cover and cook in the oven for 45 minutes or until the vegetables are tender and the chicken is cooked through.

Add the cabbage to a saucepan of boiling water, blanch for 2 minutes then drain well. Stir into the casserole, taste and adjust the seasoning if needed then sprinkle with the chopped parsley. Spoon into bowls and serve with warm crusty bread and butter.

COOK'S TIP Getting plenty of flavour in the onions in the early stages of cooking will add a lovely sweet flavour to the dish.

Long Mynd rabbit braised in Shropshire cider

Long Mynd is situated in the Shropshire Hills, an Area of Outstanding Natural Beauty covering over 800 hectares (2,000 acres). It is traditional sheep farming countryside, and many a farmer through the years has enjoyed rabbit stew gently cooked in cider.

Serves 2
Prep 30 minutes
Cook 1 hour 10 minutes

25g/1oz butter
115g/4oz onion, chopped
1 stick celery, diced
1 rabbit, cut into joints
1½ tbsp plain flour
Salt and freshly ground black pepper
1 tbsp vegetable oil
225g/8oz carrot, diced
250g/9oz potatoes, cut into chunks
500ml/18fl oz dry cider
1 tsp English mustard
Fresh chopped chives or parsley to garnish

Heat the butter in a saucepan, add the onion and celery and fry over a low heat for 5 minutes, stirring until softened and lightly browned.

Put the rabbit joints on to a plate, sprinkle over the flour then season with salt and pepper. Rub the flour all over the joints.

Heat the oil in a large frying pan, dust the excess flour off the rabbit joints then fry for about 5 minutes, turning once or twice until golden.

Stir any excess flour into the onion and celery. Arrange the rabbit portions on top then add the carrots and potato. Mix the cider with the mustard, pour over the rabbit and bring to the boil. Cover and simmer gently for about 1 hour or until the rabbit is tender. Spoon into large shallow bowls, garnish with chopped chives or parsley and serve with crusty bread.

COOK'S TIP Ask your local butcher for fresh rabbit or he may have some in the deep freeze. Rabbit meat is very lean, but there is a high ratio of bone to meat so although the portions may look huge there isn't quite as much meat as you would imagine.

Robartes pie

Life for a Victorian servant could be very hard. But unlike many country homes of the time, the Agar-Robartes family at Lanhydrock took a real interest in their servants, calling them staff and providing a good standard of living, with birthday presents and annual trips. The Servants' Hall at Lanhydrock is now the visitors' restaurant and this dish is served in homage to the family.

Serves 6
Prep 30 minutes plus chilling
Cook 1 hour

Pastry
325g/11½ oz plain flour
70g/2½ oz butter, diced
70g/2½ oz white Flora, diced
2 tbsp freshly chopped sage leaves
1 egg, beaten
1–2 tbsp cold water

Filling
2 freshly boiled potatoes (approx. weight after peeling 280g/10oz)
25g/1oz butter
Salt and freshly ground black pepper
450g/1lb tart dessert apples, quartered, cored and thinly sliced
250g/9oz Cheddar cheese, thinly sliced
175g/6oz rindless streaky bacon, diced

COOK'S TIP If you don't have any fresh sage, add 1 tsp of dried sage plus 2 tbsp fresh or frozen chopped parsley.

To make the pastry, add the flour to the bowl of an electric mixer, add the butter and white fat and rub in until fine crumbs. Add the chopped sage and beaten egg then mix in enough water to make a soft but not sticky dough.

Knead the pastry very lightly then roll out thinly on a lightly floured surface until large enough to line the base and sides of a 20cm/8in buttered springform tin. Lift the pastry over the rolling pin then press over the base and up the sides, pressing the pastry with fingertips to make an even layer.

Trim the top of the pastry level with the top of the tin then crimp the edge between fingers. Chill for 15 minutes while making the filling.

Preheat the oven to 190°C/375°F/gas mark 5 Mash the potatoes until lump free then beat in the butter and a little salt and pepper and set aside.

Arrange one third of the apple slices over the base of the pie case, season with a little salt and pepper then top with one third of the cheese slices and one third of the bacon then repeat the layers twice more, almost filling the tin.

Press the filling down a little then spoon the mashed potato over the top in a thin layer. Rough up with a fork then put the pie tin on to a baking sheet and bake for about 1 hour until the topping is golden brown and the pastry crisp and golden.

Leave to stand for 15 minutes then loosen the edge of the pastry, unclip and remove the side of the tin and transfer to a serving plate. Cut into thick wedges and serve with salad.

Vegetable tagine

Full of flavour, autumn roots and butternut squash get a little Middle Eastern magic in this tagine. Serve in bowls with warm bread and butter or with a spoonful or two of couscous flavoured with a little lemon and lime juice.

Serves 4
Prep 20 minutes
Cook 55 minutes

1 tbsp extra virgin rapeseed or olive oil
225g/8oz onion, roughly chopped
2 garlic cloves, finely chopped
½ tsp chilli powder
½ tsp turmeric
2 tsp ground coriander
½ lemon, grated zest and juice
½ lime, grated zest and juice
400g/14oz carton chopped tomatoes
250g/9oz butternut squash, peeled, deseeded and cut into chunks
250g/9oz carrots, cut into chunks
250g/9oz swede, cut into chunks
600ml/1 pint vegetable stock
2 tsp runny honey
400g/14oz can chickpeas, drained
40g/1½ oz ready-to-eat dried apricots, diced
25g/1oz sultanas
4 tbsp fresh chopped parsley
Salt and freshly ground black pepper
2 tbsp fresh chopped mint

Preheat the oven to 180°C/350°F/gas mark 4. Heat the oil in a flameproof casserole dish and add the onion and garlic; fry over a medium heat for 5 minutes, stirring until softened.

Stir in the chilli powder, turmeric and coriander then mix in the lemon and lime zest and fry gently for 5 minutes, stirring.

Add the tomatoes, squash, carrots and swede. Pour over the stock and lemon and lime juice then add the honey, chickpeas, apricots, sultanas and half the parsley. Season with salt and pepper and bring to the boil, stirring.

Cover and transfer to the oven and cook for 45 minutes. Stir well then sprinkle with the remaining parsley and mint. Spoon into bowls and serve with warm crusty bread and butter or couscous.

COOK'S TIP Chilli powder can really vary in its heat and intensity, so taste the sauce once you have brought it up to the boil and before it goes into the oven so that you can adjust the amount depending on the strength of the powder.

Cragside hodgepodge pie

Cragside was the home of inventor and armaments manufacturer Sir William (later Lord) Armstrong. It was not only the first house in the world to be lit by hydro-electric power using man-made lakes but – much to cook's delight – had an early version of a labour-saving gas stove, dishwasher and dumb waiter to take the food – perhaps including this traditional Northumbrian dish – from the kitchen up to the dining room.

Serves 4
Prep 25 minutes
Cook 2 hours 11-12 minutes

2 tbsp vegetable oil
650g/1lb 7oz mixed shin beef, shoulder of pork and lamb, diced
200g/7oz onion, sliced
200g/7oz carrots, sliced
200g/7oz turnip or swede, diced
3 sticks celery, thickly sliced
1½ tbsp plain flour
600ml/1 pint beef or lamb stock
2 tbsp pearl barley
2 tbsp mixed fresh chopped rosemary, thyme and sage or 2 tsp dried mixed herbs
Salt and freshly ground black pepper
450g/1lb potatoes, thinly sliced
50g/1¾ oz Northumbrian Cheviot cheese or mature cheddar cheese, grated

Preheat the oven to 160°C/320°F/gas mark 3. Heat 1 tbsp of the oil in a large frying pan, add the mixed meats, a few pieces at a time until all the pieces are in the pan then fry over a medium heat for 5 minutes, stirring until browned. Scoop out of the pan with a draining spoon and add to a 2 litre/3½ pint casserole dish.

Add the remaining oil to the frying pan and fry the onion for 5 minutes, stirring until softened. Add the carrots, turnips or swede and celery, cook for a minute or two then sprinkle over the flour and mix in. Pour in the stock, add the pearl barley and herbs, season with salt and pepper and bring to the boil, stirring.

Pour the stock mixture over the meat then arrange the potato slices overlapping on top. Season with salt and pepper and cover the dish. Bake in the oven for 1½ hours.

Remove the lid, sprinkle with the cheese and cook for another 30 minutes until the cheese is bubbling and golden. Serve with steamed curly kale or spiced red cabbage.

COOK'S TIP Red cabbage makes the perfect accompaniment as it can be braised in a casserole dish either next to the pie or on the shelf below for about 1½ hours. Just check that both dishes will fit in the oven before you fill them.!

Pumpkin and sundried tomato pearl barley risotto

This British version of the traditional Italian dish, risotto, is made with high-fibre pearl barley rather than white Arborio rice for a nutty flavour that complements the addition of autumnal diced butternut squash, carrots and sundried tomatoes.

Serves 4
Prep 15 minutes
Cook 45 minutes

1 tbsp olive oil or the oil from the sundried tomatoes
1 red onion, finely chopped
2 garlic cloves, finely chopped
175g/6oz pearl barley
1.2 litre/2 pints hot vegetable stock
200g/7oz carrots, diced
350g/12oz butternut squash, deseeded, peeled and diced
40g/1½ oz sundried tomatoes in oil, drained and sliced
4 tbsp white wine
1 tsp tomato purée
1 tsp balsamic vinegar
4 tbsp double cream
Salt and freshly ground black pepper
2 tbsp fresh chopped parsley
40g/1½ oz parmesan, cheese peeled into shavings with a vegetable peeler

Heat the oil in a large, deep frying pan, add the onion and garlic and fry over a medium heat for 5 minutes until softened.

Add the pearl barley and stir well until coated in the oil. Add the carrots and one third of the stock. Bring to the boil then cover and simmer for 20 minutes, stirring occasionally and topping up with extra stock if needed.

Add the squash, sundried tomatoes, white wine and tomato purée then mix in half the remaining stock. Bring back to the boil, cover and simmer for 20 minutes until the risotto is rich and thick and the pearl barley soft. Gradually top up with the remaining stock as needed to keep the barley moist and stir more frequently towards the end of cooking.

Stir in the balsamic vinegar and cream, season to taste with salt and pepper then spoon into bowls. Sprinkle with the parsley and shaved parmesan. Serve with warm bread and butter.

COOK'S TIP The pearl barley will keep on absorbing the stock as it stands, so if you are not serving it immediately, or you get a little delayed, loosen the mixture with extra hot stock just before serving.

Lyme Park braised venison with sage and onion mash

Lyme Park in Cheshire was originally a hunting lodge, and later transformed into a magnificent mansion with a 567-hectare (1,400-acre) deer park. Venison is often on the menu at the Ale Cellar restaurant or you can buy cuts of venison, venison sausages or burgers from the shop to cook at home.

Serves 4
Prep 45 minutes plus standing time
Cook 1¾ hours

Braised venison
4 venison leg steaks, each about 200g/7oz
Salt and freshly ground black pepper
2 tbsp vegetable oil
175g/6oz onion, chopped
2 garlic cloves, finely chopped
300ml/½ pint red wine
150ml/¼ pint beef stock
1 sprig fresh thyme
1 sprig fresh rosemary
1 bay leaf

Sage and onion mash
900g/2lb potatoes, cut into chunks
55g/2oz butter
115g/4oz onion, finely chopped
2 tbsp fresh chopped sage
3–4 tbsp milk

Caramelised apples
25g/1oz butter
2 Cox eating apples, cored and sliced
4 tsp light muscovado sugar
2 tbsp apple juice

Preheat the oven to 180°C/350°F/gas mark 4. Season the venison steaks with salt and pepper and leave to stand for 30 minutes. Heat the oil in a large frying pan, add the steaks in a single layer and brown quickly over a high heat for 1 minute each side. Take out and transfer to a casserole dish.

Add the chopped onion and garlic to the pan and fry in the meat juices for 5 minutes until softened. Pour in the red wine and stock, add the herbs and season with salt and pepper. Bring to the boil and pour over the venison steaks so they are covered, adding more wine or stock if needed. Cover the dish and cook in the oven for 1½ hours until the venison is tender.

To make the mash, add the potatoes to a saucepan of boiling water, bring back to the boil, cover and simmer for 15–20 minutes until tender. Drain the potatoes, return to the empty pan and heat for a minute or two to 'dry'. Add 25g/1oz butter and salt and pepper to taste and mash well. Heat 25g/1oz butter in a frying pan, add the onion and fry until softened and just beginning to colour. Stir the sage into the onions then mix into the potatoes, adding a little milk if needed. Cover and keep warm.

To make the caramelised apples, heat the remaining butter in the drained onion and sage pan, add the apples and cook over a medium heat until just beginning to brown. Sprinkle with the sugar and cook until the sugar has dissolved and is just beginning to caramelise. Add the apple juice and cook for a minute or two until the sauce is syrupy. Keep hot.

Drain the wine and stock mix from the casserole into a saucepan. Boil rapidly for 4–6 minutes until reduced and thickened to a gravy consistency. To serve, spoon the mash on to plates, add a venison steak to each and spoon over the sauce. Garnish with the apple slices.

Sissinghurst honey, walnut and cobnut tart

Here's an English version of the American favourite, pecan pie. Cobnuts can be found in the hedges and woodlands around the fields of the Sissinghurst estate in Kent. This dish also uses other locally sourced ingredients – the honey is collected from beehives in the orchard at Sissinghurst and even the eggs come from the estate farm.

Serves 6–8
Prep 30 minutes plus chilling time
Cook 45 minutes

Pastry
175g/6oz plain flour
85g/3oz butter, diced
40g/1½ oz icing sugar
2 tbsp water

Filling
85g/3oz butter
100g/3½ oz set honey
4 eggs
175g/6oz demerara sugar
100g/3½ oz walnut pieces
100g/3½ oz shelled cobnuts or hazelnuts, lightly toasted and roughly chopped

To make the pastry, add the flour, butter and icing sugar to a bowl or electric mixer and rub in the butter until the mixture resembles fine crumbs. Gradually mix in enough water to make a smooth, soft dough.

Lightly knead the pastry then roll out on a lightly floured surface until a little larger than a 23cm/9in buttered tart tin. Lift the pastry over a rolling pin, press into the tin and trim the pastry a little above the top to allow for shrinkage. Prick the base with a fork and chill for 30 minutes.

Preheat the oven to 190°C/375°F/gas mark 5. Line the tart case with a circle of non-stick baking paper and baking beans. Bake for 10 minutes, remove the paper and beans and cook the tart case for 5 more minutes.

Meanwhile, melt the butter in a saucepan, take off the heat and stir in the honey. Beat the eggs in a bowl with a whisk then beat in the butter mix and the sugar until smooth.

Sprinkle the nuts over the base of the tart case, pour in the honey mix and bake at 150°C/300°F/gas mark 2 for 30–40 minutes or until the filling is set.

Leave to cool then take the tart out of the tin, cut into wedges and serve with a spoonful of thick cream or crème fraîche.

COOK'S TIP Cobnuts have only a very short season, so when they are not available use blanched hazelnuts from the supermarket instead.

Apple crumble bake

The National Trust celebrates the autumn harvest with Apple Days across the UK, where you can enjoy nature's bounty. This is a great cake to make with ingredients you'll find in the cupboard.

Cuts into 10 slices
Prep 20 minutes
Cook 20-25 minutes

Sponge base
140g/5oz self-raising flour
115g/4oz soft light muscovado sugar
115g/4oz soft margarine
2 eggs
200g/7oz or 1 medium Bramley cooking apple, quartered, cored, peeled and diced

Crumble topping
55g/2oz plain flour
15g/½ oz porridge oats
15g/½ oz caster sugar
½ tsp ground cinnamon
40g/1½ oz soft margarine
30g/1oz mixed nuts, roughly chopped
1 tbsp soft light muscovado or demerara sugar

Preheat the oven to 180°C/350°F/gas mark 4. Line a 20cm/8in shallow square cake tin with a large square of non-stick baking paper, snipping the paper diagonally into the corners of the tin and pressing the paper down so that the base and sides of the tin are lined.

To make the sponge base, add the flour, sugar, margarine and eggs to the bowl of an electric mixer then beat until smooth. Spoon into the lined tin and spread into an even layer. Roughly crush the apples with a potato masher then sprinkle evenly over the top of the sponge.

For the crumble topping, add the flour, oats, sugar and cinnamon to a bowl then add the margarine and rub in with fingertips until the mixture resembles fine crumbs. Stir in the nuts then sprinkle over the apple and top with the muscovado or demerara sugar.

Bake for 20–25 minutes or until the cake is well risen and a skewer comes out cleanly when inserted into the middle of the cake. Leave to cool in the tin then lift the cake and paper out of the tin, peel away the paper and cut into ten bars.

COOK'S TIP You might also like to try sprinkling some blackberries over the sponge along with the apples. For those who would rather not add nuts, try adding a little grated orange rind to the crumble topping instead.

Coffee and walnut cake

This classic combination is always popular in our cafés. We use espresso coffee to flavour this cake, but instant coffee dissolved in a little boiling water works just as well.

Cuts into 8 slices
Prep 35 minutes
Cook 20 minutes

Sponge cake
175g/6oz soft margarine
175g/6oz caster sugar
3 eggs
175g/6oz self-raising flour
½ tsp baking powder
2 tsp instant coffee dissolved in 3 tsp boiling water
40g/1½ oz walnut halves, chopped

Buttercream
115g/4oz butter, at room temperature
225g/8oz icing sugar, sifted
3 tsp instant coffee dissolved in 3 tsp boiling water
100g/3½ oz ready chopped mixed nuts, lightly toasted then cooled
4 walnut halves, cut in half

COOK'S TIP When cooked and cooled the individual sponge cakes can be wrapped and refrigerated for up to 3 days or frozen up to 3 months. Decorate with buttercream when needed.

Preheat the oven to 180°C/350°F/gas mark 4. Brush two 20cm/8in Victoria sandwich tins with a little oil and line the bases with circles of non-stick baking paper.

Add the margarine and sugar to the bowl of an electric mixer and beat until light and fluffy. Gradually beat in the eggs, little by little, and beat well after each addition. If the mixture looks as if it may curdle, beat in a little flour.

Mix the flour with the baking powder then fold into the creamed mixture. Add the dissolved coffee and chopped nuts and fold together. Divide the mixture evenly between the two tins, spread level and bake for about 20 minutes until well risen and the tops spring back when pressed with a fingertip.

Leave the cakes to cool in the tin for 5 minutes then loosen the edges, turn out on to a wire rack and peel off the lining paper. Leave to cool.

To make the buttercream, beat the butter, icing sugar and dissolved coffee together until light and fluffy. Use one quarter of the buttercream to sandwich the cakes together then spread about one third of the remaining icing over the sides of the cake.

Sprinkle the chopped nuts over a sheet of non-stick baking paper then coat the sides of the cake in the nuts by holding it on its side and rolling in the nuts.

Transfer to a cake plate and spread half the remaining buttercream thinly over the top of the cake. Mark into eight portions then spoon the remaining buttercream into a piping bag fitted with a large star tube, pipe a whirl of buttercream on each portion and top with a piece of walnut.

Frosted spiced beetroot cake

A twist on a passion fruit cake, this version contains grated beetroot and walnuts and topped with a caramel frosting. Plus it's made with gluten-free flour, so even those on a special diet needn't miss out.

Cuts into 8 slices
Prep 30 minutes, plus cooling
Cook 24–30 minutes

250g/9oz pack chilled cooked beetroot in natural juices, drained well, finely grated
100g/3½ oz carrot, finely grated
40g/1½ oz walnut pieces, chopped
175ml/6fl oz vegetable oil
4 eggs
250g/9oz caster sugar
250g/9oz gluten-free self-raising flour
1½ tsp ground cinnamon
¾ tsp grated nutmeg
¾ tsp ground ginger

Toffee frosting
175g/6oz cream cheese
40g/1½ oz butter, at room temperature
115g/4oz caster sugar
2 tbsp water
2 tbsp walnut pieces, to decorate, if liked

COOK'S TIP If you don't feel very confident about boiling sugar then make up the frosting by beating the cream cheese with the butter then stir in 115g/4oz icing sugar and 1 tsp vanilla essence.

Preheat the oven to 180°C/350°F/gas mark 4. Grease two 20cm/8in sandwich tins with a little oil and line the bases with non-stick baking paper. Add the beetroot to a sieve and press out excess liquid with the back of a spoon or using hands in rubber gloves to prevent the juices staining your hands. Then mix with the carrot and walnuts.

Add the oil, eggs and caster sugar to the bowl of an electric whisk and beat for 5 minutes until very light and fluffy.

Mix the remaining dry ingredients in a third bowl. Gently fold the beetroot mix into the whisked eggs then fold in the dry ingredients. Spoon the cake mixture evenly into the tins and gently ease into an even layer, being careful not to knock out the air.

Bake for 20–25 minutes until the cakes are well risen, golden brown and the top springs back when lightly pressed with a fingertip. Leave to cool in the tins for 5 minutes then loosen the edge and turn out on to a wire rack. Peel off the lining paper and leave to cool.

To make the frosting, whisk the cream cheese and butter together in a bowl until smooth. Add the sugar and water to a heavy-based pan and very gently heat until the sugar has dissolved. Don't be tempted to stir or you may crystallise the syrup. Increase the heat and cook for to 3–4 minutes until a golden caramel. Whisk into the cream cheese mixture in a thin steady stream then cool in the fridge until thick.

To finish the cake, put one cake on to a serving plate, spread with half the frosting. Add the second cake and spread the rest of the frosting on top then sprinkle with walnuts, if liked.

Powis Castle plum and walnut cobbler

The kitchen garden, once banished from sight by Lady Violet, is once again the powerhouse of the garden at Powis, where greener carbon-neutral garden practices are top priority. Here, home-grown plums are flavoured with cinnamon and topped with a fluffy scone-like topping. Delicious served with cream, ice cream or custard.

Serves 4
Prep 20 minutes
Cook 30–35 minutes

800g/1lb 12oz fresh plums,
  halved, stoned and chopped
115g/4oz caster sugar
1 tsp ground cinnamon
225g/8oz self-raising flour
Pinch of salt
55g/2oz butter, diced
55g/2oz walnut pieces,
  roughly chopped
1 egg, beaten
4 tbsp double cream
3–4 tbsp milk

Preheat the oven to 190°C/375°F/gas mark 5. Add the plums to the base of a 1.4 litre/2½ pint shallow ovenproof gratin dish. Sprinkle over 25g/1oz of the sugar and the cinnamon and mix together lightly.

In a large bowl or electric mixer, sift in the flour with the salt. Add the butter and rub in until the mix resembles fine crumbs. Stir in the chopped walnuts and 55g/2oz of the sugar then mix in the egg, cream and enough milk to make a soft dropping consistency.

Spoon dollops of the mixture around the top of the fruit, sprinkle with the rest of the sugar and bake for about 30 minutes until the cobbler topping is well risen and golden and the fruit is soft. Serve hot, spooned into bowls with pouring cream or spoonfuls of vanilla ice cream.

COOK'S TIP The cobbler topping is also lovely spooned over blackberries and apples, peaches and blueberries or plums and strawberries.

Spiced apple and blackberry cheesecake

Gently cooked apple in a spiced red wine syrup is swirled through a lemony cheesecake with tangy blackberries for a creamy smooth cheesecake in a glass.

Serves 4
Prep 25 minutes
Cook 19–25 minutes

175g/6oz leftover sponge cake or bought Madeira cake
¼ tsp ground cinnamon
½ small star anise
25g/1oz caster sugar
100ml/3½ fl oz red wine
1 medium Bramley apple, about 300g/10oz, quartered, cored, peeled and diced
Pinch ground mixed spice
Large pinch ground ginger
40g/1½ oz butter, melted
140g/5oz canned condensed milk
140g/5oz cream cheese
150ml/¼ pint double cream
4 tsp lemon juice
100g/3½ oz blackberries

Preheat the oven to 160°C/325°F/gas mark 3. Blitz the sponge cake in a food processor until the mixture resembles fine crumbs. Tip out on to a baking sheet and spread into an even layer. Bake for 15–20 minutes until crisp and dry.

Add the cinnamon, star anise, caster sugar and red wine to a saucepan and heat gently until the sugar has dissolved. Add the apple, cover and simmer for 4–5 minutes until the apple is just tender.

Drain the apple into a sieve, reserving the juice, then pour the juice back into the saucepan and boil for a few minutes until reduced and thickened.

Mix the cooled cake crumbs with the mixed spice, ginger and melted butter then divide between the base of four serving glasses.

Add the condensed milk, cream cheese, double cream and lemon juice to a mixing bowl then gently whisk together until thick and creamy. Reserve some of the apple and a few of the blackberries for decoration then fold the rest into the cream mixture with the red wine syrup.

Spoon into the glasses then spread into an even layer. Top with the reserved fruit and serve or chill until needed.

COOK'S TIP If you don't have any leftover sponge cake and would like to use homemade then make up a quick-mix sponge with 55g/2 oz soft margarine, 55g/2oz caster sugar, 55g/2oz self-raising flour, ¼ tsp baking powder and 1 egg. Beat all the ingredients together then bake in a 15cm/6in greased sandwich tin for 15–20 minutes until the top springs back when pressed with a fingertip.

Sticky date and butterscotch puddings

Nothing beats an indulgent, warm pudding after a brisk stroll in the crisp autumnal air. But this recipe, in truth, is popular any time of year and completely irresistible if served with a scoop of good vanilla ice cream.

Serves 4
Prep 20 minutes, plus soaking
Cook 1 hour–1 hour 10 minutes

140g/5oz ready chopped dates
150ml/¼ pint boiling water
½ tsp bicarbonate of soda
55g/2oz butter
55g/2oz soft dark brown sugar
1 egg
85g/3oz self-raising flour

For the sauce
85g/3oz light brown sugar
25g/1oz salted butter
150ml/¼ pint single cream

Put the dates in a medium saucepan with the water and bicarbonate of soda and stir until the soda has dissolved. Add the butter and sugar and continue to cook for a few minutes until the dates are soft enough to beat to a purée.

Remove the pan from the heat and quickly beat in the egg and flour until well mixed.

Divide the date mixture evenly between four lightly buttered 200ml/7fl oz pudding moulds. Cover with buttered foil, put in the top of a steamer, cover and cook for about 1 hour or until well risen and a skewer comes out cleanly when inserted into the centre of one of the puddings.

While the puddings cook, make the sauce. Add the sugar and 2 tbsp of water to a small saucepan, heat gently without stirring until dissolved then boil for a few minutes until it begins to smell of toffee. Take off the heat and carefully stir in the butter then the cream until smooth.

Loosen the edges of the puddings, turn out on to plates then spoon over the sauce and serve with a scoop of vanilla ice cream.

COOK'S TIP The puddings can be cooked in the microwave in a plastic microwaveable mould or china ramekin, one at a time for 2–2½ minutes.

Hidcote apple Bakewell

The Arts & Crafts gardens at Hidcote Manor in Gloucestershire include a kitchen garden and a small orchard. You are welcome to pick up windfalls from the orchard to take home and make into our own, spiced version of the Bakewell tart. Bramley apples have been used here, but slightly sharp dessert apples would also work well.

Serves 8
Prep 20 minutes plus
30 minutes chilling
Cook 40 minutes

Pastry
175g/6oz plain flour
85g/3oz butter, diced
2 tbsp cold water

Filling
300g/10½ oz or 1 large
   Bramley apple, quartered,
   cored, peeled and diced
2–3 tbsp water
175g/6oz butter, at room
   temperature
175g/6oz caster sugar
175g/6oz self-raising flour
115g/4oz ground almonds
1 tsp ground mixed spice
4 eggs, beaten
Little icing sugar, sifted
Little ground cinnamon to dust

To make the pastry case, add the flour and butter to a bowl or electric mixer and rub in until the mixture looks like fine crumbs. Stir in enough water to make a smooth, soft dough.

Lightly knead the pastry then roll out on a lightly floured surface until a little larger than a 4cm/1½in deep, 23cm/9in buttered fluted loose-bottomed tart tin. Lift the pastry over the rolling pin and press into the tin. Trim the top of the pastry level with the top. Chill for 30 minutes.

Add the apple and water to a saucepan, cover and cook gently for 10 minutes, stirring from time to time until the apple is soft and pulpy. Set aside until cold.

Preheat the oven to 180°C/350°F/gas mark 4. Meanwhile, cream the butter and sugar together in a bowl or electric mixer. Add the flour, ground almonds, mixed spice and eggs and beat together until smooth.

Spoon the apple mixture over the base of the uncooked tart case in an even layer. Spoon over the almond mixture and smooth level. Bake for 35–40 minutes until the filling is well risen and golden brown and the top springs back when pressed with a fingertip.

Leave to cool in the tin. Take the tart out of the tin and transfer to a serving plate. Dust lightly with sifted icing sugar and cinnamon. Serve cut into slices as it is or with spoonfuls of thick cream or a drizzle of hot custard.

COOK'S TIP Tart tins vary in depth – make sure you have a deep one for this tart as the filling is generous.

Hill Top plum cake

Author Beatrix Potter bought Cumbrian cottage Hill Top in 1905, using the proceeds from her first book. This recipe was found in amongst some papers in the Beatrix Potter Collection and had been written down by Beatrix's maternal grandmother Jane Leech, who died in 1884. Although it is called plum cake, there aren't actually any plums in the cake in much the same way that plum pudding doesn't have any either.

Cuts into 24 slices
Prep 30 minutes
Cook 2½–3 hours

350g/12oz plain flour
1 tsp ground cinnamon
1 tsp ground ginger
1 tsp ground allspice
½ tsp grated nutmeg
½ tsp salt
900g/2lb mixed dried fruit with candied peel
2 lemons, finely grated zest
2 oranges, freshly squeezed or 200ml/7fl oz juice
350g/12oz butter at room temperature
225g/8oz caster sugar
4 eggs
115g/4oz ground almonds
225g/8oz glacé cherries, quartered
100–150ml/3½–5fl oz brandy

COOK'S TIP
The cake could also be topped with homemade marzipan or royal icing for a special celebration or Christmas cake. It is only 5cm/2in deep, so if you prefer a deeper cake, cook the mixture in a 23cm/9in square cake tin instead, allowing a little extra cooking time.

Preheat the oven to 140°C/275°F/gas mark 1. Line a 25cm/10in deep square cake tin with two long strips of nonstick baking paper that will go over the base and up two sides. Arrange at right angles in the tin so that the base and sides of the tin are completely covered.

Add the flour, spices and salt to a bowl and mix together. Add the dried fruit to a second bowl then add the lemon zest and orange juice and stir together.

Add the butter and sugar to the bowl of an electric mixer and beat until light and creamy. Gradually beat in the eggs one at a time, adding a little of the spiced flour if the cake mixture appears to be about to split.

Gradually beat in all the spiced flour until smooth then gradually mix in the dried fruit, lemon zest and orange juice. Add the ground almonds and cherries and stir until just mixed.

Spoon the cake mixture into the lined tin. Spread the top level then bake for 2½–3 hours until browned and a skewer inserted into the cake comes out cleanly.

Leave to cool for 30 minutes then turn out of the tin and leave to cool completely on a wire rack. Peel away the lining paper and pack into a large plastic container lined with fresh paper and store overnight. Next day, make fine holes in the top of the cake with a skewer and drizzle over 2–3 tbsp of the brandy. Drizzle over a little more brandy, day by day, until it has all been drizzled over the cake. Allow the cake to mature in the container for a week or two then serve cut into slices.

Winter

With cold frosty mornings and darker nights, now is
the time for steaming bowls of soup – try red lentil and
coconut, delicate celeriac and fennel or roasted onion
and garlic soups with home-cooked Mediterranean
bread, warm from the oven. Tuck into comforting stews
such as Churchill's slow-cooked lamb stew, steak, ale
and stilton pies with pastry that just melts in the mouth
or warming turkey and squash gratin, perfect to use
up the last of the Christmas turkey. Cosy up round the
fire and indulge in a slice of ginger and satsuma cake,
a rich gingerbread sandwiched with a light frosting,
or wonderfully festive Ightham Mote mince pie slice –
topped with a rich, nutty frangipane.

Red lentil and coconut soup

Full of mellow Indian flavours this comforting earthy soup has just a hint of coconut.

Serves 4
Prep 20 minutes
Cook 29–31 minutes

2 tbsp vegetable oil
250g/9oz onion, chopped
2 garlic cloves, chopped
½ tsp ground cumin
½ tsp ground coriander
½ tsp ground ginger
1 tsp curry powder
1 tbsp tomato purée
250g/9oz red lentils
1 litre/1¾ pints vegetable stock
200ml/7fl oz canned coconut milk
Large pinch of cayenne pepper
Salt
Few toasted coconut flakes or flaked almonds, to garnish

Heat the oil in a medium saucepan, add the onion and fry over a medium heat for 5 minutes, stirring from time to time until the onions are softened. Stir in the garlic, ground spices and curry powder and cook gently for 2–3 minutes to release the flavours.

Stir in the tomato purée and lentils then pour in the stock and coconut milk. Season with cayenne pepper and salt, bring to the boil then cover and simmer for 20–25 minutes, stirring from time to time until the lentils are soft.

Remove from the heat then scoop out half the lentils with a slotted spoon and reserve in a bowl. Purée the soup still in the saucepan with a stick blender or transfer to a liquidiser and purée in batches. Stir in the reserved lentils. Taste and adjust the seasoning and mix in a little extra stock if needed.

Reheat the soup then ladle into bowls and sprinkle with the coconut flakes or almonds. Serve with warm crusty bread and butter.

COOK'S TIP The lentils tend to swell on standing so if you make this soup in advance or have leftovers, you may need to stir in a little extra stock when reheating to thin the soup.

Celeriac and fennel soup

Celeriac is one of those underused vegetables and yet it makes the most delicious soup flavoured with just a hint of fennel seeds.

Serves 4
Prep 20 minutes
Cook 30-35 minutes

1 tbsp vegetable oil
225g/8oz onions, chopped
½ tsp fennel seeds, crushed
450g/1lb celeriac, diced
140g/5oz potato, diced
1.2 litre/2 pints vegetable
  stock
Salt and freshly ground black
  pepper

To finish
2 tbsp extra virgin rapeseed or
  olive oil
1 tsp fennel seeds, crushed

Heat the oil in a medium saucepan, add the onion and fennel seeds and fry over a medium heat for 10 minutes, stirring from time until the onions are softened and just beginning to turn golden.

Stir in the celeriac and potatoes, cook for 2 minutes then pour in the stock. Season with a little salt and pepper and bring to the boil, stirring. Cover and simmer for 20–25 minutes or until the vegetables are soft.

Meanwhile, heat the oil for the infusion in a small frying pan, add the fennel seeds and heat gently until the seeds sizzle. Take off the heat and leave to cool and the flavour of the fennel to infuse the oil.

Purée the soup with a stick blender still in the saucepan or transfer to a liquidiser and purée in batches. Taste and adjust the seasoning, if needed. Reheat then ladle into bowls. Strain the fennel oil, if liked, then drizzle a little oil over each bowl of soup and serve with warm crusty bread and butter.

COOK'S TIP The oil will keep well in a labelled jar in the fridge for two weeks.

Greys Court kale soup

The kitchen garden at Greys Court in Oxfordshire, has its roots in the Second World War 'Dig for Victory' campaign and is just as productive today. Back then the government encouraged all gardeners to grow kale as it was highly nutritious and easy for the even most novice of gardeners to grow. Cavolo nero or black kale is the main ingredient in this Italian-inspired rustic peasant soup, perfect to warm you up after a cold wintery walk.

Serves 4
Prep 5 minutes
Cook 25 minutes

2 tbsp vegetable oil
175g/6oz onion, finely chopped
3 garlic cloves, finely chopped
500g/1lb 2oz potatoes, scrubbed, cut into 1cm/½ inch dice
2 tbsp mixed fresh chopped thyme, rosemary and parsley
1 litre/1¾ pint vegetable stock
300g/10½ oz cavolo nero (black kale), shredded
200g/7oz drained canned cannellini beans

Heat the oil in a saucepan, add the onion and garlic and fry over a medium heat for 5 minute, stirring until softened and just beginning to turn golden around the edges.

Stir in the potatoes, cover and fry for 5 more minutes, stirring from time to time.

Add the chopped herbs and stock and bring to the boil, stirring. Cover and simmer for 10 minutes until the potatoes are just cooked. Stir in the kale, re-cover the pan and cook for 10 minutes.

Blend the soup in a liquidiser or leave chunky, add the cannellini beans, season to taste and adjust the consistency with a little extra stock if needed. Reheat then ladle into bowls, sprinkle with a little grated parmesan, if liked and serve with warm crusty bread.

COOK'S TIP For non-vegetarians you might like to add a little diced chorizo or bacon when frying the onions. Or for those who like their food a little on the spicy side, stir a large pinch or up to ¼ tsp hot smoked paprika in with the herbs.

Roasted onion and garlic soup

Rather than frying sliced onions here they are roasted in their skins for maximum flavour.

Serves 4
Prep 20 minutes
Cook 52-63 minutes

1 kg/2¼ lb onions
6 garlic cloves, still in their
  skins
2 sprigs fresh rosemary
2 sprigs fresh sage
1 tbsp vegetable oil
1 litre/1¾ pints vegetable
  stock
2–3 tsp caster sugar
Salt and freshly ground black
  pepper

To finish
2 tbsp extra virgin rapeseed or
  olive oil
1 sprig fresh thyme
1 sprig fresh sage

Preheat the oven to 180°C/350°F/gas mark 4. Peel the outer layer off the onions if a little dirty and trim away the root then put into a roasting tin with the garlic and half the rosemary and sage and roast for 30–40 minutes. Take the garlic out after 20 minutes or when soft and the onions when softened and just beginning to leak a little liquid.

Leave the onions and garlic until cool enough to handle then peel away the skins and roughly chop.

Heat the oil in a medium-sized saucepan, add the onions and garlic and the remaining rosemary and sage and fry over a high heat for 2–3 minutes until golden. Pour in the stock then bring to the boil, cover and simmer for 20 minutes.

Meanwhile, add the oil for the infusion to a small frying pan, bruise the herbs, add to the oil and heat until the herbs just begin to sizzle then take off the heat.

Take the soup off the heat and purée still in the saucepan with a stick blender or transfer to a liquidiser and purée in batches. Stir in sugar and salt and pepper to taste. Reheat, stirring then ladle into bowls and drizzle with some of the strained herb oil.

COOK'S TIP The flavoured oil can be made up in larger batches then strained and kept in the fridge in a small squeezy bottle. Drizzle over the soup when needed, try drizzled over just-cooked new potatoes or pasta or add to steaks or lamb chops before cooking.

Mediterranean bread

Homemade Italian focaccia bread really isn't difficult to make and the aromas while the bread bakes will soon get your family to the table. Try different toppings, such as sundried tomatoes, roasted peppers, canned artichoke hearts or mushrooms. Delicious served with a bowl of steaming soup or cold meats and salad.

Cuts into 8 pieces
Prep 25 minutes
Rising 1¼ hours
Cook 25–30 minutes

350g/12oz strong white
  bread flour
½ tsp salt
1 tsp caster sugar
2 tsp easy-blend dried yeast
250ml/9fl oz warm water

Topping
3 tbsp extra virgin rapeseed or
  olive oil
200g/7oz red onion, thinly
  sliced
4 garlic cloves, peeled and
  thinly sliced
55g/2oz pitted black or green
  olives, roughly chopped
2 stems fresh rosemary, leaves
  torn from stems, roughly
  chopped
65g/2½ oz/½ ball
  mozzarella, drained and torn
  into small pieces
Little coarse sea salt

COOK'S TIP This bread is made with easy-blend, sometimes called easy-bake dried yeast which is stirred straight into the flour. Don't confuse it with dried yeast that needs to be frothed in warm water before

Add the flour, salt and sugar to the bowl of your electric mixer. Add the yeast then gradually mix in the warm water, using a dough hook until you have a smooth, soft dough. If you don't have an electric mixer, stir with a wooden spoon then bring the dough together with your hands.

Knead the dough well for 4 minutes using the mixer or turn out on to a lightly floured work surface and knead by hand until smooth and elastic. Lightly oil the bowl, add the dough then cover the top of the bowl with oiled clingfilm and leave the bread to rise in a warm place for about 45 minutes until doubled in size.

Meanwhile, heat 1 tbsp of the oil in a large frying pan, add the onion and fry gently for 5 minutes over a medium heat until softened.

Knead the dough lightly then press into the base of a 20 x 30 x 4cm/8 x 12 x 1½in shallow rectangular cake tin with your hand. Make deep indentations in the dough with your fingers or the end of a wooden spoon. Drizzle the top with 1 tbsp oil then scatter over the onions, garlic, olives and about half of the rosemary.

Cover loosely with oiled clingfilm and leave to rise in a warm place until the bread has risen to the top of the tin. Meanwhile, preheat the oven to 200°C/400°F/gas mark 6. Remove the clingfilm from the bread, sprinkle with a little coarse salt and bake for 10 minutes then sprinkle with the mozzarella and cook for about 10–15 minutes until golden brown and the bread is cooked through. Drizzle with the remaining oil, scatter with the remaining rosemary and serve warm, cut into eight triangles.

Smoked mackerel, fennel and grapefruit salad

Winter is not all about pies and stews – this zingy and colourful salad is a healthy alternative. Deep red beetroot has been added to this lovely crisp, crunchy salad, but if you are lucky enough to grow Burpee's Golden or pink Candy Stripe beetroot then use a mix of different coloured beetroot for an even more eye-catching dish. Thinly slice the peeled and raw beetroot on a mandolin, if you have one, so that they are really thin.

Serves 4
Prep 20 minutes

1 grapefruit, peeled and segmented
1 small fennel bulb, thinly sliced
140g/5oz iceberg lettuce, torn into bite-sized pieces
100g/3½ oz trimmed radishes, thinly sliced
4 tbsp fresh chopped parsley
200g/7oz trimmed raw beetroot, peeled and thinly sliced
250g/9oz or 3 plain or peppered smoked mackerel fillets, skinned and flaked

Dressing
4 tbsp extra virgin rapeseed or olive oil
2 tsp white wine vinegar
1 lemon, freshly squeezed
3 tsp runny honey
1 tbsp freshly grated horseradish or horseradish sauce to taste
Salt and freshly ground white pepper

Add the grapefruit and fennel to a bowl. Add all the dressing ingredients to a jug and whisk together or add to a jam jar, screw on the lid and shake well to mix. Pour over the grapefruit and fennel and gently toss together.

Add the lettuce, radishes, parsley and beetroot to a large salad bowl. Spoon over the grapefruit, fennel and dressing and gently toss together then sprinkle the smoked mackerel over the top. Spoon into shallow bowls to serve.

COOK'S TIP To help prevent the beetroot staining all the other salad ingredients, soak the slices in cold water first, then drain well in a sieve and pat dry with kitchen towel.

Pulled pork and roasted vegetables

Slow roast the pork so that it is meltingly tender then shred with two forks and mix with roasted vegetables and a cheat's barbecue sauce for a relaxed supper to share with friends.

Serves 4-6
Prep 30 minutes
**Cook 2 hours 55 minutes –
3¼ hours**

140g/5oz onion, chopped
2 bay leaves
2 garlic cloves, finely chopped
1.3kg/3lb pork shoulder joint
1 onion, halved, thickly sliced
300g/10½ oz swede, cut into batons
300g/10½ oz carrot, cut into batons
2 tbsp virgin rapeseed or olive oil
200g/7oz parsnips, cut into 1cm/½ inch thick slices
140g/5oz leeks, cut into 1cm/½ inch thick slices
300g/10½ oz celery, cut into 1cm/½ inch thick slices
200g/7oz mushrooms, halved or quartered if large
5 garlic cloves, left whole and unpeeled
2–3 sprigs fresh rosemary
3 tbsp demerara sugar
3 tbsp balsamic vinegar
Coarse sea salt and roughly crushed black pepper
300ml/½ pint hot chicken stock
4 tbsp barbecue sauce

Preheat the oven to 160°C/320°F/gas mark 3. Add the chopped onion, garlic and bay leaves to a small casserole dish then tuck the piece of pork into the casserole so that it fits snugly. Cover with a lid or foil then roast in the oven for 2½–3 hours until tender.

Meanwhile, make the roasted vegetables. Add the sliced onion, swede and carrot to a large roasting tin. Drizzle with the oil then turn the vegetables to coat evenly. Add to the oven and roast on the shelf above the pork for 20 minutes.

Add the parsnips, leeks, celery, mushrooms, garlic cloves and rosemary to the part-roasted vegetables and toss together. Roast for 20 minutes. Turn the vegetables, sprinkle with the sugar, add the balsamic vinegar and season with salt and pepper. Roast for 20–30 minutes until a good colour. Take out of the oven, cover with foil and set aside.

Take the pork out of the oven, remove from the casserole dish with two forks then cut away the rind and some of the fat and thickly slice the meat. Arrange the meat slices in a second roasting tin, cover with foil and return to the oven for 20 minutes until the pork is almost falling apart.

Tear the pork into shreds with two forks then add to the roasted vegetables. Mix the stock with the barbecue sauce then pour over the pork. Cover with foil and return to the oven for 20 minutes until the vegetables are piping hot. Spoon into bowls, discarding the rosemary and serve with warm crusty bread and butter.

COOK'S TIP This is a good way to use up leftover roasted vegetables. The pork can be roasted in advance, sliced and shredded then cooled and kept covered in the fridge until you are ready to reheat with the vegetables, stock and barbecue sauce, either in a saucepan on the hob or in the oven until piping hot throughout.

Smoky turkey and squash gratin

Forget about cold turkey salad, this delicious hot saucy supper dish mixes butternut squash, parsnips and mushrooms with Christmas leftover turkey then is topped with a crispy breadcrumb, parsley and smoked cheese topping.

Serves 4
Prep 25 minutes
Cook 45–51 minutes

1–2 tbsp vegetable oil
1 garlic clove, finely chopped
250g/9oz onions, chopped
140g/5oz mushrooms, sliced
250g/9oz butternut squash, peeled, deseeded and diced
115g/4oz parsnip, peeled and diced
2 sticks celery, trimmed and diced
450ml/¾ pint turkey or chicken stock
40g/1½ oz butter
25g/1oz plain flour
150ml/¼ pint milk
Large handful of fresh parsley
Salt and freshly ground black pepper
350g/12oz cooked turkey, cut into bite-sized pieces
85g/3oz bread, torn into pieces
85g/3oz smoked cheddar, diced

Heat 1 tbsp of the oil in a large frying pan with a lid, add the garlic and fry over a medium heat for 2–3 minutes, stirring from time to time until golden.

Add the onions and fry for 5 minutes until softened and just beginning to turn golden. Stir in the mushrooms and an extra tablespoon of oil, if needed and fry, stirring, for 3 minutes. Mix in the butternut squash, parsnip and celery then pour in the stock. Bring to the boil, cover and simmer for 15–20 minutes or until the vegetables are just tender.

Preheat the oven to 190°C/375°F/gas mark 5. Drain the stock from the cooked vegetables into a jug and reserve. You should have about 300ml/½ pint – if you have a little less, make up with extra water.

Heat the butter in a medium-sized saucepan, stir in the flour then gradually mix in the reserved stock and milk and bring to the boil, stirring all the time until thickened and smooth. Chop half the parsley and mix into the sauce with the vegetables. Season to taste with salt and pepper. (If you would like to prep this ahead, you could chill the sauce and vegetables at this stage).

Stir in the turkey and bring to the boil. Tip into an ovenproof dish that is about 1.7 litre/3 pints.

Add the remaining parsley, bread and cheese to a food processor and blitz together until the mixture resembles fine crumbs. Sprinkle over the turkey mix in an even layer and bake for about 20 minutes until the topping is golden brown, the sauce is bubbling and the turkey is piping hot. Serve with mashed potatoes and roasted vegetables.

Steamed venison and root vegetable pudding

After a chilly morning walking round a National Trust garden, a steaming suet pudding is just what's needed to help you thaw out.

Serves 4
Prep 35 minutes
Cook 1 hour 25 minutes

1 tbsp vegetable oil
85g/3oz onions, finely chopped
1 garlic clove, finely chopped
½ tsp ground ginger
4 juniper berries, roughly crushed
250g/9oz minced venison
85g/3oz minced chicken
2 tsp fresh chopped thyme leaves
2 tsp fresh chopped sage
100ml/3½ fl oz red wine
250ml/9fl oz chicken stock
4 tsp cranberry sauce
20g/¾ oz stoned dates, chopped
85g/3oz carrots, cut into small
 dice
85g/3oz swede, cut into small
 dice
85g/3oz parsnip, cut into small
 dice
Salt and freshly ground black
 pepper

Pastry
350g/12oz self-raising flour
175g/6oz shredded suet
¼ tsp salt
Freshly ground black pepper
175–200ml/6–7fl oz water

Heat the oil in a frying pan, add the onion, garlic and ginger and fry over a low heat for 5 minutes, stirring until the onion is softened.

Add the juniper berries, minced meats and herbs and continue to fry for 5 minutes, stirring until the meat is browned.

Pour in the red wine and stock then add the cranberry sauce and dates and bring to the boil, stirring. Mix in the diced vegetables, season with a little salt and pepper then cover and simmer for 15 minutes.

Drain the meat mixture into a sieve set over a bowl then pour the wine mixture back into the frying pan and boil for 3–5 minutes until reduced and thickened. Return the meat and vegetables to the pan then set aside.

To make the pastry add the flour, suet, salt and pepper to a bowl and stir together. Gradually mix in enough water to make a soft but not sticky dough. Lightly knead on a floured surface until a smooth ball then cut into four.

Cut one quarter off each of the balls of dough and reserve for the lids. Roll one of the larger pieces of dough out to a circle about 18cm/7in in diameter then press into a lightly buttered 250ml/9 fl oz pudding basin or metal pudding mould, leaving the pastry overhanging the top edge. Repeat to fill three more basins then spoon in the filling.

Roll the smaller pieces of dough out to make pudding lids then moisten the edges of the pastry in the basins with water and press the lids in place, sealing the edges well, trimming off the excess pastry and crimping the edges. Cover the tops of the puddings with buttered foil, doming up the foil slightly to allow for the pastry to rise.

Put the puddings into a large steamer set over a saucepan of simmering water. Cover and steam for about 1 hour until the pastry is light and firm to the touch. Lift the puddings out with a cloth, remove the foil and serve in shallow bowls with a creamy root vegetable mash or roasted cauliflower with cumin seeds.

COOK'S TIP If your steamer isn't very big then add the puddings to a roasting tin, pour boiling water into the tin to come halfway up the sides of the pudding moulds then cover the top of the tin with foil and seal well around the tin edges. Bake in a preheated oven 180°C/350°F/gas mark 4 for about an hour.

Red lentil cottage pie

Homely and comforting, this meat-free cottage pie is an easy way to encourage the family to eat more vegetables. Make earlier in the day, then just reheat until golden and bubbling when needed.

Serves 4
Prep 30 minutes, plus 15 minutes soaking time
Cook 55 minutes – 1 hour 20 minutes

10g/¼ oz dried mixed mushrooms
125ml/4fl oz boiling water
1 tbsp extra virgin rapeseed or olive oil
250g/9oz onions, chopped
2 garlic cloves, finely chopped
1 bay leaf
1 tsp ground coriander
¼ tsp ground cinnamon
250g/9oz red lentils, rinsed and drained
4 tsp pesto
400g/14oz carton chopped tomatoes
450ml/¾ pint vegetable stock
150ml/¼ pint red wine
175g/6oz carrots, diced
115g/4oz swede, diced
Salt and freshly ground black pepper
85g/3oz spinach

Topping
850g/1lb 12oz potatoes, scrubbed, cut into chunks
55g/2oz butter
2–3 tbsp milk

Add the dried mushrooms to a bowl, pour over the boiling water and leave to soak for 15 minutes.

Heat the oil in a medium saucepan, add the onion, garlic, bay leaf, ground coriander and cinnamon and fry gently for 10 minutes, stirring until softened.

Lift the mushrooms out of the water and chop then add the chopped mushrooms and soaking liquid to the onions with the lentils, pesto and tomatoes. Pour in the stock and wine then add the carrots and swede. Season with salt and pepper and bring to the boil, stirring. Cover and simmer for 25–30 minutes, stirring from time to time until the lentils are soft and have absorbed most of the liquid.

Meanwhile, add the potatoes to a saucepan of boiling water and cook for 15–20 minutes or until soft. Drain and mash with the milk and half the butter. Season with salt and pepper.

Preheat the oven to 190°C/375°F/gas mark 5. Add the spinach to the lentils and cook for 1 minute until just wilted. Spoon the lentil mix into the base of four 300ml/½ pint individual ovenproof dishes or a 1.2 litre/2 pint dish. Top with the mashed potato and rough up with a fork. Melt the remaining butter and brush over the mash. Bake the pies for 20 minutes if individual or 40 minutes if one large one, until golden brown and piping hot. Serve with roasted root vegetables.

COOK'S TIP These cottage pies freeze well just after adding the mashed potato topping. Cool then cover with a lid or foil, seal and label and freeze up to two months. Defrost overnight in the fridge, uncover and brush with butter then bake when needed.

Herdwick mutton with salsa verde

Curved-horn Herdwick sheep have been grazing the Lake District fells for centuries. Now a rare breed, their survival owes much to Beatrix Potter, a sheep farmer as well as a writer, who left her land to the National Trust on condition that Herdwicks were grazed on it in perpetuity.

Serves 6
Prep 25 minutes
Cook 5-6 hours

1 leg of mutton, 2.5–3kg/ 5½–6½ lb
2 tbsp extra virgin rapeseed or olive oil
Salt and freshly ground black pepper

For the salsa verde
A generous handful each of mint, parsley and basil
1 small garlic clove, finely chopped
2 tbsp capers, rinsed with cold water, drained
2 tbsp Dijon mustard
2 tbsp red wine vinegar
8 tbsp extra virgin rapeseed or olive oil
Salt

Preheat the oven to 140°C/275°F/gas mark 1. Put the mutton in a large roasting tin, rub with the oil and roast for 1 hour for every 500g/1lb 2oz. Baste with the meat juices from time to time and season with salt and pepper towards the end of cooking.

To make the salsa verde, wash the herbs, dry and tear the leaves from the stems. Add the herb leaves to a blender or food processor with the garlic, capers, mustard, vinegar, oil and salt and blend until a coarse paste. Spoon into a bowl, cover and set aside until ready to serve.

When the lamb is ready, carve into wedges, starting by cutting a slice halfway between the aitchbone (hip joint) and the knuckle, then working outwards in each direction. Arrange on serving plates with spoonfuls of the salsa verde.

COOK'S TIP Herdwick mutton or mutton from other sheep breeds is difficult to come by so support your local farmers and source some good-quality lamb from your local area and follow your preferred roasting method. Generally lamb comes from sheep 4–12 months old, while mutton comes from older sheep so it has a stronger flavour but tends to be tougher and so needs long slow cooking.

Caramelised onion and goat's cheese quiche

Don't try to hurry frying the onions – you are aiming for soft, deep golden onion slices with just a hint of sweetness to complement the smooth sharpness of the goat's cheese.

Cuts into 8
Prep 30 minutes, plus chilling
Cook 50-60 minutes

Pastry
225g/8oz plain flour
Pinch of salt
½ tsp dried mixed herbs
115g/4oz butter, diced
50g/1¾ oz cheddar cheese, grated
1 egg, beaten
1–2 tbsp milk

Filling
2 tbsp virgin rapeseed or olive oil
2 tsp fresh thyme leaves
1 tbsp fresh finely chopped sage leaves
500g/1lb 2oz onions, thinly sliced
1 tbsp balsamic vinegar
2 tsp demerara sugar
4 tsp sweet chilli sauce
100ml/3½ fl oz milk
100ml/3½ fl oz double cream
4 eggs
Salt and freshly ground black pepper
125g/4½ oz pack goat's cheese, diced

COOK'S TIP
Make up double the amount of pastry and make and bake two tart cases blind then fill and use one now; cool and freeze the second empty case in a plastic box for another time.

To make the pastry case, add the flour, salt, herbs and butter to a bowl or electric mixer and rub in until the mixture looks like fine crumbs. Stir in the cheese then mix in the egg and enough milk to make a smooth soft dough.

Lightly knead the pastry then roll out on a lightly floured surface until a little larger than a 23cm/9in buttered loose-bottomed tart tin. Lift the pastry over the rolling pin and press into the tin. Trim the top of the pastry a little above the top of the tin to allow for shrinkage, prick the base with a fork then chill for 30 minutes.

Preheat the oven to 190°C/375°F/gas mark 5. Line the tart case with a circle of nonstick baking paper and baking beans then bake for 10 minutes. Remove the paper and beans and cook for 5 more minutes until the base is crisp and dry. Set aside.

Meanwhile, make the filling. Heat the oil in a large frying pan, add the herbs and fry gently for 2–3 minutes, stirring. Add the onions, mix with the herb oil then gently fry for 10–15 minutes, stirring from time until softened and just beginning to caramelise.

Add the balsamic vinegar and sugar and continue to fry for 5 more minutes until the sugar has dissolved and the onions are a deep golden brown. Stir in the chilli sauce and set aside.

Whisk the milk, cream, eggs and seasoning together in a jug. Spoon the onion mix into an even layer in the base of the cooked tart case. Scatter the cheese over the top then pour over the cream mix. Bake at 180°C/350°F/gas mark 4 for 30–40 minutes until golden brown and set.

Leave to stand for 5–10 minutes before removing the tart case and slicing. Serve with roasted root vegetables and mashed potato or with green salad.

Steak, ale and stilton pies

Pies are a great prep-ahead main course. Make up the pie filling earlier in the day, even the day before, then spoon into individual dishes and top with the pastry. Pop in the oven 20–25 minutes before you are ready to serve.

Makes 4
Prep 35 minutes
Cook 3 hours – 3 hours 5 minutes

1 tbsp vegetable oil
225g/8oz onion, chopped
2 sticks celery, diced
½ tsp grated nutmeg
650g/1lb 7oz diced braising beef
350g/12oz butternut squash, peeled, deseeded and cut into chunks
200g/7oz mushrooms, quartered
300ml/½ pint brown ale
300ml/½ pint beef stock
Salt and freshly ground black pepper
200g/7oz/½ carton chopped tomatoes
2 tsp cornflour mixed with 1 tbsp cold water

For the pastry
225g/8oz plain flour
115g/4oz butter, diced
55g/2oz stilton cheese, rind removed, crumbled
1 egg, beaten, plus extra beaten egg to glaze

Add the oil to a medium-sized saucepan, add the onion, celery and nutmeg and fry over a medium heat for 5 minutes, stirring until softened. Add the beef a few pieces at a time until all the beef is in the pan then fry for 5 minutes, stirring until evenly browned.

Stir in the butternut squash and mushrooms then add the brown ale and stock. Season with salt and pepper and bring to the boil. Cover and simmer gently for 2½ hours, topping up with a little extra stock if needed until the beef is tender.

Add the tomatoes and cornflour and mix together, stirring until thickened. Leave to cool then divide between four 300ml/½ pint individual pie dishes.

To make the pastry, add the flour, butter and stilton to a bowl or food processor and rub in the butter and cheese until the mixture resembles fine crumbs. Add the egg and bring together to a smooth dough.

Lightly knead then cut the pastry into four. Roll out each piece until a little larger than the top of the pie dish. Moisten the dish edge with water then press the pastry lid in place. Trim off the excess pastry and crimp the edge. Re-roll the trimmings, if liked, cut leaves and arrange on the pies.

When ready to bake the pies, preheat the oven to 190°C/375°F/gas mark 5. Brush the pies with a little extra beaten egg and bake for 20–25 minutes until the pastry is golden and the filling piping hot. Serve with roasted root vegetables and mashed potatoes.

COOK'S TIP If you don't have any individual oven-proof dishes then use foil freezer containers instead.

Churchill's stew

During the war, Churchill had regular Tuesday lunches with General Eisenhower at which Irish stew was always served. This tradition still continues to this day at his country home Chartwell, in Kent, where it has now been aptly renamed Churchill's stew. The lamb comes from Church Farm in Seal, just eight miles away.

Serves 4
Prep 20 minutes
Cook 2½ hours

2 tbsp sunflower oil
15g/½ oz butter
650g/1lb 5oz leg of lamb, diced
4 tbsp white wine
175g/6oz onion, finely chopped
1 carrot, finely chopped
1 stick celery, finely chopped
1 leek, white part finely chopped, green part sliced
1 garlic clove, finely chopped
1 tbsp plain flour
600ml/1 pint lamb stock
1 bay leaf
Salt and freshly ground black pepper

To finish
140g/5oz carrots cut into chunks
1 large sprig of fresh thyme
140g/5oz frozen baby onions
140g/5oz frozen peas
3 tbsp fresh chopped parsley

Heat the oil and butter in a large saucepan, add the lamb a few pieces at a time until all the meat is in the pan then fry over a medium heat for 5 minutes, stirring until the lamb is evenly browned. Add the wine and cook for 2–3 minutes, stirring to deglaze the pan.

Add the chopped onion, carrot, celery, white chopped leek and garlic to the pan. Cook for 5 minutes, stirring until just beginning to soften. Sprinkle over the flour then mix in, add the stock and bay leaf and season with salt and pepper. Bring to the boil, stirring, then cover and simmer gently for 2 hours, stirring from time to time until the lamb is tender.

Stir in the carrot chunks and thyme, top up with a little extra stock if needed then re-cover and simmer for 15 minutes. Check the seasoning and add lots of pepper and just a little salt then stir in the remaining sliced green leek, frozen onions and peas. Re-cover and simmer for 5 minutes.

Stir in the parsley then spoon into large bowls and serve with mashed potatoes.

COOK'S TIP Lamb chump chops or lamb fillet could also be used instead of boneless lamb leg steaks.

Winter spiced bake

Full of Christmassy flavours, this is much lighter than a traditional fruit cake. The sultanas are soaked in Earl Grey tea but if you don't have any to hand, you can use your usual teabags.

Cuts into 10 slices
Prep 25 minutes, plus 30 minutes soaking time
Cook 30–37 minutes

1 Earl Grey tea bag
4 tbsp boiling water
115g/4oz sultanas
55g/2oz glacé cherries, roughly chopped

Sponge base
140g/5oz self-raising flour
115g/4oz soft light muscovado sugar
115g/4oz soft margarine
2 eggs
1 tsp ground mixed spice
1 tsp almond extract

Crumble topping
50g/1¾ oz plain flour
15g/½ oz porridge oats
15g/½ oz light muscovado sugar
25g/1oz soft margarine
55g/2oz marzipan, coarsely grated
2 tbsp flaked almonds

Add the teabag to a bowl and spoon over the boiling water. Mix in the sultanas and leave to soak for 30 minutes.

Preheat the oven to 180°C/350°F/gas mark 4. Line a 20cm/8in shallow square cake tin with a large square of non-stick baking paper, snipping the paper diagonally into the corners of the tin and pressing the paper down so that the base and sides of the tin are lined.

To make the sponge base, add the flour, sugar, margarine, eggs, ground spice and almond extract to the bowl of an electric mixer and beat until smooth. Drain the sultanas and mix any remaining tea into the sponge mix. Spoon into the lined tin and spread level.

Scatter the drained sultanas and cherries over the sponge.

To make the crumble topping add the flour, oats, sugar and margarine to a bowl and rub in the margarine until the mixture resembles fine crumbs. Scatter over the fruit then bake for 25–30 minutes. Sprinkle with the marzipan and almonds and cook for 5–7 minutes more until lightly browned on top.

Leave to cool in the tin then lift the cake out, peel away the paper and cut into ten bars.

COOK'S TIP If you freeze the marzipan for 30 minutes before you need it, it will be much easier to grate and sprinkle over the cake.

Bread and butter pudding with marmalade

Bread and butter pudding can be traced back as far as 1723, and the eighteenth-century recipe often used bone marrow in place of butter. This version of the winter warmer is much more appealing – it is rich and creamy with zesty orange marmalade set in a vanilla custard.

Serves 4–6
Prep 20 minutes, plus 15 minutes soaking time
Cook 30 minutes

450ml/¾ pint milk
100ml/3½ fl oz double cream
3 eggs
1 tsp vanilla extract
6 slices of bread cut from a bloomer loaf
40g/1½ oz butter, at room temperature
140g/5oz medium-shred marmalade
70g/2½ oz caster sugar
1 tbsp demerara sugar

Whisk the milk, cream, eggs and vanilla together in a large jug and set aside.

Lay out the slices of bread on a large chopping board and spread butter over three of them and marmalade over the remaining three. Sandwich the slices together then spread the top with the remaining butter.

Cut the sandwiches into wedge shapes then arrange in a buttered 20 x 26 x 4cm/8 x 10½ x 1½in small rectangular cake tin. Sprinkle with the caster sugar, whisk the milk mixture one more time and pour over the bread. Sprinkle with the demerara sugar and leave to soak for 15 minutes. Preheat the oven to 180°C/350°F/gas mark 4.

Bake the pudding for about 30 minutes until well risen, the tops of the bread are crisp and golden and the custard just set. Scoop into shallow bowls and serve with hot custard or cream.

Chilled chocolate and orange tart

This decadent desert is incredibly rich so serve in small slices with a drizzle of cream or spoonful of crème fraîche and a light dusting of sifted icing sugar, even topped with a few raspberries.

Cuts into 8-10 slices
Prep 30 minutes, plus chilling
Cook 40-50 minutes

Pastry
225g/8oz plain flour
115g/4oz butter, diced
60g/2¼ oz icing sugar
1 egg
2-3 tsp milk

Filling
140g/5oz butter, diced
150g/5½ oz dark chocolate,
  broken into pieces
1 tsp salt
85g/3oz cocoa
4 eggs
200g/7oz caster sugar
3 tbsp whipping cream
3 tbsp golden syrup
1 medium orange, grated zest
  and juice
Little cocoa powder or icing
  sugar, sifted, to decorate

COOK'S TIP The timing in the oven is critical, as ovens vary slightly from make to make so check frequently. You are aiming for a softly set filling with a slight wobble to the centre, just as you do when baking brownies. The filling will firm up a little as it cools.

To make the tart case, add the flour, butter and sugar to a bowl or electric mixer and rub in the butter until the mixture looks like fine crumbs. Stir in the egg then mix in enough milk to make a smooth, soft dough.

Lightly knead the pastry then roll out on a lightly floured surface until a little larger than a 23cm/9in buttered loose-bottomed fluted tart tin. Lift the pastry over a rolling pin and press into the tin. Trim the top a little above the top of the tin to allow for shrinkage, prick the base with a fork and then chill for 30 minutes.

Preheat the oven to 190°C/375°F/gas mark 5. Line the tart case with a circle of non-stick baking paper and baking beans then bake for 10 minutes. Remove the paper and beans and cook for 5 more minutes until the base is crisp. Set aside.

To make the filling, melt the butter in a medium saucepan over a low heat. Add the chocolate, salt and cocoa powder and stir well until the chocolate has melted and the mixture is smooth and glossy. Take off the heat.

Whisk the eggs and sugar in the bowl of an electric mixer for 3-4 minutes until light and fluffy. Add the cream, golden syrup, orange zest and juice and mix well. Add the chocolate mix and gently fold together.

Pour the chocolate filling into the tart case and bake at 160°C/320°F/gas mark 3 for 25-35 minutes until the filling is slightly cracked around the edges and the centre softly set. Check after 20 minutes cooking then every 5 minutes so that you don't overcook the filling.

Leave to cool in the tin before removing, transfer to a serving plate, cut into thin slices and dust with sifted cocoa or icing sugar. Serve with pouring cream or crème fraîche.

St Clement's cheesecake

Creamy smooth with tangy citrus notes, this easy no-bake cheesecake is made with St Clement's curd, a mix of lemon and orange. If you can't find it in the shops then use a jar of lemon curd instead.

Serves 6
Prep 20 minutes
Cook 15–20 minutes

200g/7oz leftover cake pieces or shop-bought Madeira cake
½ tsp ground mixed spice
1 tsp ground ginger
50g/1¾ oz butter, melted
200g/7oz condensed milk
200g/7oz full-fat cream cheese
200ml/7fl oz double cream
½ lemon, finely grated zest and juice
115g/4oz St Clement's curd
Little extra grated lemon zest to decorate, if liked

Preheat the oven to 160°C/320°F/gas mark 3. Blitz the cake crumbs in a food processor until you have fine crumbs. Tip out on to a baking sheet and spread into even layer. Bake for 15–20 minutes until crisp and dry. Check halfway through cooking and stir, you may find the crumbs around the edges cook more quickly.

Transfer the cake crumbs to a bowl, add the ground spices and melted butter and stir together. Divide between the bases of six individual shallow glass dishes and press down with the back of a spoon. Chill while making the filling.

Spoon the condensed milk, cream cheese, double cream and lemon zest and juice into the bowl of your electric mixer and whisk together until thick and smooth. Reserve one quarter of the St Clement's curd then add the rest to the cream mixture and gently fold through until you have a marbled effect.

Spoon the cheesecake mixture into the glass dishes, level the tops then spoon or pipe over the remaining curd. Sprinkle with a little extra lemon zest if liked.

COOK'S TIP We often have leftover sponge cake in the café and so it makes sense to transform it into this spiced cheesecake base, but you could also use crushed digestive biscuits mixed with melted butter if you would rather. If you don't have individual dishes then make in a 1.2 litre/2 pint shallow dish instead.

Ginger and satsuma cake

Traditional gingercake gets taken to a whole new level with wafer thin slices of satsuma baked beneath the cake and a filling of gingery buttercream.

Cuts into 12–15
Prep 35 minutes
Cook 30–40 minutes

2 satsumas, thinly sliced, pips discarded
250g/9oz self-raising flour
1 tsp bicarbonate of soda
1 tsp ground cinnamon
1 tsp ground mixed spice
1 tbsp ground ginger
250ml/9fl oz milk
115g/4oz golden syrup
115g/4oz black treacle
115g/4oz light muscovado sugar
40g/1½ oz, about 2 pieces drained stem ginger in syrup, chopped
115g/4oz butter, diced
1 egg, beaten

To finish
175g/6oz icing sugar
2–3 tbsp syrup from a jar of stem ginger in syrup
55g/2oz butter, at room temperature
2 tbsp golden syrup
2 tsp boiling water

COOK'S TIP Don't boil the milk when mixing with the syrup, treacle and sugar: make sure it is warmed just enough to melt the sugar.
Why not serve two strips of cake and freeze the third strip well wrapped in clingfilm. Handy for unexpected visitors, it will defrost at room temperature in just over an hour.

Preheat the oven to 180°C/350°F/gas mark 4. Line a 20 x 30 x 4cm/8 x 12 x 1½in shallow rectangular cake tin with a large sheet of non-stick baking paper. Snip diagonally into the corners then press the paper into the tin so that the base and sides are lined. Arrange the sliced satsumas in a single layer over the base of the tin.

Mix the flour, bicarbonate of soda and ground spices together in a bowl and set aside.

Pour the milk into a medium saucepan and heat up. Add the syrup, treacle, sugar and chopped ginger and stir until the sugar has dissolved. Take off the heat, add the butter and stir until melted.

Beat in the egg then add the spiced flour mix to the saucepan and whisk well until smooth. Quickly pour into the lined tin, ease into an even layer and bake for 30–40 minutes until well risen, spongy to the touch and the gingercake is just beginning to shrink from the sides of the tin. Leave to stand for 20 minutes.

Cover the cake with a sheet of non-stick baking paper and a wire rack and turn upside down to release the cake from the tin. Peel away the lining paper and leave to cool.

Meanwhile, to make the buttercream, beat the icing sugar and ginger syrup together in a bowl or electric mixer until smooth. Add the butter and beat until light and fluffy.

Cut the cake into three strips through the long sides then cut each strip in half horizontally and sandwich back together the buttercream. Mix the golden syrup with the boiling water until smooth then brush over the top of the satsumas to glaze. Cut each cake strip into four bars to serve.

Mrs Landemare's fruit cake

Sir Winston Churchill himself laid plans for a tea-room at Chartwell, Kent, when he realised it would become a visitor attraction. Among the offerings at the tea-room was 'Mrs Landemare's fruit cake as served at No.10.'

Serves 10-12
Prep 25 minutes, plus soaking overnight
Cook 1¾-2 hours

500g/1lb 2oz mixed dried fruit
150ml/¼ pint hot tea, preferably Yorkshire tea
225g/8oz butter, at room temperature
225g/8oz dark brown muscovado sugar
280g/10oz self-raising flour
1 tsp ground mixed spice
4 eggs
85g/3oz cherries, quartered
1 tbsp black treacle
Little caster sugar to decorate

Tip the fruit into a bowl, pour over the hot tea, cover and leave to soak overnight.

Preheat the oven to 150°C/300°F/gas mark 2. Cut two strips of paper long enough to line the base and two sides of a 20cm/8in square cake tin then arrange one on top of the other at right angles to completely line the base and sides of the tin.

Cream the butter and sugar together in an electric mixer until light and fluffy, beginning on the slowest speed and working up to the highest speed. Scrape down the sides of the bowl.

Mix the flour and mixed spice together in a second bowl. Gradually beat the eggs into the creamed mixture. If the mixture begins to split turn down the speed and fold in a little flour.

Turn the mixer speed to low and gradually beat in the flour and spice mix. Gradually mix in the soaked fruit and any tea then the cherries and treacle.

Spoon the mixture into the lined cake tin, spread into an even layer then bake for 1¼ –1½ hours or until a skewer comes out cleanly when inserted into the tin. Check after 1 hour and reduce the temperature down to 140°C/275°F/gas mark 1 if the cake seems to be browning too quickly.

Sprinkle the top with a little caster sugar and leave to cool in the tin for 30 minutes. Remove from the tin and cool on a wire rack. Remove the lining paper and store in a cake tin lined with fresh non-stick baking paper. Cut into slices to serve.

COOK'S TIP This fruit cake will easily store up to one month if the cake tin is kept in a cool place.

Orange and poppy seed cake

A triple layered, zesty orange gluten-free sponge filled with orange buttercream and swirled with marmalade. Dress up with candles or small indoor sparklers for a special celebration.

Cuts into 10-12 slices
Prep 30 minutes, plus cooling
Cook 20 minutes

Sponge cake
250g/9oz soft margarine
250g/9oz caster sugar
Finely grated zest of 1 medium orange
5 eggs
250g/9oz self-raising gluten-free flour
1 tsp ground cinnamon
1 tbsp poppy seeds
2 tbsp medium-shred orange marmalade

To finish
Juice of 1 medium orange or 4 tbsp
300g/10½ oz icing sugar, sifted
115g/4oz butter, at room temperature, diced
3 tbsp medium-shred orange marmalade

COOK'S TIP If the marmalade you are using is very set, loosen with a few drops of boiling water so that it is softer to spread.
Folding the gluten-free flour through the cake mixture rather than beating it all in with an electric mixer will give a lighter sponge.

Preheat the oven to 180°C/350°F/gas mark 4. Brush three 20cm/8in Victoria sandwich tins with a little oil and line the bases with circles of non-stick baking paper.

Add the margarine, sugar and orange zest to the bowl of an electric mixer and beat until light and fluffy. Gradually beat in the eggs, one at a time, with a little flour to prevent curdling and mix until smooth.

Stir the cinnamon and poppy seeds into the remaining flour then add to the cake mixture and gently fold together with a large spoon. Fold in the marmalade.

Divide the cake mixture evenly between the three tins, spread level and bake for about 20 minutes until well risen, golden brown and the tops spring back when lightly pressed with a fingertip.

Leave the cakes to cool in the tins for 5 minutes then loosen with a knife, turn out on to a wire rack and peel off the lining paper. Leave to cool.

To make the buttercream, mix the orange juice and icing sugar together until smooth. Add the butter and whisk together until light and creamy.

Place one of the cakes on a serving plate, spread with 1 tbsp of the marmalade then spoon over one third of the buttercream. Cover with a second cake and repeat. For the top layer, spread and swirl the remaining buttercream over the cake then dot the remaining marmalade over the top and swirl with a small knife or skewer to decorate.

Cinnamon lemon buns

These are no ordinary Chelsea buns. The enriched homemade bread is rolled around a buttery, cinnamon-spiced muscovado filling then drizzled with lemon glacé icing and orange and lemon curd warm from the oven.

Makes 12
Prep 30 minutes
Rising: 2–4 hours
Cook: 20 minutes

Bread
250g/9oz strong white bread flour
115g/4oz plain flour
25g/1oz caster sugar
2 tsp easy-blend dried yeast
125ml/4fl oz warm milk
3 tbsp warm water
1 egg, beaten
25g/1oz butter, melted

For the filling
55g/2oz butter, at room temperature
100g/3½ oz light muscovado sugar
1½ tsp ground cinnamon
115g/4oz icing sugar, sifted
½ lemon, grated zest and juice
100g/3½ oz St Clement's curd or lemon curd

COOK'S TIP If you would like these buns for a special weekend breakfast, the bread dough can be made the evening before, shaped and left to rise in the cake tin loosely covered with oiled clingfilm in the fridge. Remove the clingfilm and bake as above.

To make the bread dough, add the flours, sugar and yeast to the bowl of your electric mixer and mix briefly. Mix the milk and water together then gradually beat into the flour. Gradually beat in the egg and melted butter until the dough is smooth and soft. If you don't have an electric mixer, stir with a wooden spoon then bring the dough together with your hands. Continue to beat for 4 minutes, or knead by hand.

Lightly oil a second bowl, add the dough and cover with oiled clingfilm. Refrigerate for 2–4 hours or until risen by half as much again. (The dough will rise more slowly in the fridge, so it will not be as big as if left in a warm kitchen.)

Remove the dough from the bowl, knead lightly then roll out on a very lightly floured work surface until a rectangle about 25 x 40cm/10 x 16in. Spread with the soft butter and sprinkle with the sugar and cinnamon.

Roll up, starting from one of the long edges as evenly and as tightly as you can. Cut into 12 even-sized slices and arrange cut side uppermost in a lightly oiled 20 x 30 x 4cm/8 x 12 x 1½in rectangular cake tin, leaving space between the slices. Cover the top loosely with lightly oiled clingfilm and leave in a warm place for 45–60 minutes or until the buns have risen and are touching. Preheat the oven to 200°C/400°F/gas mark 6.

When the buns are well risen, remove the clingfilm and bake for about 20 minutes until golden brown and the bread sounds hollow when gently tapped. While the buns cook, mix the icing sugar and lemon juice together until smooth. Drizzle the icing over the buns as soon as they come out of the oven then drizzle with the St Clement's curd and sprinkle with the lemon zest. Leave to cool in the tin then remove with a knife and enjoy while still warm.

Ightham Mote mince pie slice

Based on a recipe by Mrs Ginny Rogers, the housekeeper and cook back in the 1960s for the last owner of Ightham Mote in Kent, Mr Charles Henry Robinson. Any leftovers were always a favourite with the staff too.

Serves 8
Prep 30 minutes plus chilling time
Cook 45–55 minutes

Pastry
225g/8oz plain flour
115g/4oz butter, diced
60g/2¼oz icing sugar
1 egg
2–3 tsp milk

Filling
125g/4½ oz butter, at room temperature
125g/4½ oz caster sugar
125g/4½ oz ground almonds
½ tsp almond extract
3 eggs, beaten
400g/14oz jar sweet mincemeat, homemade or shop bought
50g/1¾ oz flaked almonds
Little icing sugar, sifted

To make the pastry, add the flour, butter and icing sugar to a bowl or electric mixer and rub in the butter until the mixture resembles fine crumbs. Add the egg and gradually mix in enough milk to make a smooth, soft dough.

Knead gently then roll out on a lightly floured surface until a little larger than a 23cm/9in buttered tart tin. Lift the pastry over a rolling pin, press into the tin and trim a little above the top of the tin to allow for shrinkage. Prick the base with a fork and chill for 30 minutes.

Preheat the oven to 190°C/375°F/gas mark 5. Line the tart case with a large circle of non-stick baking paper and baking beans. Bake for 10 minutes, remove the paper and beans and cook for 5 minutes.

Meanwhile, make the filling by beating the butter and sugar together until light and fluffy. Add the ground almonds and almond extract then gradually beat in the eggs until smooth.

Spoon the mincemeat into the base of the tart and spread into an even layer. Spoon the almond mixture on top then spread level with a round bladed knife dipped in hot water. Sprinkle with flaked almonds and bake at 180°C/350°F/gas mark 4 for 30–40 minutes until the topping has set and is golden brown. Check after 20 minutes and cover the top loosely with foil if the almonds seem to be browning too quickly.

Leave to cool then remove the tart from the tin and dust with the icing sugar. Serve while still warm with a spoonful of thick brandy cream or custard.

COOK'S TIP Short of time? Then cheat and use a 500g/1lb 2oz pack of good-quality readymade sweet pastry from the supermarket.

Christmas pudding scones

A few years ago in the café at Treasurer's House, York, we ran a competition for visitors to invent or suggest flavours for their special scones. The Christmas pudding scone won and has been on their Christmas menu ever since.

Makes 8-10 large scones
Prep 25 minutes
Cook 15-20 minutes

450g/1lb self-raising flour
55g/2oz caster sugar
½ tsp ground mixed spice
55g/2oz butter, diced
125g/4½ oz leftover
  Christmas pudding
250ml/9fl oz milk
1 tbsp brandy, optional

Preheat the oven to 190°C/375°F/gas mark 5. Add the flour, sugar, spice and butter to a mixing bowl or electric mixer and rub in the butter until the mixture resembles fine crumbs.

Break the Christmas pudding into tiny pieces and stir into the flour mix. Make a well in the centre, add half the milk and the brandy, if using, then gradually mix in enough of the remaining milk to make a smooth soft dough.

Lightly knead – being careful not to over-knead the dough or the scones will be heavy – then roll out thickly to a generous 2cm/¾in. Stamp out 7cm/2¾in scones with a fluted biscuit cutter and transfer to a lightly oiled baking sheet. Re-roll the trimmings and continue stamping out scones until all the mixture has been shaped.

Brush the tops lightly with the remaining milk and bake for 15–20 minutes until well-risen and golden brown. Transfer to a wire rack and serve while still slightly warm split and buttered or spread with a little brandy or rum butter, if you have some.

COOK'S TIP The secret to a good scone is to handle the dough as little as possible and roll out with even pressure from both hands so that the scones rise evenly. If you don't have any leftover Christmas pudding then use the same weight of mixed dried fruit and soak in 1 tbsp brandy for 1 hour before using. You might also like to try sprinkling the top of the glazed scones with a little ground cinnamon and caster sugar just before they go in the oven.

Conversion chart

Weights

7.5g	¼ oz
15g	½ oz
20g	¾ oz
30g	1oz
35g	1¼ oz
40g	1½ oz
50g	1¾ oz
55g	2oz
60g	2¼ oz
70g	2½ oz
80g	2¾ oz
85g	3oz
90g	3¼ oz
100g	3½ oz
115g	4oz
125g	4½ oz
140g	5oz
150g	5½ oz
170g	6oz
185g	6½ oz
200g	7oz
225g	8oz
250g	9oz
285g	10oz
300g	10½ oz
310g	11oz
340g	12oz
370g	13oz
400g	14oz
425g	15oz
450g	1lb
500g	1lb 2oz
565g	1¼ lb
680g	1½ lb
700g	1lb 9oz
750g	1lb 10oz
800g	1¾ lb
900g	2lb
1kg	2lb 3oz
1.1kg	2lb 7oz
1.4kg	3lb
1.5kg	3½ lb
1.8kg	4lb
2kg	4½ lb
2.3kg	5lb
2.7kg	6lb
3.1kg	7lb
3.6kg	8lb
4.5kg	10lb

Volume

5ml	1 teaspoon	
10ml	1 dessertspoon	
15ml	1 tablespoon	
30ml	1fl oz	
40ml	1½ fl oz	
55ml	2fl oz	
70ml	2½ fl oz	
85ml	3fl oz	
100ml	3½ fl oz	
120ml	4fl oz	
130ml	4½ fl oz	
150ml	5fl oz	
170ml	6fl oz	
185ml	6½ fl oz	
200ml	7fl oz	
225ml	8fl oz	
250ml	9fl oz	
270ml	9½ fl oz	
285ml	10fl oz	½ pint
300ml	10½ fl oz	
345ml	12fl oz	
400ml	14fl oz	
425ml	15fl oz	¾ pint
450ml	16fl oz	
465ml	16½ fl oz	
500ml	18fl oz	
565ml	20fl oz	1 pint
700ml	25fl oz	1¼ pints
750ml	26fl oz	
850ml	30fl oz	1½ pints
1 litre	35fl oz	1¾ pints
1.2 litres	38½ fl oz	2 pints
1.5 litres	53fl oz	2½ pints
2 litres	70fl oz	3½ pints

All eggs are medium. Use either metric or imperial measures, not a mixture of the two.

Length

5mm	¼ in
1cm	½ in
2cm	¾ in
2.5cm	1in
6cm	2½ in
7cm	2¾ in
7.5cm	3in
9cm	3½ in
10cm	4in
18cm	7in
20cm	8in
22cm	8½ in
23cm	9in
25cm	10in
28cm	11in
30cm	12in
35cm	14in
38cm	15in

Oven temps

Oven temperatures	Fan	Conventional	Gas
Very cool	100°C	110°C/225°F	Gas ¼
Very cool	120°C	130°C/250°F	Gas ½
Cool	130°C	140°C/275°F	Gas 1
Slow	140°C	150°C/300°F	Gas 2
Moderately slow	150°C	160°C/320°F	Gas 3
Moderately slow	160°C	170°C/325°F	Gas 3
Moderate	170°C	180°C/350°F	Gas 4
Moderately hot	180°C	190°C/375°F	Gas 5
Hot	190°C	200°C/400°F	Gas 6
Very hot	200°C	220°C/425°F	Gas 7
Very hot	220°C	230°C/450°F	Gas 8
Hottest	230°C	240°C/475°F	Gas 9

Picture credits

Picture captions

p.7
The entrance to the shop and cafe at Claremont Landscape Garden, Surrey. The cafe's design is in the style of a gardener's bothy.

p.8
Flowers and vegetables growing in the Kitchen Garden at Dunham Massey, Cheshire, in August.

p.11
Top: Clive Goudercourt at work in the kitchen.
Bottom left: Producing food for the Mulberry Tea-room at Bateman's, East Sussex.
Bottom right: The Pavilion Restaurant at Upton House and Gardens, Warwickshire.

p.12
Spring blossom at Monk's House, East Sussex. Monk's House was the country home and retreat of the writer Virginia Woolf.

pp.40–41
Rhubarb, grown in July at Llanerchaeron, Ceredigion's garden

p.56
Close up of courgettes in August grown in the vegetable garden at Sissinghurst Castle Garden, Kent.

The vegetable garden supplies the restaurant with organic produce.

p.66
Georgian Greenway in Devon was the holiday home of crime writer Agatha Christie.

p.78
A view over the kitchen garden towards Bateman's, East Sussex, in late summer. The Jacobean house was the home of Rudyard Kipling from 1902 to 1936.

p.112
An avenue of trees in November at Moleskin and Markham Hills, Bedfordshire.

pp.120–121
The Harlequin variety of winter squash and pumpkins at Wimpole Hall, Cambridgeshire.

p.130
Dawn breaks over the Long Mynd at the head of the Carding Mill Valley, Shropshire.

p.144
The gazebo, or summer house, dovecote and beehives at dawn in the Orchard at Sissinghurst Castle Garden, Kent.

p.156
Frost highlighting the delicate structure of an umbellifer seed head, on the banks of the River Wey Navigations, Surrey, in November.

p.164
Red onions grown in the gardens at Felbrigg Hall, Gardens and Estate, Norfolk.

p.173
Root vegetables grown in the community kitchen garden at Hatchlands Park, Surrey.

pp.180–181
The south front of Chartwell, Kent, the home of Sir Winston Churchill between 1924 and 1965.

p.190
A winter's day at Crickley Hill, Gloucestershire. Crickley Hill sits high on the Cotswold escarpment with views towards the Welsh Hills.

p.201
Treasurer's House in York, North Yorkshire, pictured in winter.

Index